Fragrant Rivers of Wisdom

Fragrant Rivers of Wisdom

—*An Invitation to Buddhist-Christian Dialogue*—

A. CHRISTIAN VAN GORDER

Foreword by
LAJU BALANI

CASCADE Books • Eugene, Oregon

FRAGRANT RIVERS OF WISDOM
An Invitation to Buddhist–Christian Dialogue

Copyright © 2021 A. Christian van Gorder. All rights reserved. Except for brief quotations in critical publications or reviews, no part of this book may be reproduced in any manner without prior written permission from the publisher. Write: Permissions, Wipf and Stock Publishers, 199 W. 8th Ave., Suite 3, Eugene, OR 97401.

Cascade Books
An Imprint of Wipf and Stock Publishers
199 W. 8th Ave., Suite 3
Eugene, OR 97401

www.wipfandstock.com

PAPERBACK ISBN: 978-1-7252-8726-6
HARDCOVER ISBN: 978-1-7252-8727-3
EBOOK ISBN: 978-1-7252-8728-0

Cataloguing-in-Publication data:

Names: van Gorder, A. Christian, author. | Balani, Laju, foreword.

Title: Fragrant rivers of wisdom : an invitation to Buddhist–Christian dialogue / A. Christian van Gorder ; foreword by Laju Balani.

Description: Eugene, OR: Cascade Books, 2021. | Includes bibliographical references.

Identifiers: ISBN 978-1-7252-8726-6 (paperback). | ISBN 978-1-7252-8727-3 (hardcover). | ISBN 978-1-7252-8728-0 (ebook).

Subjects: LCSH: Christianity and other religions—Buddhism. | Buddhism—Relations—Christianity. | Dialogue—Religious aspects.

Classification: BR128.B8 V36 2021 (print). | BR128.B8 (ebook).

12/07/21

Unless otherwise noted, Scripture quotations are from New Revised Standard Version Bible, copyright © 1989 National Council of the Churches of Christ in the United States of America. Used by permission. All rights reserved worldwide.

Scripture quotations marked *The Message* are taken from THE MESSAGE, copyright © 1993, 2002, 2018 by Eugene H. Peterson. Used by permission of NavPress, represented by Tyndale House Publishers. All rights reserved.

Scripture quotations marked (NIV) are taken from taken from the Holy Bible, NEW INTERNATIONAL VERSION®, NIV® Copyright © 1973, 1978, 1984, 2011 by Biblica, Inc.® Used by permission. All rights reserved worldwide.

Contents

Foreword by Laju Balani | vii
Acknowledgments | xv

Part I: Fragrant Rivers of Wisdom
  1 Wrestling the Crocodiles | 3
  2 The Thousand-Petaled Lotus of Buddhism | 13
  3 The Life of Buddha | 18
  4 Buddhist *Dharma* | 31
  5 The Four Noble Truths | 43
  6 The Mission of the Greater Path | 55

Part II: Buddhist and Christian Understandings
  7 Lord Buddha and Lord Christ | 75
  8 Dharma and Gospel | 87
  9 The Zen Teachings of Jesus? | 102
 10 Sangha and Church | 122
 11 Partnerships for Social Justice | 134
 12 Creative Interfaith Engagement | 147

Conclusion | 163

Glossary of Selected Buddhist Terms | 185
Bibliography | 191

Foreword

Professor A. Christian van Gorder has written a book whose foundations lie in his living among, and befriending, Buddhists during a decade living in Singapore and China. There is no better way to write a book on Buddhist–Christian dialogue than to have lived as a practicing Christian among Buddhists. Van Gorder writes as a committed Christian who believes that our faith can mature when exposed to other faiths.

We live in troubled times. As I write this, the coronavirus has wreaked havoc throughout our world and, as of today, August 2020, almost twenty million people have been infected by the virus with almost a million deaths. All of us are also facing a mental health crisis as we struggle with burnout, financial stress, and fears that those we love may contract the virus, while some of us have battled the actual virus itself. On the political front, world leaders have sometimes taken shelter in xenophobic nationalism even as the needy call for help or refugees seek safety. Even so-called progressives or liberals have closed their hearts to "outsiders" while some conservative Christians, Jews, Hindus, Buddhists, and Muslims become more insular—at times even intolerant and racist—instead of loving and openhearted towards others who are different. Many in this crisis have lost their moral and spiritual compass and no longer act accountable to higher ideals.

Most urgently, our world faces a pressing environmental crisis that demands clear action. Issues related to global warming and greenhouse gas emissions are only two of the challenges in this context. Indeed, the rapid extinction of nonhuman species and the disappearance of forests are causing an unprecedented ecological imbalance. Scientists warn us that if these issues are not addressed quickly, the sustainability of our world and our own existence will be threatened. We live in times of unprecedented crisis.

In this climate of fear, intolerance has also grown toward minority religious and ethnic groups, who have become victims of hateful violence. I am seeing this firsthand in my beloved India. Today, van Gorder's call for mutual respect—joining others in this call—is a refreshing glass of water for our neighbors often parched with thirst. This book is one step to encourage respectful dialogue between Buddhists and Christians. While some may see a sharp difference between the image of the crucified Christ—a "suffering God"—with the image of a calm Buddha sitting in the lotus position, the two images resonate together in our time of spiritual and relational need. Christ comes to suffering from peace, and Buddha comes from suffering to peace. Today, our task is to be loving and compassionate in the spirit of Lord Buddha and the Lord Jesus, as expressed in our various concepts. This was a theme I stressed in my doctoral dissertation, "Thich Nhât Hanh's Contribution to Buddhist–Christian Dialogue," when I noted that *love* is not a Buddhist term, although Thich Nhât Hahn uses the word *love* (as does the Dalai Lama) in order to reach a global audience.

For me, Buddhist teachings, what van Gorder calls a "pragmatic psychology focused on helping individuals use meditation practices to find freedom from suffering,"[1] have aided me in my struggles. I have found great comfort in the writings of the North American nun Pema Chödrön, Vietnamese Zen Master Thich Nhât Hanh, and His Holiness the fourteenth Dalai Lama. Chödrön, in *When Things Fall Apart: Heart Advice for Difficult Times*, testifies that the most tragic response to suffering is fear. We do all we can to avoid fear, and this is when we try temporary cures for our dilemmas. The fear of suffering manifests in various forms, especially with muscle spasms, headaches, acid reflux, anxiety disorders, and serious cases of depression that make us run to the pharmacy or our doctors for short-term cures from medications that may have serious side-effects. Instead, Chödrön suggests we need to develop an "intimacy with fear," which sounds rather intimidating.[2] By developing "intimacy with fear," Chödrön is asking us to get at the roots of our suffering and realize that our sufferings can become an opportunity for us to transform a crisis into moments of awakening. Acknowledging this reality, we can forge a new pathway and release ourselves from personal chains of fear and anxiety. For Pema Chödrön, life's inevitable sufferings are essential gateways for our healthy practice.

Van Gorder discusses the ways that we relate to our own faiths in relationship to other faiths. Thich Nhât Hanh, in *A Joyful Path: Community, Transformation, and Peace,* has observed that many people have disassociated themselves from their original spirituality traditions. He suggests that those who have estranged themselves from their mother-faith should practice the best elements of those traditions and "let the ancestors in us to

---

1. See p. 19, below.
2. Chödrön, *When Things Fall Apart*, 6.

be liberated."³ When we make peace with our past, we are able to share this deliverance from suffering to our children (and their children). He adds, "[by] doing so, we remove all limits and discrimination and create a world in which all traditions are honored!"⁴ For Nhât Hanh, when one abandons their faith tradition, they end up suffering because they have been uprooted from their ancestors.

This reminded me of my own conversion of becoming a born-again Christian in Bangalore while attending a Church of South India school as a Hindu. My conversion deeply affected my relationship with my father, who almost disowned me when he discovered that I had converted to Christianity, and when I told him I would stop praying in front of our family altar. My father, being faithful to the inclusivity of the Hindu faith, responded to my confession by suggesting that he would be happy to place a cross of Christ in our temple. This did not change my decision. My intransigence became an impediment in my spiritual relationship with my father for fifteen years. However, as I grew as a Christian, I became drawn to the practice of contemplative prayer primarily through the writings of the Trappist monk Thomas Merton. As my practice matured, I felt further rooted in my Christian faith, which helped me re-embrace my Hindu tradition. While not forsaking my Christian faith, I allowed elements of my ancestry to enrich my journey as a Christian. Van Gorder writes that those who are grounded in their faith as Christians are more apt to engage in constructive dialogue with members of other faiths. Often those who are religiously isolationist are not grounded in their faith and subsequently not interested in dialogue. For them, interfaith dialogue poses a risk of compromising their faith wrapped in concretized creeds.

Thich Nhât Hanh, in *Anger: Wisdom for Cooling the Flames*, states that we should realize that our enemies make us suffer because they are also suffering. We see that they do not intend to make us suffer, which could very well lead to reconciliation with them. In reconciliation, our enemies become our friends. This insight has enabled me to forgive those who have hurt me and has made me aware that the suffering that I caused those I loved sprang from my own suffering. I have been able to reconcile with others by admitting this truth. The Buddhist theme of compassion (*karuna*) is explored extensively in van Gorder's book. Another major theme in Buddhism that has impacted my journey as a Christian is the notion of impermanence. Everyone at their core is empty of any essence that is permanent. Instead of applying our energies pursuing possessions, which will not last, we should focus on spiritual practices that enhance our inner lives and those of our

3. Nhât Hanh, *A Joyful Path*, 15.
4. Nhât Hanh, *A Joyful Path*, 15.

natural surroundings. This truth of impermanence has enabled me not to concretize any experience, positive or negative. We may begin our day on a high note, but at the end of the day we may be visited by a crisis.

The film *Kundun* is based on the life of His Holiness the fourteenth Dalai Lama. (Tibetans refer to the Dalai Lama as Kundun, which means "the presence.") In the film, the director shows the audience a sand-art mandala where patterns are formed on a surface using a small metal tube to create the exact texture and organization of colored sand-grains. Creating this can take weeks, and shortly after it's complete, it is destroyed to illustrate the Buddhist teaching that nothing is permanent. The film switches from scenes between the Dalai Lama's travel into exile and the creation and final destruction of the sand-art mandala. This ritual sends a chill down my spine. The Dalai Lama, among the best-known figures in the world, has been forced to escape into India as the most pragmatic option for his continuation as leader of the Tibetan people in exile. As he writes in his autobiography, *Freedom in Exile*, a few days before leaving for India, the Dalai Lama stood in front of an altar of Buddhas: "The thousands of gilded Buddhas that stood flickering in the gentle light of countless butter lamps were a pointed reminder that we live in a world of Impermanence and Illusion."[5] In a recent (2019) documentary *The Great 14th: Tenzin Gyatso the 14th Dalai Lama in His Own Words*, the Dalai Lama confesses the inherent benefit of leaving Tibet. By living in freedom in India, he has been exposed to the need for democracy as a fair-minded political system and the benefits of the inherent empirical nature of scientific inquiry as a legitimate path to proving the admissibility of facts because the Buddha said never to accept his teachings out of faith but to test their relevance and applicability in our lives. By embracing the truth of impermanence, he has distanced himself from a seemingly exclusive idea of being a Buddhist. The Dalai Lama has confessed that "awareness of impermanence and appreciation of our human potential will give us a sense of urgency that we must use every precious moment."[6] And he has indeed used every chance to impact our world by embracing the gift of living in exile in a free country.

In this comprehensive study, Van Gorder also explores the fascinating similarities between Buddhist and Christian religious communities. The Buddhist and Christian faiths are the only two faiths in the world that have established monastic orders—communities available where, in silence and solitude, believers can come to ground themselves and renew their respective commitments to their spirituality. Having reached a place of spiritual

---

5. Dalai Lama XIV, *Freedom in Exile*, 125.
6. Rawcliffe, dir., *The Great 14th*.

burnout after having lost my maternal and paternal grandmothers six weeks apart, I read a book about Mother Teresa called *Something Beautiful for God*, by BBC journalist Malcolm Muggeridge—at the time an atheist. Muggeridge shares a quote from Mother Teresa that awakened in me the desire to rest in silence and solitude to revive my faith: "We need to find God, and he cannot be found in noise and restlessness. God is the friend of silence."[7]

Although I had done brief spiritual retreats in silence in the past, this time I felt the need to retreat for an extended period in complete silence and solitude to bring healing to my inner being. I was living in Philadelphia at the time and was able to arrange a fourteen-day retreat at a priory where I was also invited to attend the Daily Offices of the nuns. The day I arrived, I found the schedule and walked to the chapel and found a binder with pages marked with prayers to be recited. After each psalm was chanted, "Glory be to the Father, the Son, and the Holy Spirit. As it was in the beginning is now and forever shall be." I thought of this when I read van Gorder's claim, "The sangha and the church are contexts where ritual is integrated into daily life. Both faiths warn against separating faith from practice . . . Skeptics, bereft of visionary empathy, see rituals as contrived and superstitious activities. For critics, rituals are exclusion-making distractions and entertainments."[8] At the priory's Divine Offices, I discovered the beauty of rituals. My body prayed through bowing after every psalm; my ears and mouth prayed by listening to and praying the chants; my nose prayed by savoring the incense that was burned; my eyes prayed when I glanced at the icons I was surrounded by, and after the end of each psalm, I stood in brief silence before the next psalm. As an evangelical Protestant who ridiculed the Roman Catholic Church in India, I found that my critique of Catholicism as a liturgical and ritual-based church vanished after I was invited by a Catholic friend who lived a life dedicated to the Gospels to attend the campus mass led by a delightful Jesuit priest named Father Bischoff. Gradually I was drawn to be communed as my attendance at mass continued. I approached the priest about whether he would commune me, he called me aside and asked if I was baptized in the name of the Father, Son, and Holy Spirit, to which I admitted positively. He said I was welcome to be communed.

After experiencing healing at the priory in Philadelphia, I continued to retreat at Benedictine and Trappist monasteries whenever I found myself in times of intellectual or spiritual burnout. I would plan a weeklong retreat whenever I approached exhaustion. Just as Benedictine monasteries receive each guest as Christ, each Buddhist monastery receives guests of

---

7. Quoted in Muggeridge, *Something Beautiful for God* (1972), 66.

8. See page 127 below.

any faith as embodiments of the Buddha-nature. Thich Nhât Hanh explains that at Plum Village, his monastic center in France, when each community-member meets any person, they bow and affirm the confession "The divine in me honors the divine in you."[9]

Another interesting theme van Gorder raises is the idea that Buddhism does not teach the existence of a god similar to those confessed by Jews, Christians, and Muslims. When asked about this question after interfaith dialogue with Father Daniel Berrigan, and after having spoken with Father Thomas Merton, Dr. Martin Luther King Jr., and others, Thich Nhât Hanh clarified in his book *Living Buddha, Living Christ*, "The Buddha was not against God. He was only against notions of God that are mere mental constructions that do not correspond to reality, notions that prevent us from developing ourselves and touching ultimate reality."[10] This theme becomes important in Buddhist–Christian dialogue whenever concepts of God become more ideological and theoretical than lived and experienced in daily devotion. Some people can become obsessed with conceited notions of God, which they feel they need to defend when faced with those from other faiths who do not agree with their restricted conceptions. When I took a seminar on East Asian Religions with my beloved mentor, Dr. John N. Jonsson, this topic came up, and the point was made that the closest Christian concept of God that Buddhists could relate to came from Paul Tillich's notion of "ultimate reality." I remembered this insight later when reading Thich Nhât Hanh's book *Living Buddha, Living Christ*, where Nhât Hanh claims, "Tillich has said that speaking of God as a person is just a figure of speech. He said that God is the ground of being . . . he also said that God is ultimate reality, and that makes me remember Nirvana."[11]

The Indian Christian theologian M. M. Thomas wrote in his book *Risking Christ for Christ's Sake* that Christians should place in God their penultimate notions of truth along with the penultimate beliefs of other faiths.[12] In other words, all the faiths of the world are proclaiming their beliefs and confessions in the form of a truth that falls short of Tillich's notion of ultimate reality as long as we live in a world that falls short of an absolute notion of truth. I agree with van Gorder that Christians ought not to proclaim a compartmentalized notion of Christ, which falls short of ultimate reality. This can only occur if Christians realize that the message of Christ is not set in a concrete, static doctrine about truth but is a living reality as fluid as the river of God's Holy Spirit,

---

9. *Buddha Groove* (website), "Namaste: Meaning, Origin, and Its Use in Yoga."
10. Nhât Hanh, *Living Buddha, Living Christ*, 151.
11 Nhât Hanh, *Living Buddha, Living Christ*, 140.
12. See Thomas, *Risking Christ for Christ's Sake*.

who directs us like the waters that change course according to the terrain they meet. I have always been puzzled that Gandhi's notion was "Truth is God" and not "God is truth." I saw Gandhi's words in a new light when Dr. John N. Jonsson said that if we claim that God is truth, then we risk that extremist members of a religion can tamper with their theologies of God to suit their selfish ends to proselytize members of other faiths. However, if we say that truth is God, then what we experience as God becomes truth for us, which leaves room for renewed awareness of our experience. Experience is always open to change since life is a mystery—we need to grasp our fallibility and the unknown of what lies ahead. As one aphorism states, "Life is a mystery to be lived and not a problem to be solved."

I am grateful for van Gorder's emphasis on interfaith dialogue in the context of living friendships and the need for "Listenology." Van Gorder shares a story from a Japanese theologian that has parallels to an experience I had with two students when I was teaching at Baylor University in a course titled Religions of India, China, and Japan. Our class textbook was an anthology of the various sacred texts of India. Students had to submit a reading journal for each assignment. Sandra (a pseudonym), a devout evangelical, wrote that everything she had read in the first week was "of the devil." After I gave her a response to this dismissal, she came to my office in tears because her church had taught her to think this way about all other religions. I encouraged her to consider how Jesus showed loving respect to people who disagreed with him. How would she feel, I asked, if someone told her that the Bible she loved was of the devil? She said she would be very angry. I asked her if someone who felt the same way about their holy books would probably respond to her statement? I stressed to her that I was not asking that she change her views or agree with whatever she was reading but to simply read with tolerant respect. In contrast, another evangelical student I'll call Grace, in the same class, suggested that I share with Sandra when and how I had converted from Hinduism to Christianity—something she knew, but something I had not shared with the class.

The three of us met, and I began to tell my story. I had also met very judgmental Christians, which fostered in me no interest in their critical views. Later, however, when I was reading Mahatma Gandhi's autobiography, I saw clear parallels between what Gandhi was saying as a Hindu and what Jesus was saying as the founder of Christianity. This made me curious, and I began to talk to Christians who were kind and patient. We did not try to convert each other, but through our friendships I came to become a professing Christian. At that point in the meeting the light went on, so to speak, with Grace, who said that in high school she had tried to convert a Muslim girl by trying to befriend her in order to evangelize her but that she was rejected. Eventually, however, Grace and the Muslim girl became close friends who loved each other. Sandra responded to this story by saying she now knew what to do: simply become a better listener and a person of love. This story from my teaching echoes the emphasis that van Gorder is striking in this book—that trusting friendships open doors where we all can learn. The difference between hearing and listening is that in the first instance we hear what the other is sharing and are already preparing a counterargument. In the case of listening, we listen from the core of our being and ask questions to clarify what the other person is saying.

I also appreciate van Gorder's call for Buddhists and Christians to partner against our world's many injustices. Every faith reminds us that, if we do not care for victims of injustice, poverty, sexism, racism, ethnocentrism, and violence, then how can we claim to be devout? Yes, we live in difficult times, but it is also a wonderful time to live out the best from our wisdom and spirituality traditions by showing mercy and kindness to victims of injustice. This is not a time to judge those who are suffering. Sometimes, after a crisis someone will say that what is happening is a judgment from God. That helps and heals no one. Such statements astonish nonbelievers for their insensitivity. Such doctrines are far from the message of Jesus, who told us: "Do not judge and you shall not be judged" (Luke 6:37). Such glib views are far from the loving heart of Jesus, whose words from the cross shared healing love and forgiveness.

In conclusion, I highly recommend Professor Christian van Gorder's invitation that we dive into and swim in these two fragrant rivers of wisdom for our mutual edification and inspiration. I am grateful that reading this book has renewed my own passion to learn more from my Buddhist sisters and brothers as a practicing Christian. I will, no doubt, revisit this book in future steps along the path—come what may. Here in India, I want to learn and grow, watered from richer spirituality streams that are informed by both Buddhist wisdom and my own Christian tradition. This is how I now confess my own personal faith, as a person on the way. My daily prayer and meditation times have found welcome space for the Vedic wisdom of my sweet Hindu neighbors as well as for the rich Christian and Buddhist spirituality currents that I have celebrated. I end with one of my favorite quotes from this book: "one of the greatest benefits of interfaith engagement is the splendid opportunity to reflect on—and reframe—what we cherish within our own faith tradition."[13]

Laju M Balani, PhD
Bangalore, India

---

13. See page 158 below.

Acknowledgments

The world is a theatre of love.
—Vietnamese Proverb

I SPENT NINE DELIGHTFUL years studying and teaching in Asia. At first, I studied Chinese at the National University of Singapore. Singapore's heat reminded me I was far from my beloved Pittsburgh home. After long hours of study, I would walk to a canteen on Pasir Panjang and stop for a sweet mango-juice drink. Then, I would walk down a steep hill to my waiting family.

In 1989, our family moved to China. In June of that year, I flew to Beijing to be with student protestors calling for freedom. I will never forget those weeks. Eventually, a dragnet swept all foreigners in Beijing to the train station or airport, and before I knew it, I was on a train in the middle of the night to Ulaan Bataar, Mongolia. On returning to Singapore (via Moscow and Berlin!), I moved to Kunming, Yunnan, where I began teaching at the Yunnan University. Years in Western China provided the foundations for this study. Thanks to Zhang Zhen Hua, Xu Qin Sun, He Ting Dong, Yang Qi Kun, Zhou Zhen, and my beloved students at YunDa. Those who have lived in China and have savored the mysterious cooling warmth of Yunnan can appreciate how I feel reflecting back on my years in Kunming.

Since returning from China in 1996, I have continued studying Buddhist and Christian interactions in North America, Europe, Tibet, Nepal, Burma, Sri Lanka, Cambodia, Japan, Korea, and back to China on dozens of occasions. At Messiah College, I would like to thank John Yeats, Terry Brensinger, Doug Jacobsen, and Mac Carr. At Baylor, thanks are in order to Ralph Wood, Artyom Tonoyan, Kipp Swinney, Casey Spinks, and Samuel Otwell. Special thanks go to Buddhist scholar Elizabeth Harris, formerly

Associate Professor of Religious Studies at Liverpool Hope University and now an Honorary Fellow at the Edward Cadbury Centre of the University of Birmingham, for her careful reading and helpful suggestions in the process of completing this book.

This book is dedicated to the best from four decades of students who studied in Flint, Kunming, Grantham, Harrisburg, Lagos, and Waco: John Francis O'Magher and Carlos Emmons—who maybe never learned anything from anyone; Tim Seidel, Huan Ying, Yang Nan Gai, Mac Carr, Francisco Solórzano, Tim Laux, Dawn Baxter, Mike Mallick, John Parker, David Sonne, B. J. Schulte, Nathaniel Jung-Chul Lee, Evan Edwards, Jeremiah Scofield, Miguel Rivera, Kristi DiLascio, Gretchen Hulse, Daniel Hellfrich, Len Brown, Lily Espinoza, Hunter Moore, Winston Pollard, Jason Blazen, Bianca Morales, Adam Benner, Steve Heere, Nate Hempel, Sheena Styles, Renee Leverette, Kitto Lafeya, Keelan Downton, Justin Shorey, Femi Akkinabe, Bin Xiong, Mo Jing Hua, Patrick and Sarah Green, and—partner in righteous crimes—Philip John Bert.

I am blessed with five daughters, Keegan, Tatijiana, Gretchen, Grace, and Clare. One of them, Keegan, even shares my joy of learning from Buddhists. The day Keegan was born in Hilversum, the Netherlands, the entire country celebrated with cookies and song! My daughters are all now bubbling, intelligent artists filled with irresistible graces and infectious enthusiasms. I remember, however, as if it was yesterday when each of them were little "Buddha-babies" with pudgy cheeks and porky legs. They are now all blossoming black swans filling the world with their graces. No matter their chosen wanderings, I pray each of them will learn their truest Buddha-nature and walk beside a poor Galilean carpenter along the road as they follow their hearts. I love you, little treasures, more than words can say.

PART I

Fragrant Rivers of Wisdom

Who in the world am I? Ah, that's a great puzzle. I'm sure I'm not Ada. // It might lead you to know my going out altogether, like a candle. —I wonder what I should be like then.
—Lewis Carrol, *Alice in Wonderland*

Dreams are true while they last. Do we not live in dreams?
—Madhyamika School

On we'll plumb the depths, whatever befall // For in the Emptiness // I trust to find the All.
—Goethe, *Faust*

Just as the lotus born in water, bred in water, overcomes water, and is not defiled by water, even so I, born into world have overcome the world.
—Siddhartha Gautama

Buddhism, unlike Judaism and Christianity, is not frantically concerned with being good; it is concerned with being wise and being compassionate . . . [with] all the ignorant people who don't know that they're it but who are playing the very far-out game of being "you and I."
—Alan Watts, *Buddhism*

1

Wrestling the Crocodiles

THIS BOOK HAS MODEST objectives: There is no need for grandiose summations of how Buddhism and Christianity differ or share common ground. Instead, I write to share a few insights shared in warm friendships with Buddhist practitioners.

Crocodile Dundee was a movie about an off-balance adventurer, Mick Dundee, who gained his nickname by wrestling with crocodiles in Australia's swampy outback. Similarly, any book exploring Buddhist–Christian relations might be akin to wrestling with crocodiles: Sharp teeth can fly in all directions and there can be a lot of frantic thrashing in fetid waters. Generalized comparisons between Buddhism and Christianity provide ample opportunities for crocodile-wrestlers to be chewed up or swallowed alive. Indeed, interfaith dialogue can be as exciting as wrestling crocodiles—you never know what might happen next.

To shift to another metaphor, hidden quicksand pits can often entrap nonchalant passersby, unsuspecting of dangers beneath their feet. Arrogant religious practitioners sometimes set quicksand pits of assertion that sabotage respectful interfaith relations by promoting polarizing, isolating identities—framed in exclusionary language. The very choice to identify with any religion is also, inherently, an act of exclusion. This is especially true if you define *religion* as a "form of life that is comprehensive, incapable of abandonment and of central importance."[1]

Today, there is no benefit from continuing to strive in religious competition. While an insecure devotee may shout that they alone know where truth resides, they cannot also prove claims that the faiths of others are

---

1. Griffiths, *Problems of Religious Diversity*, 7.

deficient. For those with open hearts and a willingness to learn with a fresh mind, it becomes obvious that the faiths of others are able to provide deep foundations for personal authenticity and strong commitments for relational warmth.

Encouraging paths of mutual respect among people of different faiths would seem to be of obvious benefit. Yet, implicitly, or explicitly, some backward-looking tribal guardians, filled with their own sense of self-importance, call on the faithful to be careful about becoming polluted by the differences of others. Guardians of truth sometimes shout because they are unable (or unwilling) to fathom any ideas beyond their own boundaries. Questions become challenges. It is safer not to question and not to learn and live, with blessed assurance, that they alone know what questions can be asked and how they can be answered. In contrast, interfaith engagements are not encouraged because they cannot be controlled. Entrenchment is preferred to exploration. Those who are intransigent assert that isolation defends orthodoxy—as if it were threatened. All that matters is a zero-sum game—the *Wahrheitsfrage*—the question of who has the only truth.

Those drunk with the strong brew of religious certainty have no need to ask questions because they have already captured the truth like a criminal captures a hostage. The self-assured, framing religious smugness as righteousness, only paint with black and white and suspect anyone using a rainbow palette. They have all the answers and none of the questions. The righteous have no need to learn about the wisdom of others except as a means to better advance predatory, apologetic strategies that misrepresent views to tally points against those deceived by falsehoods. Religious isolationists are blighted by a soulfully cancerous pre-existing condition: They are right and everybody else is wrong.

But, self-appointed guardians of our communities have no authority. Those who aspire to have open hearts can encourage genuine interfaith engagements as a refreshing "series of retrievals" from a landscape often polarized and intellectually and spiritually paralyzed. While the smug live in mazes of their own invention and assume that these mazes shelter a minotaur somewhere in the shadows, we can be "bold as lions."[2] As my father, a lawyer, always said, assertion is not proof. Beatrice Bruteau sees the need for "cross-traditional studies" that find shared conversational spaces with others of goodwill.[3] She calls us to "travel abroad and read from an expanded

---

2. Keller, "Scoop Up the Water," 107, 102.
3. Bruteau, *What We Can Learn from the East*, 2.

family bible of human faith."[4] Some view such ambitions as a betrayal of Christ—sold again by liberal traitors for thirty cold pieces of silver.

RELIGIOUS ISOLATIONISTS

Religious isolationists burrow down for comforting refuge under dank rocks of ideology. Buddha taught: "The world in general grasps after systems and is imprisoned by dogmas and ideologies."[5] Dulling toxins of self-assertive ideologies objectify adherents of other faiths and force them into dead-end alleys of preconceived expectations.[6] Whenever a sincere question arises, it is quickly smothered in the cradle of dogmatic certainty. Towering castles of unchallenged religious assertions are guarded by impassable moats of grandiloquent invectives against others. Religious authorities—who rarely know someone from another faith—invariably prefer theatrical performances instead of open-ended and genuine responses of interrelational trust.

Self-proclaimed religious tribal chiefs claim they alone hold the truths about the true God. They ask us to take their word on this even though there's no empirical proof beyond their assertions. The God they worship, in fact, is a god of their own conception; controllable, shrunken down, and recast in to their own image. Filled with self-importance, these god-creating men seem to have an apparent need to dismiss the views of others.

Stodgy assertions make the invocation of creative engagement even more urgent. Nothing less than the global reputation of our traditions—as contexts of healing embrace—is at stake. It is necessary, finally, to expose religious gatekeepers and call their followers to abandon arthritic intransigence for a higher path of love—free and transparent. We do not have to agree to defend prisons of religious self-isolation.

---

4. Bruteau, *What We Can Learn from the East*, 3.

5. Jones, *The New Social Face of Buddhism*, 59. Jones notes the Nazis reached the "sharp end of ideology" as soon as their armies entered Poland. He quotes Norman Davies in *Heart of Europe: A Short History of Poland*: "The Nazi Gestapo followed racial-guidelines consigning some two million Polish Jews to closed *reservaten* or ghettos. In the Extraordinary Pacification Campaign of 1940 some 15,000 Polish priests, teachers, and political leaders were transported to Dachau or shot in the Palmiry Forest. The first experiments were made in euthanasia, in the selection of children for racial breeding, in slave labor schemes, and in gas chambers" (59).

6. Jones, *The New Social Face of Buddhism*, 60. Related to ideology, Jones talks about the role of education and literature: "The publications of ideological movements consequently tend to have a repetitive, formulaic quality about them no matter what the subject. Their main purpose is to confirm the faithful in their beliefs and loyalties and to attract new supporters" (60).

Nonrelational arrogance is sad coming from a Christian perspective, which, without apology, begins as a missionary faith committed to engaging each person on their own terms and preconditions. This same relational priority at the genesis of faith explains why Buddhism is also a religion of missionaries. Followers of the Buddha and the Christ should meet others in a spirit of healing openness—not defensive alienation. Our first task is to share.

TASTING STRAWBERRIES

People of goodwill should seek spiritual freedom, creativity, appropriate humility, and exploration. We should be learners—confident in meeting the other on their own terms and without prejudgments. We can explore that which is not familiar without fear. We should embrace—with an open heart—whatever is true, honorable, just, pure, pleasing, and commendable (Phil 4:8), wherever its source, without fear.

When Buddha and Jesus began to teach, there were no such things as Buddhists or Christians. Instead, early followers aspired to become "inner beings" who embodied the values they preached. To use another analogy, Buddhists and Christians are called to emulate hard-working vendors at a farmer's market who encourage others to sample the sweetness they have on offer. Once a shopper savors fresh strawberries, they can then reach their own conclusions. Instead of the theoretical ideas of strawberries, people should enjoy the actual deliciousness of fresh strawberries. Instead of stale ideologies, we should live out our truths in a multiprismatic way—with mind, emotion, and action. Zen Master Seng advised: "Do not search after the truth but only cease to cherish opinions."[7]

INTELLECTUAL TRASH COMPACTORS

Is the goal of meeting those of other faiths the promotion of tolerance? *Toleration* is an oft-used term which has limitations.[8] Austria's Cardinal Franz Köning (an architect of Vatican II) warned,

---

7. Jones, *The New Social Face of Buddhism*, 62

8. Michael Jinkins writes, "The limitations of the concept of toleration have led some scholars to test new terms. Henry Hardy has suggested 'radical tolerance' and 'acceptance,' the first of which is intended to express greater openness to difference than is assumed in the older word, with its Enlightenment associations; the second goes a step further, implying a willing reception in a multicultural society of different or conflicting ideas, though not necessarily an endorsement of them" (Jinkins, *Christianity, Tolerance,*

> Formal tolerance automatically accepts different points of view without question and often springs from indifference and is negative because prejudices and contradictions remain and can result in ignorance and ostracism.[9]

What Cardinal Köning calls "real tolerance" means loving others from a sincere heart that moves us beyond mere acceptance to engage with others in mutual respect. Invariably, those involved in interfaith interactions will encounter any number of misunderstandings. Between Buddhists and Christians problems arise when adherents from one group expect the other faith to be an unchanging tradition that they have read about or heard mentioned. But no spiritual community is static. It is fine to read books that summarize another's faith, but it makes more sense to learn about the changing experiences of those practitioners who aspire to live faithful to their convictions.

In religious studies, a term used to describe the empathetic process of learning about the multivalent experiences of others is *phenomenology*. The goal of the phenomenologist of religion is to gain as far as is possible a participant's appreciation of faith. What sometimes happens instead is that people try to categorize the experiences of others into tidy boxes. This leads to focusing on the tangential—and the easily dismissible. Those who are certain they alone have the truth often paint with a broad brush instead of meeting others with immediacy, and directness. Critics of other religions assemble an inaccurate—but a self-satisfying—circus hall of mirrors filled with distortions. Critics "detour religious teachings around the heart and not through it."[10]

The minds of the close-minded are *trash compactors* who take everything and scrunch it down into something they can throw away. They frame—in a negative light—the experiences of others, using the bricks and mortar of their own traditions.[11] The ideas of others are most easily attacked when not understood. Straw-men are easy to assemble and even easier to destroy. The judgmental hermetically seal those they do not valorize in a

---

and Pluralism, 175).

9. König, *Open to God, Open to the World*, 97.

10. Raymaker, *Buddhist-Christian Logic of the Heart*, 155.

11. George Sumner explains, "Christians have spun understandings of other religions off from a wide variety of their own primary doctrines—the Trinity, grace, the economy of salvation, eschatology, creation, etc. Furthermore, the church has cast the religions in a wide variety of roles derived from different Biblical types—preparer of the coming of the gospel, ordained restrainer of evil, rod of God's wrath, exemplar of legalism, recipient of secret wisdom or inarticulate faith, etc." (Sumner, *The First and the Last*, 15).

static world of condescending judgments. False religions are simplistically caricatured in contrast with The Truth. The smug assume that others who think differently have nothing to offer, and so they are incapable of meeting others without presumptions.

INVENTING BUDDHISM

How old is Buddhism? Thousands of years? According to Tomoko Masuzawa, the first European missionaries invented the term *Buddhism* to describe those who followed the teachings of the Buddha. She explains:

> Buddhism's countenance reflected in the European imagination and was marked by what might be called a series of bipolar characteristics, or a jumbled contradiction of striking extremes. Buddhism was unquestionably foreign and archaic, but it was also unexpectantly modern and resonant with current conditions.[12]

According to Masuzawa, the early Western conception of Buddhism was devised as a rhetorical event by Europeans, eager to encapsulate—and thus dismiss—what they did not understand. The term *Buddhism* became a tabula rasa, a blank canvas, on which they could create their own version of faith. As Europeans realized that the world consisted of more than Christians, Jews, Muslims, pagans, and idolaters, a series of neologisms were invented to contain the dynamism of the unknown "other." A founder had to be identified, and a gaggle of texts had to be boxed into a manageable canon. Prefabricated categories of Buddhisms were agreed upon and an unquestioned metanarrative origin-story emerged that claimed that Buddhism was a reform of the Vedic traditions. Buddhism was "discovered" as a nonnational religion, a *Weltreligion*. This claim by Masuzawa, that Buddhism was "invented," provides an instructive starting point for interfaith conversations.

Since the first interactions between Buddhists and Christians, a host of themes have been debated. In fact, both the static Buddhism and the Christianity of categorical frameworks are quite distinct from the lived experience of everyday adherence. The Buddhist faith is primarily an experience of helping people live lives with balance.[13] The conviction of the "otherness" and the distance between Buddhists and Christians seems set in stone even before adherents meet. Yet, one who lives inside Buddhist or Christian communities might find it impossible to tell them apart until dogmas are

---

12. Masuzawa, *The Invention of World Religions*, 121.
13. Berzin, *Developing Balanced Sensitivity*, 15.

articulated. There is a collective echo throughout humanity where our experiences resonate with those of others. There is plenty of room to build links that articulate mutual questions and explore our common ground.

FRESH THINKING

Perhaps interfaith engagements best begin, not with words, but in sharing spaces of prayerful, meditative silence. Alexander Pope said, "Words are like leaves ; and where they most abound, / Much fruit of sense beneath is rarely found."[14] The Dalai Lama has noted, "Something is touched in sharing deep silence together that words can point to but never quite express."[15] One Zen practitioner mirthfully described a scholar as someone who uses words to "make waves where there is no wind."[16]

Jewish scholar Martin Buber, speaking of Christians, claimed it was the mission of the church to share a sustaining "life-breath."[17] For Christians, *mission* means witness to Christ expressed in both words and silence. For Buddhists, a mission also means witness to Buddha both in words and actions. Seven years living among Buddhists in Yunnan (and two years in Singapore) gave me a profound respect for Buddhism in practice, as well as a willingness to share the joys of my own faith as my interest increased in learning more about their perspectives. Both faiths originally flourished in contexts where there was already a set religious path. Both faiths have often dealt with the religious "other" through searching for common ground as opposed to relying on initial assumptions of incompatibility. Neither religion began with black-and-white declarations of a dogmatic assertion.

This last statement is vigorously contested by some Christians. In fact, Christ's message was experienced before it was transcribed. The vibrancy of the early church was personal and relational before it was creedal and universal. Christian theology was launched as a local missiological and relational fulcrum before being a universalizing agent for compartmentalization and contention. The unity of the first Christians was a grandiloquent statement about the viable merit of their convictions. While controversies appear among the first Christians, they had a remarkable degree of unity rooted in love for God and for one another While some Christians have drifted from these moorings, Paul Tillich writes that "early Christianity did not consider itself as a radical-exclusive, but as the all-inclusive religion in the sense of

---

14. Pope, "An Essay on Criticism" (1711).
15. Dalai Lama XIV, *The Good Heart*, 3.
16. Shrobe, *Don't-Know Mind*, 1.
17. Shenk, *Who Do Men Say That I Am?*, 13.

the saying: All that is true anywhere belongs to us, the Christians."[18] Over time, arguments surfaced about who was heretical and who had twisted a faith originally rooted in ethical and relational priorities.

A goal of this book is to encourage creative thinking about how Buddhists and Christians can best relate to each other. Tillich explained that he wrote to "challenge my readers to take what I have written and to be driven by it and through it to something creative, something deep, something that will illumine, enliven and make meaningful the time and place in which they find themselves."[19] Another goal of this book is to provide a resource for those who want to interact with Buddhists with a greater sense of cherished respect. In this task, Jacques Dupuis explains our goal should be to "understand others as they understand themselves and not as we, often according to our stubborn traditional prejudices, think we know who they are."[20]

I will use the spellings of Sanskrit, Pali, Chinese, and Japanese terms as they appear in *The Shambala Dictionary of Buddhism and Zen*. I write as a Christian hoping to encourage interfaith interactions that help others better grasp some of the theological and relational challenges that Christians among Buddhists often experience. What is my point of reference? While profoundly touched by a vision for incarnational service as expressed by the Catholic Worker Movement, I am now midstream in the Anabaptist and African American church traditions. My life's passion is to challenge and to be challenged by the ways that the faith meets the faiths.

My hope is to evangelize my immediate North American context out of glib assertions. I am wearied by pat answers and the reductionistic bumper-sticker-ology. Those who know less and less are becoming more outspoken. Why do people listen to those who have nothing to affirm in those unlike themselves? What might Jesus or Buddha say? Gentle reader, no one religion has a monopoly on wisdom or spirituality. Interfaith explorations should not be based upon the need to control the old theological thermostats of our comfortability. The alternative to healthy interfaith engagement seems to

---

18. Tillich, *Christianity and the Encounter of the World's Religions*, 22. Tillich feels that the idea of universalism is "in the air" at the time of Christ and is a central idea for Greeks, Romans, and even for the Jews. This idea of universalism, to use Tillich's term, does not negate the centrality of Christ. He explains, "This astonishing universalism, however, was always balanced by the criterion which was never questioned, either by the orthodox or by the heretical groups: the image of Jesus as the Christ, documented in the New, and prepared for in the Old Testament. Christian universalism was not syncretistic; it did not mix, but rather subjected whatever it received to an ultimate criterion" (23).

19. Paul Tillich, quoted in James, *Tillich and World Religions*, 157–58.

20. Dupuis, *Christianity and the Religions*, 7.

be stagnation into nonrelational isolationism. Many Christians write about interactions between Buddhists and Christians by first erecting high walls of rhetorical defense. A sage scholar, whom I had the privilege of meeting once, Dr. Wilfred Cantwell Smith, encouraged students to learn from others and at the same time adhere—as best as possible—to the guiding ethical ideals of their own faith. Our goal is to "find common ground and areas of agreement between the religions so that mutual suspicions and hostilities can end."[21] Simply, our goal is to listen, learn, and love as our faiths teach.

Respectful listening is central to a faithful witness of Christ's Great Commission (Matt 28:20). Interfaith interactions can be seen in this way: When we study another language, we rarely feel the need to find commonalities between languages. Few are clamoring for a one-size-fits-all language, such as Esperanto: Why do we expect this in a vast world of faiths?

Sadly, some Christians have co-opted interfaith discussions to become another tool for covert, result-focused, evangelism. In contrast, it would seem to be the duty of any person of faith to be transparently honest in interpersonal interactions: There is no room for deceptive sleights of hand. While Christians are called to be witnesses of faith, a call to evangelize should never be expressed as an aggressive tool to denigrate others. To be a faithful adherent of a faith would seem to logically include loving authenticity and relational humility.

When we listen to those of other faiths, we also gain the potential to learn more about our own traditions. Rita Gross explains, "The chief purpose of interreligious interchange is one's own growth, the challenge it can provide to one's own assumptions and conclusions."[22] Rudyard Kipling mused, "What do they know of England who only England know?"[23]

Asian Buddhists have been interacting with non-Asians for centuries. Early American revolutionaries—such as Jefferson and Franklin—showed a basic familiarity with the teachings of Buddha. During the nineteenth century, a few Buddhist texts were translated into English and were quoted by the Transcendentalists Ralph Waldo Emerson and Henry David Thoreau.[24] Emerson mistakenly wrote that the *Bhagavad Gita* was "a much renowned book of Buddhism."[25] He also wrote that "a Buddhist is a Transcendentalist because of the conviction that every good deed cannot possibly escape its

---

21. Gross and Ruether, *Religious Feminism and the Future of the Planet*, 11.
22. Gross and Ruether, *Religious Feminism and the Future of the Planet*, 8.
23. Kipling attributed this quote to his mother.
24. Lai and von Bruck, *Christianity and Buddhism*, 198. Unitarians, along with other Protestants, had a role in launching the 1893 Parliament of the World's Religions.
25. Ralph Waldo Emerson in Fields, *How the Swans Came to the Lake*, 60.

reward."[26] Still today, Buddhism is sometimes seen as a uniformly Asian faith when in fact it is a global community. I love the description of Buddhism as a "thousand-petaled lotus" because it emphasizes its rich diversities of expression. In the next chapter, we will introduce some of the major themes and movements within the Buddhist wisdom tradition in hopes of helping non-Buddhists gain a more nuanced perspective on this wide-ranging tradition.

---

26. Fields, *How the Swans Came to the Lake*, 61.

2

The Thousand-Petaled Lotus of Buddhism

On my best days, a generosity of spirit bubbles up and with it a deep willingness to just be in each situation. Life becomes more improvisational, less planned. The need for rules disappears because every situation calls for a different response. The world changes in an instant. None of us is safe.

—Geri Larkin, *Tap Dancing in Zen*

A TRANSFORMATIVE HOPE

ABOUT A BILLION PEOPLE worldwide, mostly in Asia, call themselves Buddhists. From the commanding lamasery at Karakoram on the vast Mongolian Steppe to latticed stupas lording over the fertile volcanic Javan plains of Indonesia, individuals throughout Asia—and around the globe—find comfort in the teachings of Buddha. His message explained both the cause and cure of suffering as he "preached another alternative to the ritual-oriented Brahmanism of India."[1] Every day, before a colossal bronze Daihatsu Amida in the glades of Kamakura or in an unpretentious shrine in London's Hyde

---

1. Fisher, ed., *An Anthology of Living Religions*, 135.

Park, the faithful offer flowers, gifts of foods, and flickering candles in honor of our hopes and as a reminder of our fleeting impermanence.

Expressions of devotion vary throughout Buddhist communities. For many, the weathering tests of life are dealt with by stopping midstream in frenzied days to bow silently for a moment. Buddhists in Sri Lanka pilgrimage up Adams Peak to revere a miraculous footprint of Buddha. The faith continues to adapt to new contexts with fresh ways of expressing ancient teaching. Practitioners in Brazil sometimes make offerings of rice and flowers at a butsudan complete with a picture of the Virgin Mary.[2] Young Buddhists in Hawai'i seek to earn a dharma patch in local chapters of the Buddhist Boy Scouts of America.[3] Buddhists circumambulate sacred trees or temples while others pilgrimage to shrines or prayer wheels.

Disparate cultures—Indian, Korean, Japanese, Chinese, Indonesian, Tibetan, Southeast Asian, and others—express both Buddha's message and their own unique cultures. Buddhism is a prismatic rainbow of bright color and gentle intention. The teacher's ashes, remains of his bones, and even his chipped begging bowls are scattered under stupas across Asia. But all Buddhists everywhere recite an ancient trinity of convictions: "I take refuge in the Buddha. I take refuge in the teachings. I take refuge in the community."

Buddhism is the "first world religion known to history."[4] Little is known with certainty about Buddha because early accounts of his life were written centuries after he lived. Five centuries before Jesus, and during what Karl Jaspers called the Axial Age—when Zoroaster taught in Persia; Socrates, Plato, and Aristotle tutored in Greece; prophets preached in Israel; and Master Kung taught in China—at the foothills of the Himalayas a begging monk named Siddhartha Gautama began to preach. He wrote no books and established no government, and yet he changed history. Just as Christianity was born from Judaism, Buddhism probably sprang from the context of Vedic traditions we now call Hinduism. Although Buddha's teachings reject the limitations of the Brahmanic caste system, it would be

---

2. Rocha, *Zen in Brazil*, 163. The entire chapter, "Doing Zen, Being Zen: Creoling 'Ethnic' and 'Convert' Buddhism" (153–92), focuses on Brazilian Buddhism. She notes that some Buddhists performed "baptisms" and tells of one woman who requested a baptism: "Neither her nor her husband's family is Buddhist, but they did not oppose the ceremony. They thought it was important that they were baptized, but it did not matter to them in which particular religion" (180).

3. Hunter, *Buddhism in Hawaii*, 201. Many of the first Japanese were barbers, woodworkers, tailors, and blacksmiths: "Some of them thought they were going to India; some thought China; others referred to their destination as *Tenjiku*, the resting place of the Buddha. A few expected to travel back and forth from and to Yokohama with ease" (22–23).

4. Kennedy, *Zen Spirit, Christian Spirit*, 24.

misleading to suggest that his ideas were primarily a reformation of Hinduism. His teachings presented an entirely new cause-and-effect scenario in humanity's quest to overcome suffering.

How many different types of Buddhist traditions are there? The answer depends on how you frame the question. There are many kinds of Buddhisms, which are related to a vast family of religious expressions. A famous parable is told of blind men who are asked to define an elephant: "Depending on which part of Buddhism you grasp, you might identify it as a system of ethics, a philosophy, a contemplative psychotherapy, a religion. While containing all of these, it can no more be reduced to one of them than an elephant can be reduced to its tail."[5] There are as many as eighty-four thousand different paths that a Buddhist can follow to achieve enlightenment.[6] It is a pluralistic faith with no central organization, primary text, or agreed-upon rituals. The term *Buddhism* fails to fully express the "breadth of the movement."[7] Philosopher Karl Popper argued that we should move away from broad categorizations of knowledge and a list of definitions and towards reflections on basic questions that facilitate certain beliefs or worldview assumptions.[8] Using this approach, the central focus of Buddhism is liberation: "As the sea, though wide and deep, has only one taste, the taste of salt, said Shakyamuni, so my teaching, though extensive and profound, only has one message."[9] Different expressions of Buddhism are ways to share that one refuge of truth in contrasting cultures and periods of time, and these different forms are a clear "mark of its success."[10]

BUDDHIST SCHOOLS

What are the major schools of Buddhism? Buddhism in Southeast Asia is often labeled Theravada (Orthodox) Buddhism. In Northeast Asia, most subscribe to Mahayana Buddhism, meaning "The Big Boat" or "Greater Path," which offers a more accessible way to follow Buddha's message compared to what Greater Path Buddhists called Hinayana, "Small-Boat Buddhism."

---

5. Batchelor, *Buddhism without Beliefs*, 19.

6. Taitetsu Unno, quoted in Suzuki, *Buddha of Infinite Light*, 11. Suzuki first gave this book as a series of lectures at the American Buddhist Academy in New York in 1958. The reference to the number 84,000 comes from a poem by the Japanese monk Saicho, "84,000 delusions / 84,000 lights / 84,000 joys abounding" (11).

7. Vroom, "How May We Compare Ideas of Transcendence?," 68.

8. Quoted in Gombrich, *How Buddhism Began*, 1.

9. Corless, *The Vision of Buddhism*, 287.

10. Corless, *The Vision of Buddhism*, 287.

People outside Asia are most likely to meet Greater Path Buddhists, a term first used around 100 CE in India, from the Chinese Chan (Zen) or Western Chinese, Tibetan traditions.

Followers of the Greater Path claim their beliefs provide hope to the widest possible number of people. Salvation is not only for holy saints but is available to everyone. This new creed criticized literalists, who seemed "compulsively bound to imitate one aspect of the Buddha's life."[11] The Greater Path put the needs of the masses first and made Buddha's teachings obtainable to all—a goal in keeping with Buddha's loving heart. Anyone can attain the truth, not just the devout. In the same way that Martin Luther claimed that he was reclaiming a more inclusive approach in Saint Paul's preaching of salvation by grace, the Greater Path announces that anyone who seeks Buddha can find salvation: "While the vast array of Buddhist religious cultural forms define the breadth of the experience of Buddhism, its profound quest for enlightenment . . . define the depth of Buddhist experience."[12]

One Greater Path parable echoes Christ's parable of the prodigal son. In the Buddhist version, a young person travels to the other side of the world only to land in poverty and problems. One day, after a long search, the child's father finds his child begging on the street. The child, however, does not recognize the father and assumes that the stranger encountered is a king. Being gentle, the father sends his associate to offer the child a job to clean trash from the street. Over time, the father makes sure that his child is promoted and eventually becomes the father's trusted accountant. Even then, the child does not realize that it is the father's anonymous love that is helping him. Finally, when the child is stable, the father reveals who he is and welcomes the child back into full fellowship. In the same way, Buddha hides among humanity as a humble teacher so we can learn from him about our soul-condition.

At the Sixth Buddhist World Council (Rangoon, 1955–1956), participants focused on how missionaries could take the Buddhist message worldwide. Long before that conference, however, Buddhists had been resident in Europe and North America. There were Buddhist societies in England as early as 1906, and today every major city in Europe and North America has Buddhist shrines and followers. What flourishes today is a wide breadth of experiences of meditation, devotion, philosophy, ethics, and faith in practice. The expanse of those who practice Buddhism is an untamed stallion

---

11. Matthews, *World Religions*, 118.
12. Mitchell, *Buddhism: Introducing the Buddhist Experience*, 1.

bristling beyond the constraints of analysis. As one Taoist scripture claims, "Those who know don't talk. Those who talk don't know."[13]

Any quest for the historical Buddha is impossible to achieve using modern historiographic standards. Buddha's life is shrouded in the thick fog of devotion, myth, and parable. The study of Buddha's life, however, is not about what happened in history but about how the teachings of Buddhism have been expressed in various cultures worldwide. It can be said with certainty that Siddhartha Gautama was one of the four or five most influential people in history. Entire civilizations have been affected by his message.

Christmas Humphreys compares attempts of those who have tried to categorize Buddhism: "As difficult as describing London. Is it Mayfair? Is it Bloomsbury—or the Old Kent Road? Or, is it the lowest common multiple, or is it all of them and something more?"[14] This book offers an introduction for learners from a non-Buddhist background who are willing to enjoy the airy fragrances of Buddhism's thousand-petaled lotus. It is hoped, in the process of description, that words will not crush underfoot the flowers of cherished devotion or muddle the sensual aromas of sublime wisdom. My hope is that all of us who are not Buddhists will be met with graciousness by our Buddhist sisters and brothers.

---

13. Tao Te Ching, 1:1 (in Novak, *The World's Wisdom*, 152).
14. Humphreys, *Buddhism: An Introduction*, ii.

3

The Life of Buddha

The Great Buddha at Kamakura—not at all does he blink an eyelid as hailstones fall.

—Muraoka Shiki (1867–1902)

But the Buddha is also a challenge because He is more radical than most of us . . . In His view, the spiritual life cannot begin until people allow themselves to be invaded by the reality of suffering, realize how fully it permeates our whole experience and feel the pain of all other beings.

—Karen Armstrong, *Buddha*

MAHAYANA (GREATER PATH) DOCTRINES OF THE BUDDHA

BUDDHIST SCRIPTURES ARE CALLED the "fathers/mothers of the faith" because they explain the teachings of Lord Buddha.[1] Richard Dobrich notes, "Buddha, whom we regard as a historical figure, is but one of an infinite

---

1. Cole, *Text as Father*, 26.

series of Buddhas."[2] When Christians draw parallels between Buddha and Christ, this ahistorical nature of the Buddha should be kept in mind. There are no original writings from the time Buddha lived. Further, theological categories such as revelation, theism, atheism, and polytheism convey much more about Christianity than they do about Buddhism. The faith of millions of Buddhists should be defined on its own unique terms.

Is Buddha considered a god? The Dalai Lama explains, "From the philosophical point of view, the theory that God is the creator, the almighty, and the permanent is in contradiction to Buddhist teachings."[3] Such a view, however, is more agnostic than atheistic because the question is of little concern for Buddhists. Instead of who is responsible for the creation, the real question is, how is life best lived? Buddhism is a pragmatic psychology focused on helping individuals use meditation practices to find freedom from suffering.

Buddha is given the honorific title Lord as a term of respect, but it has a different meaning from its use in Christianity. Buddha insisted he was not a prophet or an expression of God, but only a teacher who had become awake. He was a pathfinder who taught that anyone could find what he had discovered. Buddha did not seek to be worshiped but instead offered himself as a tour guide through life's dangerous jungle.

Sometimes the term *Buddha Nature* is used to describe what people in other religions refer to as God: a powerful, energizing source that sustains life. The entire world is filled with the Buddha Nature. When a person is filled with the Buddha Nature, they are enlightened, free from suffering. Buddha's nature exists on three levels. First, the Buddha is a historical being in an earthly form. Second, Siddhartha Gautama gained the Buddha Nature and therefore transcended the limits of human ignorance. A popular Greater Path text, the *Lotus Sutra*, explains that the Buddha Nature has existed for eons of time. Across time, the Buddha Nature has manifested to liberate humanity from this world of wearying, ego-grasping bluster, and illusion.

Third, the Buddha exists in nirvana—a state of complete oneness with all that is true. For non-Buddhists, the concept of nirvana can be hard to grasp because it describes something that cannot be described—a void without distinctions, a unity of essence beyond explanation. The *Lotus Sutra* explains that Buddha chose to delay entry into nirvana—pure bliss—in order to teach others the true path. A person who does this is called a *bodhisattva*, a term when translated into Tibetan means, "one who has

---

2. Gombrich, *How Buddhism Began*, 5.

3. Dalai Lama XIV, *Answers*, 13. The quote ends, "The variety of the different world religious philosophies is a very useful and beautiful thing" (13).

exchanged themselves for another (*dark-shen-jay-wa*)."[4] A bodhisattva vows to dedicate themselves to using their own "awakening for the sake of others."[5] Bodhisattvas are guides, as numerous as the sands of the sea, who lead people, step by step, into insight. They are eternal "incarnations of enlightenment."[6]

Buddhist mythologies describe many bodhisattvas including one angel, Samantabhadra, who swaggers across the skies on a fierce, white elephant looking to help people in times of need. Another supernatural being, the devilish Kshitigarbha, is a brutish master over hell whose mission is to torture all evildoers for crimes. One of the most famous bodhisattvas is Maitreya, who will one day return to earth. Maitreya (Metteryya or Jampa in Japan)—is "the world teacher" who will arrive at the perfect time to serve all believers the elixir of enlightenment. Maitreya springs from the "body of the dharma" (Sanskrit: *dharmakaya;* Pali: *dipamakara*), which exists as true reality.[7] This messianic figure's return, only for a brief visit, will be humanity's finest moment. He will distribute vast quantities of fragrant rice and fill deserts with lush lotus ponds. In Maitreya's kingdom, there will be ten yearly harvests, and each person will live at least eight thousand years. Women will not be compelled to marry or bear children until after they are five hundred years old. When women go into childbirth, it will be as easy as floating freely in a soft, gentle breeze.

BIRTH AND CHILDHOOD

Indian poet Ashvaghosha wrote that before entering humanity, Buddha waited in a heavenly realm where each day lasted over four hundred years.[8] Finally, Buddha entered the womb of his mother, Maya, and was born among the Sakya Tribe near the Ganges River in modern-day Nepal. Siddhartha's father, Sudha Dhana (meaning "pure rice"), was a benevolent rajah who ruled the small kingdom of Kapilavista (Kapilavatthu), one hundred miles north of Benares (Varanasi). Although the king was wealthy, he was miserable because his wife (aged forty-five) was unable to provide a male heir. Finally, on the day of a full moon in May, the kingdom celebrated the supernatural birth of Siddhartha Gautama (meaning "superior cow"—alluding

---

4. Corless, *The Vision of Buddhism*, 41.
5. Batchelor, trans., *The Path of Compassion*, 4.
6. Carmody and Carmody, *Serene Compassion*, 14.
7. Kinnard, *The Emergence of Buddhism*, 60.
8. Each being in this realm, according to Corless, lives for four thousand Tushita years, which would be 576 million human years (Corless, *The Vision of Buddhism*, 33).

to a high status). It was a miracle because his parents had not had sexual relations.[9] The year of his birth is often cited as 623 BCE.[10] Others cite 560 or 448 BCE as the year of his birth.[11]

Tragically, Siddhartha's mother died seven days after her baby was born. One version of the story poetically asserts that Queen Maya died at childbirth, and her son emerged from the midst of her jewel-covered casket.[12] Another account explains that the queen was fated to die because she was overwhelmed by the matchless glory of her newborn. In any event, the care of the prince fell to the queen's sister, who raised him as if he was her own.

After his birth, one priest observed that the newborn took seven steps in the seven directions and announced that he had been "born for enlightenment and the good of the world."[13] The baby's feet were pretattooed with a dharma wheel, and a dharma circle of hair grew on his forehead. On the first day of Siddhartha's life, the sky smelled of sandalwood, and fragrant flowers rained from the heavens. Soothing gentle music could be heard filling the entire kingdom.[14]

When Siddhartha was five days old, the king summoned a hundred sages to pay homage to the boy and predict his future. Most prophesied that the prince would expand his father's kingdom with glorious military victories. One of the pundits, however, Asita (or Khodanna) prophesied that Siddhartha would either become a great king, or, if exposed to suffering, would renounce wealth and become a wandering teacher who would turn the dharma wheel of truth.

Asita's prophecy disturbed the king, who decided to shield his son in an "ivory tower" of seclusion where it would be impossible to see suffering. Anyone who was sick was not allowed in Siddhartha's presence. Even when a flower wilted in the garden it had to be removed. Further, Siddhartha's chariot driver was forbidden to take the boy outside the palace walls. One lesson from this story is that we cannot shield those we love from the harsh realities of life. The father was guilty of trying to trap his son into an unawakened lifestyle upheld by illusions.[15]

---

9. One account claimed that the father named the boy Siddhartha after an uncle, a Brahman priest, who lived in the area.

10. Dhamma, *The First Discourse of the Buddha*, 1.

11. Lefebure, *The Buddha and the Christ*, 5.

12. At death, she becomes a goddess. She dies so her womb never holds another life (Corless, *The Vision of Buddhism*, 6).

13. Lefebure, *The Buddha and the Christ*, 7.

14. Luz and Michaels, *Encountering Jesus & Buddha*, 10.

15. Armstrong, *Buddha*, 31–32.

Siddhartha was provided every comfort, including an umbrella to always shield him from the harsh sun. He was carried through his father's rice fields in a lavish palanquin befitting a prince, moving to a different mansion each season. Each palace was filled with lavish perfumes and harems of dancing maidens. The prince could beckon musicians at any time and enjoyed skilled chefs cooking the most delicious foods imaginable. He excelled in swimming, wrestling, fencing, archery, hunting within forests of mango and tamarind trees, and fishing in crystal mountain streams. He also received lessons in literature and the arts of warfare. His teachers were amazed that the prince knew more about the subjects being taught than his teachers.

When Siddhartha was about twelve (like Jesus), he was taken to a temple to be dedicated to God: a scarlet thread of devotion was placed around his wrist. When he was sixteen, his father arranged a marriage with a girl of fourteen, Bashundhara (meaning "possessor of radiance"), who was a stunningly beautiful maiden of the warrior class. The king gave lavish gifts to the couple, including three new palaces.

THE GREAT GOING FORWARD

Inevitably, Siddhartha disobeyed his father's order not to leave the palace-grounds.[16] His tranquil life was filled with boredom, and he felt restless to know what was being hidden from him. In a series of adventures, the prince escaped the palace and saw the *four passing sights*. The prince first saw a feeble, senile old man. Second, he saw an invalid racked with pain and deformity. Third, he saw a somber funeral procession filled with weeping mourners, who taught the boy that, in Shakespeare's words, "A man can die but once. / We owe God a death."[17]

The fourth sight was of a group of begging sages renouncing the world in search of the truth. Siddhartha realized that what had been presented to him about life was an empty façade, and that all his possessions were distractions that slowed his search for truth. He was impressed that these monks had turned their backs on everything he had enjoyed, and so he joined their efforts to "explore the realms of the spirit."[18]

---

16. In alternative readings, the king also made sure that all the villagers cheered his son as he passed. One senile man, however, broke through the cordon and smashed the façade of order.

17. Shakespeare, *King Henry IV, Part 2*, act 3, scene 2, lines 242–43.

18. Armstrong, *Buddha*, 10.

At age twenty-nine, deep longings swelled in Siddhartha's heart, and his mind steamed to a boiling point. Everything inside of him cried out for change, and even the natural world seemed to crave transformation—as the poet Rumi explains, "Grapes cry out to turn into wine."[19] For Siddhartha, past sensualities now felt like constricting chains, and the luxuries of life crowded his soul, making his heart heavy.[20] The prince reached a breaking-point of despair when his wife gave birth to a son named Rahula (meaning "to be chained"). When he told his father of his desire to become a wandering monk, the king replied that he could follow that path only after he had met all his responsibilities as a father. He felt like a choking boa constrictor gripped his heart.

One night, when all the "dancing girls lay strewn about the floor snoring and drooling, all of their enchantments gone," Siddhartha fled the palace.[21] His final act as a prince was to enter his wife's bedroom and kiss her and his baby. He had decided to leave all that was familiar and not return until he found peace. The prince cut his hair and left the palace in search of a teacher. This event is called the *great going forth* or *renunciation*. One poet relates that the next morning when his wife realized what had happened, "she fell on the ground like a duck who has lost its life-mate."[22] She refused all comfort and began to die of a broken heart.

On his first day of exile, the prince met a beggar who exchanged his rags for the prince's silk robes covered in jewels. Siddhartha was beginning a spiritual search similar to the one undertaken by father Abraham, who also fled the comforts of home in an uncertain quest. As was true of Jesus and Muhammad, the path of prophetic destiny often begins when a person decides to forsake the bustle of pedestrian life and choose a path of revolutionary effort. It is an ancient story: each person walks from the womb to the tomb, but for most, life's journey is rarely marked by introspection. Siddhartha realized the truth asserted by Jesus that if we want to find ourselves we first have to lose ourselves (Matt 10:39; 16:25).

Siddhartha spent the next six years wandering with a group of monks who lived in the jungle—exposed to the extremes of heat and cold, sleeping on the ground or on beds made of thorns. One scholar explains, "Gautama went either naked or clad in the roughest hemp. He slept out in the open during freezing winter nights, lay on his breath for so long that his head

---

19. Kornfield, *After Ecstasy, the Laundry*, 3. Kornfield quotes Albert Camus on the topic of human searching (10): "A man's life is nothing but an extended trek through the detours of art to recapture those one or two moments when his heart first opened."

20. Armstrong, *Buddha*, 1.

21. Corless, *The Vision of Buddhism*, 8.

22. Kinnard, *The Emergence of Buddhism*, 9.

seemed to split and there was a fearful roaring in his ears. His hair fell out and his skin became black and withered."[23] He ate so rarely that his "gaunt ribs became like crazy rafters of a tumbledown shed."[24] Most of his time was spent meditating and studying the Vedas. Siddhartha entered long trances and practiced various techniques of *yoga* (meaning "to bind"), which tethered spiritual power to human effort. It was at this time that his father and wife sent priests in search of the prince to plead that he return home. When they found him, they reported that Siddhartha was already dead to the world.

ENLIGHTENMENT

After many years, even though Siddhartha had perfected every skill in meditation, he was no closer to his goal of enlightenment. All his efforts left him unsatisfied, filled with a sense of failure and lack of liberation. He was only weakening his own health, pushing himself to an early death. Siddhartha, now thirty-eight years old, decided he would no longer fast and said farewell to his company of monks. At his departure, they questioned his level of commitment.

Siddhartha walked to the edge of the Nairanjana River and decided to rest. Soon, a village woman approached him with an offering of rice milk, which he accepted.[25] Wayworn and alone, Siddhartha had made no spiritual discovery. The next day, he wandered into the village of Badh Gaya in North India where he rested under the arms of an ancient fig tree along the banks of the Phalgu River. It was the day of the full moon in May 544 BCE.[26] Siddhartha plopped down against the Bodhi tree's trunk and faced eastward, deciding not to move until he gained spiritual wisdom. The tree was to become as vital to Buddhists as is the cross to Christians.

While waiting in meditation, Siddhartha encountered many temptations. The devilish goddess Mara (meaning "destruction") counseled him to deny all wasted efforts and return to a quiet life of wealth and ease at the palace of his father. Mara was a cunning foe who was trying to lead Siddhartha astray with different stratagems. In one of Mara's most subtle attacks,

23. Armstrong, *Buddha*, 63.

24. Fisher, ed., *An Anthology of Living Religions*, 137.

25. Ross (*Buddhism*, 14) says she had prepared this dish in advance because of a vision that she would meet a great soul. When Buddha finished eating, he threw the golden bowl into the river and it miraculously floated upstream—symbolic that his teaching was "against the ordinary flow of men's minds." The golden bowl came to rest at the dwelling place of the Serpent King (12).

26. Ross, *Buddhism*, 14.

Mara tried to persuade Siddhartha that the new ideas he had discovered were too complicated to be grasped by ordinary folks, so he should keep them to himself.

Other attacks were more direct. Mara launched ten armies of horrid demons with the faces of boars, fish, horses, camels, tigers, bears, and elephants to swirl around Siddhartha.[27] One oozing, puss-faced demon had hair blazing with fire, and others had many mouths or only one eye. Even the Serpent-King, Malinda, appeared with his raised, menacing cobra hood.[28] When these efforts failed, Mara sought to seduce Siddhartha with visions of dancing maidens. Then Siddhartha realized that even these beauties were only bags of bone and excrement who would invariably decay into old hags before transforming into rotting corpses.

Each attack spawned a new revelation into the passing nature of life. Siddhartha saw "himself and all of life as a vast process, an ever-moving stream of becoming and extinctions, and he recognized as ridiculous the idea of the existence of an individual ego."[29] In a moment of insight, Siddhartha touched the ground with his hand. This grounding of life, this contact with the truth of solid earth, forced the demons to flee from Buddha. Enlightenment was a victory over evil, a triumph of soul and spirit over the body. Siddhartha realized in the stillness of his heart that "spiritual enlightenment was not a gift from some divine being."[30] His motionlessness became the revolutionary pivot-point of history. Siddhartha Gautama became Lord Buddha. Past lives flashed before him; he viewed all the world's suffering and was filled with compassion.

Later, on the first night in this exalted state, Buddha received the first truth as an enlightened soul: From good must come good, and from evil must come evil. He saw the universality of suffering. All ritual prayers, incantations, and devotional sacrifices were pointless. Suffering came from attachment and desires. The social caste system was invalid, and the Hindu teaching that the world was created by Brahma was false: The world never began, and it would never end. Desire could be quenched, and a path was available towards freedom.

---

27. Each of these ten armies represented an evil such as sloth, fear, sexual desire, thirst, and so on.

28. According to Ross (*Buddhism*, 17), Mucalinda was not threatening Siddhartha but was there to protect him: "And when Mara, desperate sent raging storms to force the Buddha from his meditative pose, a Serpent King, Mucalinda, issuing forth from the roots of a nearby tree, wound his body in coils under the serene figure and raised his protective cobra hood until the storms abated."

29. Ross, *Buddhism*, 16.

30. Kinnard, *The Emergence of Buddhism*, 1.

For the next days, Buddha sat silently and received revelation. Now empty of himself, mind, soul, and heart were filled with wave after wave of purifying insight. On the second night, Buddha received a revelation that life is a constant cycle of birth and rebirth. During the third night, Buddha received the Four Noble Truths and the Eightfold Path, which would lead people to nirvana—a state of existence where it is like a person is able to cool off after a fierce fever.

These moments of enlightenment brought Buddhism to birth. Supreme wisdom had entered a mortal and changed that man into something more than a mere mortal. Nature responded with enthusiasm: "the flowering trees bloomed; the system of ten thousand worlds was like a bouquet of flowers sent whirling through the air."[31] In a moment, enlightenment tore down false notions that each of us is separate, incomplete, and imperfect.

A MISSION TO TEACH

Lord Buddha withdrew into the jungle where he again confronted Mara, the evil one. This devilish embodiment suggested that Buddha pass immediately into his rightful reward of bliss without teaching because humanity was incapable of understanding his message. Mara tempted Buddha to turn the Himalayas into gold and to perform other miracles. Buddha responded by touching the earth once again, and once again the temptress Mara fled.

Buddha stayed beneath the tree of enlightenment for seven weeks where it would have been easy to linger within the warm glow of peaceful realization. Instead, he decided to teach. This decision was, in a profound sense, counterintuitive. Chinese painters have long celebrated the journey of the "Walking Buddha" as he begins his ministry. One painting portrays a "tired, thin, shabby, even sad and anxious man standing on a windy slope, gazing down . . . into the valley toward which Buddha must travel to begin his mission."[32]

After traveling to Varanasi (Benares), Buddha sought out the five monks he had known from his wanderings, and he found them three miles north of the city, at the Deer Park. When his friends recognized him, they called him by the name Siddhartha and assumed he had returned to them as a weak-willed backslider. Instead, Buddha told him that his new name was

---

31. Armstrong, *Buddha*, 92. The quote continues, "The ocean lost its salty taste, the blind and deaf were able to see and hear, cripples could walk, and the fetters of prisoners fell to the ground."

32. Ross, *Buddhism*, 19–20.

now Tathagata, the "Truth-attained One."[33] The term Buddha was widely used at that time to describe a great teacher, and this became the name people used to honor his message.

The wheel of Buddhism was set in motion with his first sermon at the Deer Park. The message that he preached led to his first follower, Khodanna, to gain a "steel-eyed dharma-eye," which enabled him to gain a glimpse of nirvana and to enter the stream toward truth. Four other former monks also began to follow Buddha. From those first five "stream-enterers" came fifty-five other saints who became *arhats*, attaining enlightenment. Now, 2,500 years later, it is intriguing to think that anyone passing this group of six monks conversing in the cool of the evening at the Deer Park in Varanasi was watching the launch of a new world religion.

Buddha expounded another lesson that became known as the Fire Sermon.[34] This sermon, explaining human nature, was repeated by followers as they dispersed to persuade others. Soon, thousands of new believers embraced the Four Noble Truths and the Eightfold Path. Even Buddha's earthly father and family joined the embryonic community.

For the next forty-five years, Buddha wandered up and down India's Ganges valley delivering eighty-four thousand sermons that addressed life's eighty-four thousand distinct problems. At first, his disciples lectured in every season until some Jains criticized them for "trampling down the new grass, distressing plants, and hurting many little creatures."[35] Because Buddha agreed with the Jain doctrine of ahimsa, to "do no harm" to any plants or animals, he instructed followers only to preach during the warmer, drier months. During the wet, monsoon season (June to October), Buddha led followers on an extended retreat of meditation and daily teachings. The Buddha's orations were so gripping that listeners never once coughed or even cleared their throats.

Powerful critics emerged who attacked the new message. Religious leaders noted it was scandalous that he had left his wife and children to become a wandering teacher. One of his early followers, sometimes known as the Buddhist Judas Iscariot, even tried to assassinate Buddha (perhaps

---

33. According to Thich Nhât Hanh (in *The Raft is Not the Shore*, 43), the other nine names are *Arhat*—"worthy of respect," *Sammasambuddha*—"perfectly enlightened," *Vidyacaranasampana*—"endowed with insight," *Sugata*—"one travelling happily along the path," *Lokavida*—"one who knows the world well," *Anuttarapurusadamyasarathi*—"leader of those being taught," *Sastadevamanusyanam*—"teacher of gods and humans," *Buddha*—"enlightened one," and *Bhagavat*—"blessed one."

34. This sermon was given at Elephant Rock near the Rajagriha Valley where a jungle-fire was burning (Simpkins and Simpkins, *Simple Buddhism*, 13).

35. Armstrong, *Buddha*, 139.

out of jealousy): he made many attempts, including trying to crush him with a huge boulder and trying to get him trampled by a raging elephant.[36]

Women also became interested in Buddha's teachings and requested that nunneries be established. Although this request was granted, one dubious tradition claims that Buddha hesitated before allowing for this development. This will be discussed further in a later chapter.

After traveling on foot for over four decades across India, Buddha's body had worn out like an old cart stuck in the mud. He retired to a monastery to spend the rest of his life in teaching and meditation. Even then, Buddha's tireless teaching style was energetic. One of his strengths was the ability to adapt instructions to each audience by telling stories and sharing parables. Whenever Buddha was given a question, he always answered with patience. As an educator, Buddha spoke to both friends and enemies; even to the fierce mass-murdering thief Anguilla (of the "thousand-fingered necklace").[37] As a drummer with a singular focus, Buddha tirelessly beat out the drumbeat that the thick darkness of our age could be overcome by hearts filled with loving compassion.[38]

ENTERING NIRVANA

When Buddha reached eighty years of age, his body bore the marks of a wearying struggle. *Pari nibbana*, his time to enter the ultimate nirvana, was

---

36. Armstrong (*Buddha*, 168) reports when Nilgiri the elephant "saw his prey, he was overcome by the waves of love that emanated from the Buddha, lowered his trunk and stood still while the Buddha stroked his forehead, explaining to him that violence would not help him in the next life. Nilgiri took dust off the Buddha's feet with his trunk, sprinkled it over his forehead, and retreated backward, gazing yearningly at the Buddha" before returning to his stable, "a reformed beast from that day forth."

37. There are countless variants on the conversion of Angulimala to Buddhism. In one account, Angulimala at birth was first named Ahimisaka, meaning "harmless." At his birth, all the weapons in his hometown flashed with light, and a holy man warned that the boy should be killed at birth. Instead, he was spared and began a killing spree where he vowed to kill a thousand people. He basically killed anyone in his path to fulfill this vow. He lost track of how many he had killed and decided to cut off one finger from each victim to keep a tally. Unfortunately, some of the fingers were eaten by vultures and others were lost. Still others decomposed. His decided to make a garland of fingers, which is how he got his name Angulimala, meaning "thief-garland." He collected 999 fingers but could not kill a final victim and vowed that whoever he next met would face his sword. This happened to be his mother, but Buddha intervened, and Angulimala decided to kill him instead. A miracle happened where the killer could not catch Buddha even though he was running and Buddha was walking very slowly, barely moving. He then became a follower of Buddha (Armstrong, *Buddha*, 138–51).

38. Carmody and Carmody, *Serene Compassion* 19.

drawing near. At the end of his final three-month teaching mission, and when he laid down on a chair placed between two trees, the trees miraculously bloomed out of season. When a farmer unintentionally gave Buddha some rancid, poisonous mushrooms, he accepted the offering, sent word to forgive the farmer, and told his students that it was time to abandon his earthly body.[39]

Buddha's final homily ended by announcing, "I have taught you things that I have experienced fully for myself."[40] Buddha's earthly work was done, and he had no need for any further births. A community had been launched that would continue sharing the creed to those hungry for freedom from deceptions. With his final breath, Buddha told his close friend, "All individual things die. Seek your liberation with diligence."[41] He then lay down in the lion-pose among a grove of mango trees.[42] Buddha fell into a deep trance-like coma and left this life.[43] Even his death was an impartational event, showing followers how to die with grace and dignity. A wealthy disciple paid for the body to be cremated and buried beneath a towering monument (*stupa*). After cremation, some of the remaining bones were thoughtfully distributed to various monastic communities as an act of loving respect.

A LIFE GIVEN AS A GIFT

Anglican bishop Stephen Neill (1900–1984) affirmed that in the life of Lord Buddha compassion breathes and takes form. The focal point of devotion for millions, Buddha is misunderstood if seen as "some type of superman or extraterrestrial alien that just appeared on the earth endowed with superhuman qualities."[44] Each of us has the potential to fully express our inner

---

39. Armstrong, *Buddha*, 178.

40. Armstrong, *Buddha*, 178. Ross explains, "Pig or boar's meat was regarded by all Indians of that time as unclean and unwholesome and would, under no circumstances, or by anyone on whatever social level, have been offered to a respected teacher and an assembly of monks. In this view, the repast offered the Buddha would most certainly have been truffles" (*Buddhism*, 34).

41. Armstrong, *Buddha*, 187.

42. The river is not named. Ross notes, "He lay down on his right side in the attitude of a lion with one foot on the other. This was the same pose in which he was soon to die, a pose which can be seen today in a gigantic rock-hewn statue from the twelfth century lying in awesome quiet in the open green countryside at Polonnaruwa in Sri Lanka") (*Buddhism*, 33–34).

43. Technically, he did not die because that would imply that he would return to the earth again.

44. Dragpa, *Uniting Wisdom and Compassion*, 11.

Buddha Nature. Buddhism's central tenet is that his experience of truth can become our reality.

Many Hindu and Jain teachers recognize Buddha as an avatar of Krishna. Many Jews, Muslims, and Christians recognize that Buddha was a great teacher and prophet of moral virtue. Buddha is not a god, but also not an ordinary man. To borrow Christian terminology, Buddha was an eternal *logos* of truth. To use Jain and Vedic language, Buddha was a *Jina*, or conqueror, because he overcame the world's evils. To use Jewish and Muslim language, Buddha was a prophet who spoke with clarity from the heart. Whatever terms are used to describe him, there should be no essentialized summation that rips the thousand-petaled lotus of Buddhism into little pieces. The life and message of Buddha are vaster than the oceans—a gift to all humanity.

4

Buddhist Dharma

On the temple bell has settled—and is glittering—a firefly.
—Masaoka Shiki (1867-1902)

WORLDVIEW ASSUMPTIONS

THE DECLARATION "I TAKE refuge in the teaching" is a foundation of Buddhism. The term *Buddha dharma* describes a seamless link between Buddha's life and message. Buddha taught, "whoever has seen me has seen the *dharma* and whoever has heard the *dharma* has seen me."[1]

In this book, I try to avoid some technical religious terms (often in Sanskrit or Pali) that might blur Buddha's teachings. Distinctions about context and content certainly have their place, but my hope is to provide as much clarity as possible for those not familiar with such terms, often difficult to translate from ancient languages. One starting point might be to emphasize what the Buddha dharma does not teach. For example, non-Buddhists should appreciate that Buddhism does not teach us to worship Buddha as if he were a god. Instead, Buddha's teachings are a driving force that expresses itself in different ways and at different times. The Buddha dharma is best learned not by studying books but by practicing with mentor-teachers, through lived experience. The shifting currents of life are the only place to learn the truths of Buddhism. Truth must be lived in order to be the

1. Ruland, *Imagining the Sacred*, 91.

truth. The direction one takes when starting a journey determines where a journey will end. This is also true when thinking about how the Buddha dharma relates to our lives. If we approach Buddhism with defensive fears, we are unlikely to be able to appreciate its transforming, healing message.

Alternatively, one should embrace a posture of humility and heuristic openness to learn. I am reminded of a story from Arabia about a man who was once wrongly accused of a crime and sent to prison. A friend promised that he would help him escape. But when the friend visited the prison, instead of providing the prisoner with a saw to cut his lock he gave a prayer mat. At first, the prisoner was confused (and even angry) at this gift. Since he had time on his hands, however, he decided to use the prayer mat to pray. Every day, as he bowed down, he became aware that the designs on the prayer mat held a message. Eventually, he realized that woven into the rug was a diagram of the prison's lock, and, following its directions he was able to unlock the door and escape into freedom. In the same way, Buddhism teaches that often we may not find what we need by looking outward or by relying on past experiences. Instead, we need a sense of openness to see what is already inside us and to appreciate what we already possess.

Long before there were Buddhist scriptures, there was already the Buddha, the teachings, and the community. The written texts arose from a specific context and were not originally compiled into a singular tradition. Over time, texts emerged from a spoken tradition, but its purposes were practical, not for analytically detached evaluation. Many texts were first written in the Pali of common people before being later translated into the formal Sanskrit of the elite. While many Christians concern themselves with how their scriptures relate to divine revelation, Buddhists view their scriptures as practical study tools. The issue of the perfection or imperfection of the texts is not a concern for Buddhists. Additionally, even the notion of an authorized collection (canon) of scripture is a concept rooted in Christian assumptions about sacred texts. Buddhist views of holy books have more in common with Hindu and Jain understandings of the role of writings from the elite passed down throughout history.

A BUDDHIST CANON

Shortly after the earthly life of Buddha, followers met to discuss what scriptures were reliable. They recalled from memory some of the key teachings emphasized by Buddha. Over time, other convocations took place in Sri Lanka and in other communities as followers decided what writings to use and which to avoid.

One such conference in India, around the time of Christ, lasted over nine months, and the chosen texts became known as the Pali Canon. In Japan, a collection of scriptures about monastic life known as the Taisho Edition was given the status of an authoritative text.[2] More than a century after Buddha, the great king Asoka organized a gathering of scholars to agree upon a standard collection of scriptures. Even later, about eight hundred years after the life of the Buddha, another conference was held to consider these same issues. Sometimes different versions were used among followers of the Mahayanan and Theravadan schools.[3] Although some writings were added and others were subtracted, one of the most used texts, known as the *Dharmapada*, or "The Way of the Buddha's Teachings," managed to survive every edit. Claiming to present the actual words of Buddha, this small book, with only 422 verses, still provides a practical path for how best Buddhists should determine are the most central teachings of Buddhism.

One piece of writing commonly used among Buddhists is the *Three Baskets (Tripitaka)*; because some of the writings were first written onto palm leaves and preserved in specially woven baskets (*pitaka*). One collection, the *Basket of Monastic Order (Vinaya Pitaka)* offered practical guidelines for how to organize a monastic community. Another collection is called the *Basket of Higher Teachings (Abhidharma Pitaka)*, which includes sections on philosophy, psychology, and the subtleties of the law. Another collection, the *Basket of Discourses (Sutra Pitaka)*, consists of biographical facts about 547 earlier lives of Buddha before his final incarnation. One of the most famous of these biographies is the *Book of Great Events*, which dates from the fourth century CE.[4] In this text, Buddha is shown to appear in past lives as a miracle worker, king, scholar, slave, crafty thief, gambler, and as many animals. In one story, Buddha came to earth as a rabbit in order to throw himself into a fire to save a holy man, starving in the forest.

SCRIPTURES

As Buddhism spread across China, Tibet, Japan, Korea, and Southeast Asia, the scriptures used also changed to address local needs. The word used to describe chapters of sacred writings is *sutras*. There are also commentaries

---

2. Buddha made few rules about monastic communities because "the historic Buddha personally considered all ritual of any kind superfluous" (Ross, *Buddhism*, 36).

3. East Asian Buddhists generally follow the *Dhaarmaguptaka* tradition.

4. Luz and Michaels, *Encountering Jesus & Buddha*, 4. Another book he mentions is the *Lalitavistara* or "Complete Description of the Game" (the "Game" refers to life) from the fourth century CE.

on the sutras called *sastras*. One of the most popular sutras among Greater Path Buddhists is called the *Sutra of the Lotus of the Good Law* which describes, in poetic language, the perfection of wisdom. One of the devotional practices from this book is the mantra *om mani padme hum*, which literally means, "the jewel in the lotus" and refers to the Buddha's loving heart of compassion for the world.

Finally, there are tantric writings intended to be esoteric passages often written in a coded language and which require the explanation of a guru. Sometimes, these writings are filled with mysterious charms and spells, and sometimes, obscene language is used to shock us into deeper levels of insight. One translator critical of these writings disparaged that they included, "thousands and thousands of pages filled with statements about cosmic tortoises and sky dogs, about gods dressed in fur coats and tiger skins living in iron palaces or copper fortresses."[5] As unusual as such teaching methods might seem, the goal was simply to use language to turn the world "upside-down in order to challenge assumptions among those unwilling to embrace tantric truths."[6] Tantric teachings assume that everything has a secretive and spiritual dimension. Even the human body embodies a "code" for deeper truths. Therefore, some tantric teachings promote heterosexual and homosexual practices, alcohol, and drugs as vehicles to gain wisdom insights.[7]

ORTHODOX THERAVADAN PERSPECTIVES

What are the main differences between the Orthodox Theravadan and Greater Path (Mahayanan) Buddhist traditions? Both teach that the Buddha dharma provides the pathway to eternal peace. Both advocate mindfulness and meditation.

For Orthodox Buddhists, we enter the stream of enlightenment in a progressive way after consistent training and mastery of meditation practices. We must strive to comprehend vast quantities of knowledge and to avoid mental distractions before we gain enlightenment. Our example is Buddha himself, who won the Path after years of exertion and intense concentration. Orthodox Buddhists assume anyone seeking enlightenment will need to go through levels of membership in a monastic community. Only a selfless person can smash the thick chains of selfishness that imprison us.

---

5. Conze, ed., *Concise Encyclopedia of Living Faiths*, 266.

6. Davis, "Religions of India in Practice," 45.

7. Of the detachment of some people with their bodies, James Joyce describes one of the characters in one of his novels as "Mr. Duffy lived a short distance from his body" (Kornfield, *After the Ecstasy, the Laundry*, 175).

Enlightenment is not given; it is achieved. The heavy karma wheel of actions is lifted off our shoulders, not by grace from the gods, but through practicing ego and mind cleansing in community. Education is stressed because we should cherish knowledge (*anna*) and attack ignorance. Success or failure can be determined by even the slightest moral lapse. Every misdirected thought is like a water droplet falling on a priceless masterpiece—ruining the work.

GREATER PATH PERSPECTIVES

The Greater Path is the largest expression of Buddhism worldwide—practiced widely in China, Tibet, Japan, and Korea. The goal for Mahayana is to remain true to the Buddha dharma without becoming caught up in dry rituals and complex theological formulations.

The Greater Path worldview emphasizes that everything is cyclical, with no idea of an original creation or a final apocalypse as taught by Christians and Muslims. The passing of time is explained with a parable about a community of monks dedicated to polishing away a huge mountain by stroking the side of the mountain every hundred years with a single swipe of a cloth. Even as everything is changing, nothing is changing quickly.

Further, "everything that exists implies everything else."[8] Nothing can be separated from anything else, and everything is interrelated. Each of us is only a small piece of a vast universe, and each of us can be compared to a blind sea turtle bobbing in a huge ocean, who, by chance one time, is able to put her head through a floating ring randomly drifting across the waves. The complexity of everything is far beyond our ability to understand life's profundities; death, heaven, hell, past, present, and a world swarming with an uncountable number of spirits (*deva*).[9] Whether such beings exist or are only representations of ideas is an irrelevant question. Even though in Asia anyone can easily observe artwork or rituals that suggest a person's afterlife in heaven or hell, such ideas are fundamentally irrelevant to Buddhism. While Orthodox critics claim the Greater Path practice of focusing on supernatural beings shows they have strayed from truth into an endless quagmire of mythological folklore, Greater Path teachers counter that their first missionaries into East Asia allowed for these already existing views to help listeners eventually grasp more vital truths.

---

8. Watts, *Buddhism*, 45.

9. In one conversation I had at a Buddhist monastery in Yunnan, China, the monk said that there were at least twenty-six different heavenly realms.

Greater Path missionaries were familiar with Vedic ideas about the laws of karma. Instead of rejecting these views, Greater Path Buddhists used these ideas to convey deeper meanings. The law of karma teaches that each event is like a snowball that can lead to an avalanche of other events. Buddhists refashioned this idea to teach that what had been called karma were really actions that could not be carried over from one life to another.

When missionaries encountered local views, they did not cast aside long-held assumptions. For example, before Buddha, Indians believed that the world was a vast range of seven concentric squares of golden mountains called *Meru* (or *Sumeru*).[10] Early missionaries felt no need to disabuse their listeners about previously held ideas of a hellish place of torment for those caught in blind, egoistic sensuality and lustful, insatiable debauchery. Because Buddhism is clear that there is no afterlife, such notions remained only as effective morality fables. Indeed, Buddha's "Fire Sermon" taught: "How can there be laughter, how can there be pleasure when the whole world is burning?"[11] The Chinese idea that adulterers, for example, would be boiled alive in a steaming cauldron in hell for thirty thousand years was allowed to remain because it was effective in scaring people from adultery. Traditions from before Buddha which taught that evil people would be boiled, roasted, burnt, cut, frozen, eaten, or pierced with sharp red-hot swords for repeated millennia by flesh-hungry ghost-monsters and fiendish demons were also allowed to remain to serve the greater purpose of keeping people away from actions harmful to others.

When non-Buddhists conflate practices criticized and not crticized by Buddhist missionaries, they come to misunderstand efforts to win people over to Buddhist principles. As a missionary religion, Buddhism accepts a degree of syncretism to advance larger objectives. In the same way, observers

---

10. Corless, *The Vision of Buddhism*, 138. Each world-system is 1,200,875 *yojanas* in diameter. A *yojana* is one day's march and is set at nine statute-miles, thus the system is about 10,807,875 miles across. Corless writes: "In the Great Ocean are four continents, each with a different shape and color. The northern continent is *Uttara-Kuru*, which is "square in shape and dark blue or green in color. Life is pleasant, relaxed and bucolic. There are no villages and people are 48 feet tall and live 2,000 years." On *Aparagodana* (also called *Godaniya*) to the West, life is more hurried. The continent is circular and red and the villagers, who have round red faces, are about 24 feet and live 500 years. *Purvavideha* (*Videha*) to the east is semicircular and residents have white, half-moon-shaped faces, are twelve feet tall and live 250 years. The continent of *Jambudvipa*, to the South of *Meru* is our world. It is shaped like a triangle with its point toward the south and is golden in color. Our sky is sapphire or lapis lazuli blue, but we are about 5 or 6 feet tall and we live a maximum of 100 years. In the center of our land is a cosmic *jambu* or rose-apple tree, from which we get our name *Jambu-dvipa*, 'Rose-Apple-Tree' Continent" (138–39).

11. Lefebure, *The Buddha and the Christ*, 20.

who point out dimensions of myth that seem antiscientific remaining in Buddhism fail to appreciate this dynamic. In fact, there has never been any scientific insight which poses any "serious challenges to Buddhism's worldview in general or to Buddhist practice."[12]

Unlike the Christian tradition, which speaks of a vast metanarrative, the Greater Path claims that there is no such metanarrative. Each of us is as limited in understanding our world as is a miniscule ant on a vast anthill the size of the universe, to understand theirs. It is absurd to suggest that any category of knowledge can explain that which is unlimited. Further, we should not assume that there is a difference between the seen and the unseen. It is impossible to explain the vastness of everything.

PERSONHOOD

Unlike Christianity, Buddhism teaches that there is no continuous nature of a human being. Rejecting the idea that we are distinct individuals is a first step towards an accurate view of personhood. Zen Master Mumom taught that enlightenment is "the moment of total self-oblivion, of knowing without knowing and seeing without seeing, in which being is born out of nothingness."[13]

How do we experience the world if we are not a distinct self? Buddhism teaches that we perceive the world through five aggregates (*skandha*) which vaguely approximate the five senses. The five *skandha*, located in our minds, are our sensations, predispositions, or "preconditioning" (*samskara*), perceptions (*sanna*), and feelings (*vedana*). Our body (*rupa*) and an intuitive, hidden sense, like our sense of consciousness (*vijnana*), also define our experience of this temporal world.

These ideas evoke the views of philosopher Edmund Husserl (via Kant), who rejected the dualistic subject/object model of earlier philosophers, and who taught that humans live in a private "life-world" of phenomena. Phenomenology articulates that the experience of living in the world is constructed, not individually, but in a historical context. As the ideas of phenomenologists developed, new explorations by thinkers such as the deconstructionist Jacques Derrida and the postmodernist Emmanuel Levinas taught that all knowledge is fragmentary and intersubjective. Reality, to be grasped, should be deconstructed, and decentered away from socially created assumptions and linguistic assertions.

---

12. Ingram, *Buddhist–Christian Dialogue*, 75.
13. Dumoulin, *Christianity Meets Buddhism*, 49.

Think of your life (and yourself) as an ever-developing story or composition. Like a book, you exist as part of something larger—language and literature—that existed before you, and that will exist after you. When you embrace this assumption, you are free from any delusions about individuality. Just as a book is fundamentally a collection of words, paragraphs, and pages, so a person is fundamentally a collection of experiences that come together and eventually come apart. The Dalai Lama explains that what we think of as our lives are a collection of "many causes and conditions" that are interdependent.[14] What we call our "individual lives" are nothing more than the interplay of one's *skandha*. How we feel, think, dream, and hope are constantly giving us a false sense of our individuality. Experiences come together to make who we are. Once we cease to exist, these experiences also cease to exist. Another way to think about our identity is to consider a car, which is not a single reality but a collection of parts that eventually breaks apart.[15] In the same way, the disparate "parts" (*skandha*) of our lives are what make up our experience of existence.

T. S. Eliot, in "The Dry Salvages," the third of the *Four Quartets*, writes about a man waiting for a train; the poem's speaker observes that the man waiting for the train is not the same person as the man who will eventually board the train and read the newspaper. The person who exists in the present does not exist in either the past or the future. Zen Master Dogen explained, "Spring does not become Summer. First, there is Spring and then there is Summer. Each season stays in its own place."[16] Everything happens in the present, and who you are is not your past, but actually only what you are doing right now.

Understanding this view frees us from illusions about the past or the future that can cause suffering and keep us from living in the present. Everything changes from moment to moment. What is past can never be recaptured. We are not a distinct individual but a collection of many things, a kaleidoscopic conglomeration of feelings, experiences, ideas, and thoughts. When we grasp that "life is a condition of transiency and flux is unarguable," we will be freed from anxieties about what has happened or might happen.[17]

---

14. Dalai Lama XIV, *Essence of the Heart Sutra*, 115.

15. Quoted in Ross, *Buddhism*, 29. David Hume writes: "For my part when I enter most intimately into what I call myself, I always stumble on some perception of the other. . . I can never catch myself at any time without a perception . . . What we call mind is nothing, but a heap or bundle of different perceptions united by certain relations," a concept interestingly like that of *Skandhas*.

16. Watts, *Buddhism*, 5.

17. Ross, *Buddhism*, 30.

We are deceived into a prison of our own making whenever we fixate on our inevitable decay or live with a nostalgia for what can never return.

For Christians, the ideas of a permanent self and distinct identity are assumed. In contrast, Buddhism explains that such views lead to wasted lives. Nothing is final: Everything is in the process of either becoming or dissolving. All that is in the world is a composite (*sabbe sankkhara anicca*). We are like cherry blossoms that flourish in the morning and wither a few hours later in the frosty dusk of the same day. Our lives are like the wake of a hulking ship at sea, which, as soon as it can be traced, vanishes back into the current. Just as the laws of thermodynamics teach, everything—including our lives—are in a state of constant flux.

Because nothing in this world is permanent (and there is no such thing as a permanent soul), nothing intrinsically unchanged can transmigrate from one body to the next or ascend to a heaven. There can be no validity to concepts such as the idea of an unchanging God behind the universe. Death is merely a constructed boundary—arbitrarily assigned to describe the transition between one set of events and another set of events.

NON-SOUL

Buddha taught that the self is not unique—having no specific beginning or ending. This doctrine of "no-self" (*anatta*) does not negate our value as a person because there is no personhood to negate. We are like a river—constantly changing. What is real about us is that we are empty (*shunyata*) of something distinct. Just as a shadow—with no substance—follows us in the twilight, so the idea of individuality follows our collection of experiences. In the same way that clothing takes shape only when it is worn, we have an identity only when we fill the present with our experiences, feelings, and ideas (*skandha*).

By contrast, Christians rarely question the idea of a distinct self because the individual is the focus of God's care and attention for all eternity. To hold to such views makes us feel significant—putting us at the center of our worlds. We take comfort in knowing there is something eternal about who we are. Christians exposed for the first time to the Buddhist idea of no-self may argue that accepting such an idea makes life meaningless. From a Buddhist perspective, however, the opposite is true. The doctrine of no-self allows us to be more naturally compassionate, alive to our actual genuine sense of fundamental interrelatedness.

When we embrace the idea of no-self, we need not struggle with a false idea. The truth of being a non-self also means that it is absurd to focus on our self-worth. Freed from such illusions, we are freed from a downward spiral of suffering tied to egoism, attachment, and worry about something illusionary. A belief in a distinct self is a self-imposed ball-and-chain fixation on selfish needs and desires. Accepting the truth of no-self makes it easier, it is argued, for us to be ethical, generous, and moral in our actions towards others.[18] According to the Dalai Lama, this truth is an absolutely affirming, and in no way a negative, principle.[19] He expounds: "When we say that all phenomena are void of self-existence, it does not mean that we are advocating non-existence, or that we are repudiating that things exist."[20] What is being negated is the false view that anything exists independently.

How do our actions relate to our identity if we do not have a distinct self? Just as a child bears little resemblance to an adult and is only linked to that person through experience and causes, so our past is only superficially linked to our present. Science teaches that even the physiological components of our bodies are totally changed many times over within our lifetime from childhood to adulthood. In our deaths, there is nothing that continues except in the minds and thoughts of others. Some might feel that this view is depressing, but it is only so perceived because it destroys false notions of a permanent identity and an eternal soul. The rejection of our individuality is not a rejection of being human and being interrelated through our individuation with all of life.[21]

WOMEN AND BUDDHISM

Buddhism teaches that everyone is of equal worth. In Buddhism, unlike in Christianity, there are no statements comparable to the biblical verses that women should "be subject" to men (Eph 5:22; 1 Pet 3:1) or are the "weaker sex" (1 Pet 3:7). There is no Buddhist claim that women were created after men or that humanity has been marred with a sinful nature because of the disobedience of a first female ancestor. Along with rejecting the caste system, Buddhism rejects all forms of gender bias. Such views make no intellectual sense and therefore have no basis of support.

Sadly, this egalitarianism does not usually filter down to the experiences of men and women in Buddhist-majority countries. As in most of the world, patriarchy and sexism often bind women to a wheel of domestic duty, childbearing, childcare, and second-class citizenship. The anvils of

---

18. Guenther and Kawamura, trans., *Mind in Buddhist Psychology*, 44.
19. Dumoulin, *Christianity Meets Buddhism*, 169.
20. Dalai Lama XIV, *Answers*, 31.
21. Preece, *The Wisdom of Imperfection*, 74.

sexism and paternalism have often oppressed women in Buddhist societies. Further, the history of many Buddhist-majority societies is written by men and, thus, is decidedly about men. One sexist legend attributed to Buddha depicts him hesitant to ordain women because, "if only men had been admitted, the reign of the true dharma would last for one thousand years," but because women were to be allowed to join Buddhism would only survive for five hundred years.[22]

Because of Buddhism's early monastic character and its Brahmanic predispositions, early Buddhists were unsure about how to define the role of women in religious communities. As is true in many sexist contexts, it would have taken courage for men to support the practical outworking of Buddhist teachings that everyone is equally able to gain enlightenment. The fact that any woman could become a monastic must be appreciated in the larger context of an India where few women became ascetics. Indian society was a place where women were naturally self-effacing before men.

Certain Buddhist misogynistic texts taught that women are inferior to men. One tradition even asserts that "women are envoys of hell" who often try to seduce men away from enlightenment.[23] One sexist proverb states that although women have bodies that are angelic, they have minds that are demonic.[24] Some teachers have warned men not to "squander their parents' wealth and betray their filial duties by seeking sensual pleasures with women" who keep people from Buddhism.[25] Other teachers have conveyed a well-known Indian proverb, "Even though you look at a large snake, you must not gaze at a beautiful woman."[26]

Although progress has been made, few Buddhist women have become recognized teachers. That is also true today in many Buddhist-majority cultures. Of course, women are working to change the status quo but still face hulking obstacles. Going forward, tenacity will be needed to tear down sexist barriers. Within some orders "institutional prejudice runs deep and

---

22. Coleman, *The New Buddhism*, 141.

23. Warner, "What Do Lesbians Do in the Daytime?," 113.

24. Warner, "What Do Lesbians Do in the Daytime?," 113.

25. Quoted in Ueki, *Gender Equality in Buddhism*, 3: "A woman is a great Devil-King. She would often eat everyone. She is a cause of evil passions in this life and in the future life will become a loathsome enemy."

26. Florida, *The Buddhist Tradition*, 159 [Buddha]: "The first fault of men is that they are addicted to desire, insatiably looking at women for their own self-indulgence." Sexual attachment is a strong chain to be overcome, and when monks have sexual thoughts, they should superimpose in their imaginations an image of that same person when they become a rotting corpse. Florida quotes a poem: "Fools lust for women like dogs in heat / They do not know abstinence. / They are also like flies that see vomited food. / Like a herd of hogs, they greedily seek manure."

has prevented many from having access to these wonderful teachings."[27] Opposing such sexist views, Rita Gross warns against "quoting only part of the record" in order to "easily paint a portrait of Buddhism as hopelessly negative to women."[28] Not only did Buddha accept women into monastic orders, but he also told men to "practice passivity and a loose softness" in order to "open freely the gates of nature and let the hidden and the mysterious forces of this world penetrate into them."[29]

Buddhism continues to change worldwide as women gain more social opportunities. Noticeable progress has been made in many countries to address gender-based injustices. A sisterhood is linking together to face shared concerns. Among North American Buddhist women there is a "flow of universal energy that comes through our practice. We can use that flow of blessings to aid other beings who are suffering."[30] When asked about sexism among Buddhists, the Dalai Lama replied, "Oh, that's just culture. That's not the dharma."[31]

---

27. Ueki, *Gender Equality in Buddhism*, 4.
28. Florida, *The Buddhist Tradition*, 163.
29. Florida, *The Buddhist Tradition*, 165.
30. Northrup, *Ritualizing Women*, 95.
31. Gross and Ruether, *Religious Feminism and the Future of the Planet*, 67.

5

The Four Noble Truths

The awakening of critical consciousness leads the way to the expression of social discontents precisely because these discontents are real components of an oppressive situation.

—Paulo Freire, *Pedagogy of the Oppressed*

ALL LIFE IS SUFFERING

BUDDHA'S FIRST SERMON EXPLAINED there are Four Noble Truths (or Four Truths that Make us Noble). These are not concepts espoused by a mystic. They are observations about the nature of experience taught by a healing physician of troubled souls. Buddha's first message could have been about anything, but he began by explaining suffering. One teacher said Buddha could have "started with a focus on human aspirations . . . but he started with the opposite view—with suffering."[1]

The truth of suffering may not be what we want to hear, but it is what we need to hear. It is to our benefit to see how suffering affects us. Humanity has always suffered. There is no reason to think this will change. Ask your grandparents if you will you get old. Can we stop the aging process? Will life be better when we are old? It is only a matter of time before sickness, aging,

---

1. Tashi Tsering, *The Four Noble Truths*, 29.

and death come to us. We should be ready for—not anxious about—such inevitabilities. We should prepare for what is certain.

We all want happiness. Even in dreams we solve problems. The truth that life is suffering lifts our veil of ignorance and helps us accept life on life's terms instead of living in a fantasyland of illusions. This first truth explains exactly where problems in life are coming from. We may glimpse happiness in moments, but such feelings are fleeting—framed by the fact that all of us will die one day. Wisps of happiness are mixed with moments of pain and sadness. While the sun may shine for a few moments, at another time there will be clouds and darkness. While a flower may blossom, it will eventually wither and die. Birth, old age, sickness, grief, and death are universal. Friends and lovers will die, and bodies will age and come to an end. No one escapes these facts. Yet, many live in a dreamlike slumber, preoccupied like sleepwalking zombies heading over a cliff. One Zen proverb explains that many of us are like fleas on a hot griddle: "the fleas that fall must jump and the fleas that jump must fall."[2] For the unawakened "there is something inherently frustrating" about life that is not "accidental or coincidental. At the core, people feel a free-floating anxiety, which has no particular object but can plug into any problematic situation."[3]

One disciple met a remarkably savage death that seemed unfair until Buddha taught that this fate was the fitting result of an earlier life when the man had cruelly slain his parents. Buddha might have recast Descartes's axiom as *Doleo mihi, ergo sum*—I suffer, therefore I am. Once self vanishes, then suffering vanishes because it has nothing, like the notion of individuality, to attach itself to: No self, no suffering. The Sanskrit term *duhkha* (Pali: *dukkha*) cannot be easily translated, and other terms are often used instead of "suffering." In common speech, *dukkha* can mean discomfort, illness, sadness, or a sense of feeling unsatisfactory. Because it is the starting point of experience, *dukkha* is also sometimes referred to as "the origin." The First Noble Truth is that to experience life is to experience a "notorious inability to be happy."[4] Life is suffering, and suffering is life.

SUFFERING COMES FROM DESIRE

Some of us want to be famous, rich, or healthy while our lives may be far different from such desires. Many hope for nothing to change or for everything to change, but either way cannot accept life on life's terms. Experience is

---

2. Jones, *The New Social Face of Buddhism*, 3.
3. Loy, *The Great Awakening*, 19.
4. Loy, "Dead Words, Living Words, and Healing Words," 35.

often defined by what William Blake called our own "mind-forged manacles" that keep us from the truth.[5] Many harbor wrong ideas about what causes suffering. The Second Noble Truth explains that there is a healthy way to respond to the fact that all of life is suffering. The arising (*samudaya*) of suffering comes from the mental afflictions of attachment (*upadana*), craving (*raga*), greed (*lobha*), and desire or thirst (*tanha*). At our core each of us is a bottomless pit of desires that often surrenders to lies about our true identity.[6]

Some of us are unhappy because we wish for "something other than what is and want to change [ourselves] into someone else."[7] Suffering is fed by our minds. There is a difference between being sick and suffering from being sick. When does sickness turn into suffering? What makes aging bad? Does it have to be bad? If a car breaks down or a computer crashes, the problem is with the computer or with the car. It does not need to be your problem unless you choose to make it your problem. If your employer yells at you, then the origination of suffering is not with you but with your employer. We are deluded if we think that the origin of suffering is from outside when it is an inner problem. Some of us have spent our lives striving to solve an unending parade of outer problems while we do not focus on solving inner problems: the stress problem, the fear problem, or the anger problem.

A primary, originating source of mental afflictions or cravings is feelings (*vedana*). Feelings sometimes lead us to misunderstand a situation that we are experiencing. Any doctor will explain that we cannot cure a disease by eliminating the symptoms caused by a disease. Healing means getting to the root of the problem. If the root of the problem is not treated, then the problem will continue. We may have many symptoms, but we have only one root problem. We set up defense mechanisms that project blame onto others when in fact blaming others is really a mirror to the crisis of our shared humanity.

The way desires work parallels the way a monkey can be trapped in a cage. A hunter can hollow out a coconut, put a hole in it, and put some food inside the hole. The hole may be just large enough for the monkey to put his hand in to grab the food, but once the monkey reaches through the hole, the grasping hand is unable to be free unless it first is relaxed, which will mean

---

5. Jones, *The New Social Face of Buddhism*, 212.

6. Loy, *The Great Awakening*, 27. Loy explains: "The problem is not that I am unreal but that I keep trying to make myself real in ways that never work."

7. Lefebure, *The Buddha and the Christ*, 20.

losing the prize. Eventually, the hunter captures the foolish monkey who has refused to loosen his grasp and let go the food.

We can grasp tightly to noble as well as to ignoble desires. When desire takes control of our lives, it has an obsessive, addictive quality. A consuming fire rages inside us that cannot be explained. Some feel anxious and threatened as their constant attachments to desires increase. All desires are rooted in an inaccurate view of what it means to be human. At the core, "the source of our incessant agitation is deep-rooted self-centeredness. It is normally hidden from our sight but becomes apparent when we try to lead the highest moral life."[8] A craving often exists even for knowledge or insight. Buddhism is like a raft necessary to cross a river but is of no use (and can be discarded) once safely at the other side of the stormy waters of churning delusions.

Instead of looking inward, we turn outward and either judge others or feel dissatisfied with our lack of peace and become jealous of those who seem to be less agitated by life's struggles. Cravings create more desires and become more entrenched until we cannot distinguish our cravings from our identity. Anguish and desire become the expected norm. We try to manipulate what cannot be controlled—the realities of life—while we refuse to control what we can manage—our own responses to life. Because desires are transitory, living our lives to satisfy them will result in disappointment.

When this is related to sexuality, the issue becomes need. We are sexual and can practice our sexuality, but we should not need sex in a way that is compulsive and grasping, that controls us in the same way that animals are gripped by appetites. There may even be times when we should sublimate or redirect our sexual energy toward other drives. We should overcome lower urges and strive to nurture inside of us that which is wise and compassionate.

SUFFERING CAN BE EXTINGUISHED

The Third Noble Truth is that craving can be extinguished. The revolutionary and optimistic idea of Buddhism is that suffering will disappear when the root cause of suffering is eliminated. The cessation of suffering comes when we confront the cause of suffering and, free of all existence, we enter nirvana. To know that there is a solution is the first step. This is the great, hope-filled message at the heart of Buddhism.

Buddhism is not pessimistic, because of the truth that future suffering can be avoided. We can prepare for what we cannot avoid. We need to be "reprogrammed" from the bad habits of choosing to suffer. Old habits can

---

8. Unno, *River of Fire River of Water*, 66.

be reversed. We can stop multiplying our problem-generating responses to whatever comes. If we suffer because of the anger delusion, we should meditate on patience. If we suffer because of the pride delusion, we should meditate on humility. If we suffer because of the fear delusion, we should meditate on truth. We have trained (accustomed) ourselves to suffer instead of training ourselves to live with awareness that problems are internal instead of external. For example, anger is a state of suffering. Why choose anger? When are we angry and happy at the same time? Prepare now, for example, for the next time we are cut off in traffic.

Liberation cannot be explained with words or concepts. We become free when we deconstruct what is false and experience the extinguishing of desire, the end of hatred, and the cessation of illusion. If there is no solution to our problem, then Buddha would teach a message of despair. There is hope, however, because we can destroy that which keeps us from freedom. *Tanha* is eliminated by dousing the three fires inside us: greed (*lobha*), hatred (*dosa*), and illusion (*maya*). Embracing suffering teaches us about the true nature of reality and helps us appreciate the way things really are in life. We can be happy—not in the delusion of hedonistic or ascetic searches for what is missing—but through experiencing what is real, already present, and already inside ourselves.

THE EIGHTFOLD PATH

How do we realize the cessation of suffering? We can take specific steps toward this objective—explained in the Fourth Noble Truth or the fourth law. This path (*marga*) of training, the fourth law, is called the *Eightfold Path*, where we gain enlightenment through mental discipline. The fourth law offers a systematic pathway, the Middle Way—because it stands between the extremes of hedonism and self-mortification. It is a proven path, and liberation is the result of walking this journey (*magga*). The Eightfold Path is a system of habit training where discipline builds a better self. When we follow this path, we realize that all other avenues are misleading delusions. We will not waste time in this brief life chasing illusions and shallow hopes. Old assumptions are cast aside, and unwholesome emotions are controlled in the experience of discovery. Life's garden becomes free of the irksome weeds as we experience freedom from the limitations of self-centeredness.

Impermanence is a fact of life: No matter what you have gained, "you are either going to lose some of it or spend the rest of your days guarding what you got and scheming how to get more. And you are going to die, and you lose everything. It is all transitory."[9] Because experience is impermanent, we need to focus on experiences that encourage spiritual purification.[10] When we travel the path, we become the path. These teachings provide guidelines for insight and morality.

The order of the Eightfold Path varies slightly among Buddhist traditions. In one model, the first three steps of the path deal with our mindset. The problems we experience will be solved as we think about them in an accurate way. To begin, "right-understanding" is required along with "right-aspirations." Without "right-thought" we will drift in the wrong direction. What we say and do are governed by our inner being. If our minds are defiled, we suffer because suffering grows in delusional thought just as a "chariot follows a horse."[11] Thoughts are not facts. Just because you choose to think that the world is flat does not make it flat. Neither are expectations, or feelings, of disappointment (Kipling's two imposters, "triumph and disaster") anything but marauders of delusional thinking.[12] Right-thinking is free from a result-orientation that seeks a specific outcome. Anger, bitterness, or self-centered fears (described by Alcoholics Anonymous as the "fear that we would lose something we already possessed or would fail to get something we demanded") are examples of wrong-thinking.[13] Right-aspirations lead to experiences of a life that is clear, relaxed, simple, fresh, and open.

The third, fourth, and fifth guidelines of the Eightfold Path deal with morality. "Right-speech" means avoiding slander, idle chatter, and lies. Speaking harshly, or gossiping, or using words for self-promotion are self-defeating and harmful. I once saw a T-shirt that read, "Always Tell the Truth—There's Less to Remember." Right-speech is not dishonest. Lying springs from an inauthentic heart. Similarly, malicious slander or morsels of gossip are futile attempts to build ourselves up by putting others down. Whenever we use harsh or false speech, we hurt ourselves. Words should promote harmony.

"Right-action" is predicated on living the first three steps of the Eightfold Path. Right-action is not stealing or being greedy. Right-action is not misusing intoxicants that dull our ability to be mindful. The goal of right-action is to be a person who has a comprehensive understanding. Right-action

---

9. Smith, *The Beginner's Guide to Walking the Buddha's Eightfold Path*, 23.

10. There are seven stages of purification: 1. Moral purification; 2. Mental purity; 3. Purity of perspective; 4. Purity that comes when one overcomes doubts; 5. Purity where one can determine what is the correct path; 6. Purification through knowledge about devotional practice; and 7. Purity through insight.

11. Fisher, ed., *An Anthology of Living Religions*, 142.

12. Kipling, "If," 432–33.

13. Smith, *The Beginner's Guide to Walking the Buddha's Eightfold Path*, 56.

is being intentional about what we buy and generous with what we have. While we may know it is wrong to kill an animal, we still might eat meat. On the other hand, someone like Adolf Hitler, a vegetarian, may be protecting animals while at the same time killing millions of people.[14]

"Right-livelihood" means we will not earn money through selling liquor, slavery, the abuse of women or children, or anything that has to do with the taking of life. Our work should never harm others. A job is who you are and not only what you do. We should not choose a career based only on a desire for wealth or fame, but out of a sense of calling.

The sixth guideline of the Eightfold Path is "right-effort," where we develop alertness as well as inner awareness. The path is not for the lazy, the careless, or the passive. A disciplined life of truthful vigor expresses excellence. There is no room in right-effort for dullness, ignorance, restlessness, or stress. One teacher explains that there is not enough leather to cover our rough world to make it smooth, but if we wear leather shoes on our own feet, then the world's roughness will become smooth.[15]

The seventh guideline is "right-mindfulness." Liberation comes through directing the mind into a constant awareness of the truth. Teachers often encourage us to take a daily walk of mindfulness. Instead of observing what is around us, or listening to our own breath, we often choose to be distracted. Listen to your feelings, bodies, and minds with awareness. Sometimes our minds are like jungles filled with scurrying monkeys ("the monkey mind"). Even if circumstances are chaotic, we can live with skillfulness centered in a calm knowing of what is meaningful. The *Dhammapada* explains: "Check your mind. Be on your guard. Pull yourself out as an elephant from the mud."[16]

Buddha gained awareness while in meditation. *Meditation* (Pali and Sanskrit: *bhavana*) literally means to cultivate or develop spirituality. Right-meditation opens the padlocked doors of life sealed by the iron grip of countless misconceptions. Silence is at the heart of meditation. When a clear forest pool is perfectly still, it can reflect the trees that surround it, but when it is shifting or troubled, it reflects nothing. Meditation helps us live along a proven middle pathway of healthy freedoms. Insatiate egos, once they are fed, become accustomed to material comforts, physical treasures, and fulfilled desires, which eventually lead to feelings of loss. Ego is the enemy of discovery. Meditation provides a steadying practice through life.

---

14. Alan Watts, when asked why he was a vegetarian, said, "Because cows scream louder than carrots" (quoted in Smith, *The Beginner's Guide to Walking the Buddha's Eightfold Path*, 91).

15. I no longer have the source for this anecdote.

16. Fisher, ed., *An Anthology of Living Religions*, 143.

We do not meditate in order to speak with a god. We meditate to deepen the richness of our lives. We often experience life through our two eyes and five senses while meditation invites us to experience life with the third eye of the spirit. This makes our minds more stable and peaceful. Right-meditation helps us to "sidestep the bureaucracy of rigid intellectual processes and experience ourselves directly."[17] Hongzhi Zheng Jue explains:

> The practice of true reality is simply to sit serenely in silent introspection. This empty wide-open mind is subtly and correctly illuminating. Spacious and content, without confusion from inner thoughts of grasping, one effectively overcomes habitual behavior and realizes the self that is not possessed by emotions.[18]

Right-meditation is an entranceway into insight. Meditation chisels away mental misconceptions that barnacle our inner world. It helps cultivate self-awareness. Mind control (*samadhi*) inhibits, and then stops, distracting sensory reactions.

Meditation often begins when we sit down with some aid, such as an object like a stone or a basket. Next, we concentrate on the object intensely and try to exclude other thoughts. As we relax from distinguishing the shapes around us from the object in front of us, the process begins. Sometimes statements can help focus our mind. One phrase sometimes used is "Everything is infinite space—infinite consciousness—there is nothing." Repeating such phrases calms restlessness. Resting our minds allows us to lift worries away. When we are mindful, we live in the present moment.

NIRVANA

German theologian Wolfhart Pannenberg (1928–2014) claimed every religion is centered on one main idea (*integrationskraft*), around which all other beliefs revolve.[19] In the vast mountain ranges of Buddhism, there remains one shared goal. Buddha announced, "As the great ocean has only one taste—the taste of salt—so also, the dharma and sangha have only one taste—the taste of freedom."[20] Enlightenment does not come from being good but from being aware of what is true.[21] Paths to liberation begin with

---

17. Chögyam and Dechen, *Roaring Silence*, 3.
18. Hongzhi, "Cultivating the Empty Field," 15.
19. See Pannenberg, *Theology and Philosophy of Science*; and Pannenberg, *Systematic Theology*, vol. 1.
20. Watts, *Buddhism*, 3.
21. Watts, *Buddhism*, 3.

the Eightfold Path expressed in philosophy, ethics, and spiritual disciplines. Eventual release from human suffering is the result of practicing the Buddha dharma. To enter enlightenment is to transcend into another dimension.

Buddha's path helps us gain clarity of mind. Buddha said little about nirvana even though it is the end result. Nothing is gained if you understand the concepts of enlightenment in theory but do not experience it in life. This message is so practical that some do not think it is accurate to call Buddhism a philosophy or a religion.[22] Enlightenment is more than a remote promise of a heavenly peace beyond death. *Nirvana* means "to exhale," as in the releasing of a breath.[23] Nirvana, literally "the state of the snuffed-out candle," is the end of all searching for paths.[24] Human nature, bound by delusions, is blown out like a candle blown out in the wind. Just as the smoke of a snuffed-out candle "wafts away" so also all suffering, delusion, and anxieties "waft away" when entering nirvana. "What preoccupied Gautama and his contemporaries was not so much the possibility of rebirth as the horror of re-death. It was bad enough to have to endure the process of becoming senile, or chronically sick and undergoing a frightening and painful death once, but to be forced to go through this again and again seemed intolerable."[25]

No definition of nirvana can be precise. It is a reality of spirit and heart more than a geographical center. One teacher explained that nirvana can be described as a "cool cave, a place of bliss, emancipation, liberation, the supreme, the transcendent, the calm, the immaterial, the imperishable, the abiding, the supreme joy."[26] Nirvana annihilates that which must be destroyed; the flames of ill-will, delusion, and sensuality. Suffering need not be repeated.

Is nirvana the desire to be extinct or the opposite of self-fulfillment, as critics suggest? Peace means freedom from worry about the future. Nirvana is the result and not the goal to be sought. When one fixates on desires for nirvana, one becomes incapable of achieving it. Humanity is stuck in a traffic jam on life's freeway and needs to exit through the gateway of truth away from the binding limitations of ego. Everything grasping is illusionary and impermanent. In nirvana, the clamoring wheel of the grinding cycles of life is finally silenced.

22. Loy, *The Great Awakening*, 23

23. Watts, *Buddhism*, 24.

24. Pieris, *Fire and Water*, 19: "In Tibetan Buddhism *nirvana* is referred to as *paramasukha* or supreme bliss."

25. Armstrong, *Buddha*, 9.

26. Kinahan, *A Deep but Dazzling Darkness*, 68.

What of an individual remains to enjoy bliss after death if the doctrine of nonsoul (*anatta*) is true? It might be easier to explain to a non-Buddhist that nirvana can be savored only in the present tense. Buddhism is for now: Siddhartha gained nirvana in this life because nirvana is not synonymous with extinction. Nirvana is attained in this life, and overcomes a world inflamed by the destructive fires of steaming lust, blind delusion, and spasms of hatred. All these fires will be doused by the cooling blessedness of nirvana.

Buddha refused to describe the material reality of a place called nirvana. If it is a place, then it is a realm of serenity, passionlessness, and happiness. Once nirvana is experienced then it eludes all further description. Nirvana, however, is not an end, but the beginning of enlightenment. For Buddha, nirvana began under the Bo tree, where he experienced the liberation of continued serenity, lasting until his physical demise. It is both void and fullness. When one enters nirvana, one does not exist, but nirvana exists. There is no longer any struggle to either exist or not to exist because, in truth, nothing else matters.

BODHISATTVA IDEALS

Bodhisattvas—discussed earlier—are loving teachers who widen the path of deliverance. They intercede to assist us. Mahayanists note that bodhisattvas are loving hearts (*Maha-karuna-citta*) who spread compassion and take us into their arms. Although they have great merit, they share that merit with "all who turn to them for help."[27] While the Buddhas and *arhats* are beyond us, the bodhisattvas are ready to help any who call on them. They hear us and see our plight. In the *Diamond Sutra*, there is a description of a bodhisattva who remained free of malice even as evil forces hacked him to pieces with a sword while he was in meditation.

The most renowned of all the bodhisattvas is Avalokitesvara, "the one who looks down on the world." While this bodhisattva is revered worldwide, in China she was transformed into the goddess of mercy, Guanyin, "the "Virgin Mary of East Asia."[28] Guanyin gives blessings to all in need. All who call on the Avalokitesvara Buddha will find deliverance from their sufferings through the merit of this loving power of ultimate compassion.

Avalokitesvara is one of the most popular bodhisattvas and appears in many forms, including as Guanyin in China; Quan Am in Vietnam; and Kannon, Kansan, or Kanjizai in Japan. He reigns with his female counterpart, Tara, in a realm of miracles called the Potalka. The Potala Palace in

27. Amore and Ching, "The Buddhist Tradition," 245.
28. Amore and Ching, "The Buddhist Tradition," 247.

Lhasa gets its name from this legend. In Tibet, a manifestation of Avalokitesvara is the thousand-armed Chenrezig or the fierce Mahakala with his black head covered in skulls. Avalokitesvara is an androgynous figure often represented in renderings as having eleven different heads, ten of which were able to explode and to split into different locations in order to care for all who suffer (ten heads are, evidently, better than one).

Each bodhisattva embodies a distinct trait we should aspire to cultivate. For example, Manjushri is the "bodhisattva of wisdom and insight, who penetrates into the fundamental emptiness, universal sameness, and the true nature of all things."[29] Citizens of Nepal consider Manjushri their nation's founder. In Japan, his image often appears in meditation halls because of his power to awaken insight. Tibetans honor his spirit in Yamantaka, who went to hell to defeat Yama the King of Death. Manjushri is also the bodhisattva of poetry because he empowers language to bring insight. He is a protector for those who cannot help themselves. He is a lover of science and is often portrayed as a beggar focused on knowledge. Humans who express the attributes of Manjushri, according to Taigen Daniel Leighton, include Albert Einstein, James Joyce, and Winston Churchill because of their communication skills.[30]

Samantabhadra is the bodhisattva who works to translate ideas into action. He is often represented as riding the back of an elephant because this massive animal has the forceful ability to make things happen. Paintings show him with many arms, holding tools and weapons to get things done. He performs acts of charity in secret by living "incognito in the bustle of the marketplace or humbly 'under a bridge,'" sometimes even acting like an imbecile.[31] Notable people that Taigen Daniel Leighton feels embody the forceful actions of this bodhisattva include activists Martin Luther King Jr., Mahatma Gandhi, William Blake, and baseball great Roberto Clemente.[32]

---

29. Leighton, *Bodhisattva Archetypes*, 93.

30. Leighton, *Bodhisattva Archetypes*, 112–20. Leighton notes that Einstein, like *Manjushri*, often wore unkempt clothes. He also lists Gertrude Stein, Gloria Steinem, Mark Twain, Margaret Mead, and Bob Dylan of examples of people who fulfill the Manjushri archetype.

31. Leighton, *Bodhisattva Archetypes*, 138.

32. Leighton, *Bodhisattva Archetypes*, 141–57. Speaking of Clemente, Leighton writes, "I had the privilege of watching [him] regularly while growing up in Pittsburgh. Clemente was an exceptional hitter, both for average and power, and an excellent fielder who defined outfield defense for a generation of ballplayers. A few times Clemente used his amazing, lightning-like throwing arm to toss out batters at first from his position in right field after they had singled and taken too wide a turn around first base. Among his victims was a dumbfounded Willie Mays. But Clemente is considered a great hero for his charity as well as his athletic prowess . . . Beyond charitable works and his heroic

Kshitigarbha (Jizo in Japan and Dizang in China) is called the monk-hiding-as-mother-earth. She is the protector of children and travelers, including those traveling through the afterlife. Jizo followers in Japan show their devotion during the Obon ceremonies held every August. Although artistic renderings portray a shaved monk, Jizo is a nurturing mother figure, and the Japanese term means "earth-storehouse" or "earth-womb." Statues show Jizo carrying a staff in one hand and a "wish-fulfilling gem" in the other. Jizo cares for those who are suffering just as a loving mother cares for her children.

Bodhisattva Vimalakirti is called the "Thundering Silence of the Unsurpassed Layman" because he was once a commoner who gained enlightenment. Unlike other bodhisattvas, he began as a human but over time gained supernatural powers. He uses these to awaken spiritual insight. Vimalakirti also teaches through "thunderous silence," which expresses his serenity. His name Vimalakirti means "undefiled glory" because his actions bring glory to the Buddha.

Finally, many Buddhists await the coming of the Buddha Maitreya. Sometimes representations of him in China are of a Zen monk named Budai; in Japan he is called Hotei. There are many mountains in Japan, China, and Korea that serve as pilgrimage sites in his honor. His name means "the Loving One," and his presence promises hope for a brighter future despite present problems. The "Not-yet Buddha" is a messiah who bestows merit from a vast celestial treasure-ship to end social injustices.

---

death, Clemente most reflects Samantabhadra simply for his dynamic presence and pride in his own playing. . . His was a constant intensity, as fiery and as concentrated as any of Samantabhadra samadhi's . . . In Pittsburgh and Puerto Rico, Clemente is remembered as 'The Great One,' an apt translation of the Sanskrit epithet *mahasattva, great being*, used customarily for bodhisattvas" (Leighton, *Bodhisattva Archetypes*, 151–52).

6

The Mission of the Greater Path

Mahayana was the outcome of the Buddha's thought, the germ of which can be found even in the Pali Canon ... The real object of Mahayana Buddhism is to obtain enlightenment, to get rid of delusion, and to benefit others without hope of reward.

—Beatrice Lane Suzuki, *Mahayana Buddhism*

A GOLDEN AGE

BUDDHA'S TEACHINGS SPREAD RAPIDLY across northern India. An increased reception to Buddhism coincided with a wave of urbanization leading to greater social mobility and openness to newer ideas. Buddhism was attractive because it allowed for the intermingling of social castes and genders in a way Hinduism did not approximate. In addition, Buddhists formed monasteries that became models of egalitarian community where people from all social strata lived together.

Two hundred years after Buddha's life, a bloodthirsty dictator underwent a dramatic conversion to Buddhism.[1] King Asoka (*Ashoka*) in central

---

1. The claim about his cruelty comes from himself. Archeologists found a rock carving where he repents that in Kalinga "150,000 people were deported, 100,000 were killed and many times that number died. But after the conquest of Kalinga, the Beloved of the Gods began to follow the Righteousness of the *dharma*, to love Righteousness, and to give instruction in Righteousness. Now the Beloved of the Gods regrets the conquest,

India (r. 273–232 BCE) became known as the Dharma King and one of the most devout king-patrons of any religion in history. Asoka established a host of public works, including digging countless wells and planting many groves of trees. During his reign, a golden age of Indian Buddhism flourished.[2] Asoka gave vast tracts of land and treasure chests to monastic orders and sent missionaries to Sri Lanka and Burma. He was the first leader to establish a corpus of holy texts and train monks for cross-cultural missionary work. Asoka stopped spending money on lavish hunting expeditions and began funding missions outreaches. According to Clement of Alexandria, monks traveled to Syria and Egypt through the patronage of this "Constantine of Buddhism."

Asoka never forced citizens to embrace Buddhism. Because of his sponsorship of missionaries, Buddhism spread throughout Southeast Asia and gained a ready audience among the animist tribes of Siam (present-day Thailand). Temples were built wherever missionaries traveled. When missionaries encountered local gods (such as Kataragama in Sri Lanka), they were rechristened as lower-level spirit-helpers. Temples were also built to house sacred relics—such as Buddha's tooth at Kandy, Sri Lanka, or a lock of hair or a footprint of the Buddha in southern India. These became centers of pilgrimage. Asoka set up pillars at crossroads throughout his kingdom carved with messages of morality. Asoka's death in 232 BCE was a turning point that set the stage for a new school of thought—*Mahayana*, or Greater Path Buddhism—to emerge.

THE RISE OF GREATER PATH BUDDHISM

While Orthodox (Theravada) Buddhism in Southeast Asia held close to the strict disciplines of the Buddha, Greater Path missionaries in China, Tibet, Mongolia, Korea, and Japan stressed that the compassion of Buddha's truth embraces everyone as was also taught among early Buddhists. The spread of the Greater Path led to a host of often wildly syncretic variations. In one, the infamous tyrant of Mongolia, Genghis Khan, was proclaimed as a merciful bodhisattva. Greater Path Buddhism swings from the Tibetan expressions of mystical ritual to the Japanese Zen focus on emptiness full of possibilities.

---

for when a country is conquered and people are killed, they die, or are deported, and that the Beloved of the Gods finds painful and grievous" (from the Thirteenth Rock Edict, quoted in Amore and Ching, "The Buddhist Tradition," 224).

2. Inscriptions from the period of his life cite his name as Devanampiya Piyadasi, which means "He who is the beloved of the gods" (Kinnard, *The Emergence of Buddhism*, 37).

The Mission of the Greater Path

In its flexibility and its emphasis on compassion, the Greater Path has made a vital contribution in reinterpreting Buddhism. It has carried the message of Buddhism across India to the vast reaches of the treeless Gobi Desert and the frozen, windswept taiga of the Siberian Steppe. Ritual practices metamorphosed dramatically as missionaries swept in ever-widening concentric circles from the fringes of the Himalayan Mountains. The Orthodox tradition came to bear little resemblance to the Greater Path. At the same time, the Buddha, the teachings, and the community unite both movements at the core. The main differences between them spring from differing cultural contexts.

The Greater Path is more accessible to a greater number of people. Most of us cannot afford to lay down the pedestrian yokes of work or family responsibilities, to live in a monastery. The Greater Path preaches we can attain enlightenment without extreme commitment. Theravada critics felt that there was an otherworldly quality to the Greater Path that leads to error. The further one strays from orthodoxy, they argued, the further one embraces mysticism. Orthodox monks also claimed that the Greater Path was wrong in asserting that the world is a "sphere of unconditional potentiality—a dimension of emptiness"—where truth is found in the "emptiness of emptiness."[3] This led to the overemphasis, according to the Orthodox, on the supernatural instead of on disciplines and moral exactitude. Another argument against the Greater Path was that its followers accepted rituals without precedent in earlier practices. In Tibet one can see, for example, widespread acceptance of shamanistic, occult practices—an emphasis on magic, miracles, spells, and chants for protection from evil spirits—that springs from Bon Shamanism. Especially from the third century CE, a host of rituals, magical circles, and astrological charts were used in Tibet to deal with evil spirits.

GREATER PATH MISSION MOVEMENTS

Greater Path missionaries spread the Buddha's teachings with an unceasing willingness to adjust to the cultures they were trying to reach. Their objective was to present eternal truths dressed in the local clothes of cultures they encountered. They also advanced their message through business and medical means, using any tool at hand to create receptivity to their teachings. Once they gained an audience, they did not burden listeners with strict expectations that ran counter to local practices. They shared a simple message which strove to lessen differences between Buddhism and indigenous

---

3. Chögyam and Dechen, *Roaring Silence*, 96.

folk traditions. One missionary, trying to reach the meat-eaters of Mongolia, knew that telling Mongolians that they could not eat meat would cancel any chance that they would receive his message, so he chose to sit with them and eat meat, all the time knowing that this sin would probably land him in hell. He gained their trust, and the carnivorous pastoralists of Mongolia became devout practitioners of the Buddha-path.[4]

Along with Zoroastrians, Buddhist itinerant preachers were the world's first missionaries. Their communities ethically modeled the meaning of their message and made skeptics more receptive to their teachings. When the first monasteries were established as mission stations, they functioned without any cultural or economic distinctions. All members of the communities saw one another as sisters and brothers in a united family. This helped their message find a ready reception across an Asia hungry for equitable social change.

The first Buddhist missionary was Lord Buddha, who set the example by teaching tirelessly for over four decades. Compassion motivated Buddha to share what he had discovered. Dedicated missionaries followed Buddha's example and lived in abject poverty, thinking little about their own comfort or safety. Missionaries would join military and business caravans. Many were killed in dangerous missions to some of the fiercest tribes in history. Acts of charity often won the day with hostile audiences. They would walk tirelessly for months or years in the hopes of reaching as many as they could with their message. Because committed missionaries were willing to adapt their message to any audience, they became skillful in diplomacy and students of human nature and social psychology. They were known for respecting the faiths of others; such an attitude fostered in listeners a willingness to consider their message. Missionaries sought to "tame" local gods and overlook religious superstitions to help people come closer to Buddhism.

MISSIONS IN CENTRAL ASIA

In the seventh century, Greater Path missionaries reached Tibet where their beliefs became wedded to the resident phantasmagoria of ancient mystery rituals.

At this same time, Muslim interventions into northern India conquered the initial base of Buddhism. Buddhists who survived the Muslim onslaught either fled northward into Tibet and China or widely coalesced back into Hinduism, which began to see Buddha a venerated avatar of Lord Vishnu. While Buddhism was gaining followers in other parts of the world,

---

4. I no longer have a source for this anecdote.

it became almost extinct within India by the thirteenth century. There were no major revivals of Buddhism in India until the twentieth century, when social activists for outcasts led by Congress Party politician B. R. Ambedkhar chose en masse to convert to Buddhism as a stratagem to protest the stagnant, entrenched Hindu caste system.

Greater Path missionaries became active on the broad steppelands of central Asia but were only able to establish themselves within Tibet, Mongolia, and Siberia. Because Islam was unable to extend into Southeast Asia (with the exceptions of Malaysia and Indonesia), most of this area remained under the sway of Orthodox Buddhist monks. The Chinese and Japanese had relatively few encounters with Islam and remained largely supportive of Buddhism.

THE DIAMOND PATH

Om Mani Padme Hum! "O! Jewel of the Lotus! Amen!" Trekking across the commanding hills of Tibet, one sees waves of flags with this prayer fluttering inarticulately in bold, blue skies. Rewritten repeatedly on scrolls, banners, and thick-sheaved prayer-wheels, this hymn is recited by local devotees to gain merit. Tibet's very topography lends itself to wild flights of imagination. The air is pure, and expansive tracts of endless steppe lift into looming mountains, which stand as testaments to the power of the natural world. The veil between the visible and the unseen, between the real and the unreal, in Tibet, is as fragile as the thin mountain air.

There are many stories about how the Buddhist message came to Tibet. Sangharakshita writes: "Tibetan Buddhism is essentially the complex Buddhism of the Pala Dynasty in Northeastern India transported bodily from the subtropical plains and forests of Bengal and Bihar across the commanding and forbidding barriers of the Himalayas into the icy, windswept tablelands of Tibet."[5] Missionaries arrived in Tibet at the invitation of local kings. The most famous missionary was Guru Rinpoche ("precious teacher"), who arrived between 755 and 810 CE.[6] One account claims that Rinpoche spent 111 years establishing Buddhism in Tibet.[7] Tibetan king Songtsen Gampo (615–656 CE) was converted to the message by his Nepali wives. At that time, the advent of the practice in Tibet was vehemently opposed by local

---

5. Sangharakshita, *Alternative Traditions*, 125.

6. Dalai Lama XIV, *Opening the Eye of New Awareness*, 105 cites this date.

7. The most famous of these is the *Padma bKa'I Thang's*, and many biographies, such as the *Life and Liberation of Padmasambhava*, tell stories about his many lives as the bringer of dharma.

rulers, who were comfortable following their favored shamans of the *Bon* (meaning "truth") religion.[8]

The most effective Greater Path Tibetan teacher was Milarepa (*Mila*), born in a small town in 1052. Milarepa was first a shamanistic wizard with sensational powers including the ability to create "devastating hail-storms," before converting to the path taught by Buddha.[9] Milarepa miraculously survived many trips to India and became a saint and poet who gained legendary status in the hearts of his people. He gained the honorific title *Milarepa* after the *repa*, an austere robe he wore while living in the caves of the desolate mountains of southwestern Tibet and western Nepal, far from his wife and children. His compassionate nature and humorous, wisdom-filled practical stories garnered a huge following among the masses even though he strove to avoid fame.

Tibetan Buddhism emerged as a mixture of the indigenous Bon Shamanism, tantric practices with their symbolic rituals and esoteric meditations, and the teachings of missionaries. Bon Shamanism is an animistic tradition—rooted in Tibetan and Persian sorcery—designed to overcome evil forces by channeling the subtle energies of the body to transform both the inner mind and the external world. Because the Mongols ruled Tibet from 1222 until 1238, they played a key role in bringing Bon Shamanism to Central Asia. The Mongols imagined the world filled with spirits who lurked everywhere, even underneath layers of human flesh and inside the flow of human fluids such as blood and semen. Bodily fluids were seen to have mysterious powers and were sometimes used in Bon rituals. Contemporary adherents seek to contact both good and evil forces to enlist them for protection and their psychic powers. This combination of two traditions is practiced today throughout Tibet, Nepal, Bhutan, Ladakh, Sikkim, and Mongolia.

Tibetan Buddhism developed into four major schools of practice.[10] The largest of these not only revered Buddha but also honored the most revered goddess in the Bon pantheon, Khandro (Sanskrit: *Dakini*), which

---

8. Ching and Amore, "The Buddhist Tradition," 256: "We have only fragmentary information concerning it [Bon], but scholars are in general agreement that its ritual objectives included the safe conduct of the soul of a dead person to an existence in a land beyond death. To get the soul to that realm, the Bon priests sacrificed an animal such as a Yak, a horse, or a sheep during the funeral ritual."

9. Milarepa, *Drinking the Mountain Stream*, 6.

10. The four schools are the Nyingma school and the new (Sarma) schools, which include the Kagyu school, the Sakya ("Grey Earth") school, and the Gelug ("System of Virtue") school.

The Mission of the Greater Path 61

means "sky-goer" or "traveler-in-space."[11] Missionaries accepted these other beings because the Tibetans were certain that the high peaks of the Himalayas were home to cruel demons and bloodthirsty vampires who needed to be appeased through various incantations. Vile spirits were consulted by shamans through ecstatic trances and ritual possession ceremonies. One of the most venerated of these is the terrifying Vajrakilaya, a ferocious and ravenous deity who "manifests himself in an intensely wrathful yet compassionate form" to confront any obstacles that arise against the dharma.[12]

With this foundation in mysticism, the scriptures that gained the largest following in Tibet were the doctrines of Tantric Buddhism. Tantric texts reveal how one can perform magical ceremonies to ward off evil spirits and avert disasters.[13] There are also prayers for the dead that are consistent with

---

11. Campbell, *Traveller in Space*, 38. She is also invoked in some Tibetan rituals as Ma Namkha, which Campbell says means "Mother Sky." Practitioners often sought to become one with her through taking a "wife" (*songyum*), "sexual partner," or in local terms a "secret mother." Campbell, who served in a lamasery for years as a songyum, notes the women were called "receptacles for holy *tulkus* (monks)" (99). Women were "necessary ingredients in the process of birthing and sexual activity" (113). The highest-ranking tulkus could do whatever they wanted, "including rape and battery," because such acts would "ultimately be for the benefit of all beings" (107–108). Campbell was told that if she spoke about her liaisons, she would suffer "madness, trouble, or even death" (103). Secret collusion was a "test of faith" (103). Another term to describe them was *dakinis*, which translates as "women who dance in space or women who revel in the freedom of emptiness" (101). Publicly, women were a threat to spiritual progress and were excluded from religious ceremonies. Privately, monks would often arrange "secret meetings and liaisons with the mothers or sisters" of monks (102). Campbell reports "while a lama would, to all intents and purposes be viewed publicly as celibate, in reality he was frequently sexually active, but his activities were highly secret" (98). Milarepa, considered one of the founders of Tibetan Buddhism, "reiterates the necessity of sexual relations for the practicing yogi" (112). Several tantric texts, paintings, and statues publicly describe the "philosophy and methodology of sexual ritual" (111). Paintings often portray men as white and women as red because of the color of semen and menstrual flow (120). One teaching is that sexuality of opposites "is an experience similar to death, and also to divinity—two experiences which, by definition, are impossible to achieve in the human form" (117). Campbell quotes Miranda Shaw, author of *Passionate Enlightenment*, that "Tantric Buddhism displays the conviction that all the powers of the universe flow through and from women" (123). Other teachings emphasize the health benefit of the man retaining his semen (*ojas*) during intercourse. Campbell reports that teachers had "determined that semen (Tibetan, *tigle* or essence) had to be driven upwards along the spine to the head...the more *ojas* in a man's head the more powerful he is, the more intellectual, the more spiritually strong" (116). Campbell states, "The semen in the head becomes *changchusem*, literally meaning the mind of enlightenment" (119).

12. Namdrol, *The Practice of Vajrakilaya*, 7.

13. Tantric adherents were also influenced by Saivite Tantra and were concerned not only with warding off evil spirits but also with paths to enlightenment.

the Bon tradition. The *Tibetan Book of the Dead*, originally known as the *Bardo Thodol* (or *Liberation by Hearing on the After-Death Plane*), is a series of prayers to be read to the dying as they prepare to journey into the worlds beyond.

The hidden doctrines of Tantric Buddhism are decipherable only with the assistance of a *lama* (or *agura*, "superior one"). Gurus (*lamas*) provide prayer wheels to help gain favor with the gods. Teachers also transcribe magical mantras that bring safety and, ultimately, the celestial reward of nirvana. Lamas directed the monks (*crela*) into elaborate yoga rituals and other mystic formulas to control the powers of supernatural forces.

For Tibetans, visual art, music, and chanting are pathways that one can open to enter spiritual truth. Art is not only explanatory—it is also transformational. Art from the heart empowers as it calls observers to the noble path. Truth can come through the imagination and not only through cognition. One participates inside the energizing force of the art as creation becomes recreated internally. One moves from one spiritual realm to another through viewing art and through chanting. One of the most renowned forms of Tibetan art is the mandala, which is a many-sided symbolist diagram or work of literature used to explain cosmic revelations. Mandalas serve as "maps" to enter an inner, spiritual "transformed environment."[14]

Dreams were also interpreted in séance sessions with spirits, demons, fairies, and ghosts. Tantric Buddhism relied on ritual trances that carried devotees into heightened mystical states of ecstasy. Tantric Buddhism created an entirely new system of yoga that emphasized physical gestures (*mudra*) as sacred movement. This led to the most infamous of yoga practices, *shathism*, which employed sexuality for the cause of enlightenment. Another practice often equated with Tibetan Buddhism is the use of prayer-flags and prayer wheels for meditation. These meditation tools create a serene environment that releases positive spiritual energy. Perhaps one reason that Tibetans place prayer wheels in temples is to evoke the memory of the actual *Potala* Pure Land, which is cherished in their hearts. Practitioners using prayer wheels claim that their use leads to "more peaceful, joyful, and virtuous mental states."[15]

Major Tibetan Buddhist writings are divided into two portions: the *Kanjur*, which consists of 108 volumes, and the *Tanjur*, which has 225 volumes. These esoteric texts are accessible only to the initiated because they are written in code. Tantric writings contain "magical spells, descriptions of

---

14. Tshongkhapa, *Tantric Ethics*, 15.

15. Lardner, *Wheel of Great Compassion*, 5. Related to this there is a Buddhist proverb that if you put a beautiful cloth on dung it will soon smell like dung, but if you cover incense with a beautiful cloth the cloth will soon smell like the incense.

The Mission of the Greater Path

divinities, and sets of incantations arranged for meditation and ritual use, instructions in worship and in the bestowing of consecrations."[16]

In Tibetan Buddhist cosmology a host of lesser gods, fiends, demons, ghosts, and blithe fairies live in the underworld as well as in Tibet's mountains and rivers. These lowest of the spiritual beings are often described in travel tales. Spiritual forces are both good and evil with the king of darkness and evil being Yamantaka (*Yama*), the "Lord of Hell and Death." He is portrayed with the head of a bull, and his myriad hands are often depicted gripping human skulls. Religious theater and art portray Yamantaka as a being who lives by consuming vast sums of human flesh, and particularly raw cranial gray matter, for his dining pleasure. King Yama is surrounded by a phalanx of blood-gorged demons with bodies of men but the heads of birds and beasts. Their depictions are so grotesque that young children are often afraid to look at them.

Tibetan Buddhism is also referred to as Vajrayana Buddhism or Diamond Buddhism. (The word *vajra*—"thunderbolt"—is a synonym for the Vedic god Indra.) These terms and images are used because diamonds are indestructible and precious, while a thunderbolt is a fierce expression of power that sometimes comes as a surprise. Because Tibetan Buddhism is so unique in its various rituals, it is sometimes classified as entirely separate from the Greater Path. One method of training, called "crazy wisdom" (*ye shes chol ba*), for example, advocates that lamas should use "wisdom-eccentricity" to smash "the small fishbowls of intellectual vision" where people are bound by illusions.[17]

Of the four schools of Tibetan Buddhism, the two major groups are the Gelugpa and the Nying Mapa ("the Ancient Ones"). The Nying Mapa school is distinguishable by the red hats that priests wear. Nying Mapa, predominant in Ladakh, is the oldest (and least widespread) form of Tibetan Buddhism. The second group is called the Gelugpa or "Virtuous Ones." Their priests wear yellow caps; hence the Gelugpa have been termed "Yellow-hat Buddhists." This is the largest group of Tibetan Buddhists and is presently led by His Holiness the Dalai Lama. The Dalai Lama downplays the differences among these various groups by comparing them to different types of aircraft that exist to serve varying aviation needs.[18]

With the advent of Yellow-hat Buddhism in Tibet, politics and religion were welded together to create a ruling class of monks. Although he has officially retired, the Dalai Lama remains the de-facto political head over twelve

---

16. Harvey, *Introduction to Buddhism*, 206.
17. Dorje, *Dangerous Friend*, 68–69.
18. Dalai Lama XIV, *Opening the Eye of New Awareness*, 105–6.

million Tibetan Buddhists, while the Panchen Lama (currently presumed held captive in China) is designated as the spiritual leader. Each Dalai Lama is a manifestation of Buddha Avalokitesvara and is more than a mere human. Other Buddhas have appeared at different times across Tibet. Buddha Avalokitesvara has appeared thirteen times as the ruler of Lhasa, while the Buddha Maitreya has appeared seventeen times in Urga (Mongolia).

While there are dramatic differences between Tibetan Buddhism and other forms of Buddhism, Tibetan Buddhism is like other forms of Buddhism in significant ways. For example, right-meditation (Tibetan: *bsam gtan*), according to the Dalai Lama, has the exact same meaning in Tibetan Buddhism as in other traditions. Tibetan Buddhists, though isolated from other Buddhists as the reclusive snow leopard is from other animals, draw their desire for independence from the thin, rocky soil of their ancient homeland.

CHINESE BUDDHISM

Greater Path missionaries came to China over the daunting triple barriers of mountains, deserts, and oceans five hundred or six hundred years after the passing of Buddha, before the first century CE. By this time, Buddhism had already undergone many changes. One legend claims the emperor Ming Ti (who ruled from 57 to 75 CE) had a vision of a huge Buddha asking China for assistance. In response to this dream, he sent for gurus from India to teach Buddhism in China. At the same time, the first missionaries to the Middle Kingdom joined merchants arriving on the Silk Road from the remote plateaus of Central Asia. The Chinese initially scorned these odd, celibate monks with shaved heads. Both celibacy and abandonment of the family were anathema in Chinese traditional culture. Further, a shaved head was a sign of mourning, not appropriate for anyone but a grieving family member.

The people these first missionaries encountered were ripe for conversion. Confucian-Taoist traditions had devolved into philosophies that did not deal with the otherworldly worries that common folks had about the afterlife. Buddha's ideas became a viable alternative for the political elite because the Han Dynasty was crumbling, and leaders were looking for new ways to consolidate control. Part of the chaos in China originated from the fact that Confucian overlords were in disarray, and the fabric of unifying cultural traditions had weakened. The ruling class held to Confucianism while commoners turned to the magical rituals of Taoist priests to channel the power of spiritual forces.

The combination of Taoist philosophy and Confucian ethics provided an ideal context for the welcome reception of Buddhism. Both Taoism and Confucianism dealt with issues of this life and did not speculate on the afterlife. There were also similarities between Taoism-Confucianism and the Greater Path's ways of seeing the world. Taoism-Confucianism, in concord with Buddhism, teaches a quietist path where insights are gained through contemplation. Wise monks paralleled ways the Chinese viewed sages as adherents of disciplined meditation.

While Buddhism began partly as a response to the rigid class system of India's Vedic traditions, early China had a less stratified society, which helped Buddhism take root in China under the direct patronage of various rulers.[19] The most difficult hurdle that Buddhism had to vaunt in China was its oft-proclaimed rejection of materialism, which flew in the face of China's pragmatic trinity of values: survival, wealth, and family. Confucian scholars feared that Buddhism's antimaterialism would hinder the Confucian goal of establishing a unified state.

Buddhism's spread across China was slow but steady. By the fourth century, large monasteries had been established, serving as centers for teaching and social outreaches. By the fifth century, translations of key texts were completed which provided Confucianists with clear paths to study Buddhism. Monks won over fearful bureaucrats wary of rebellion by building strong, loyal alliances with local authorities. Coexistence between the Buddhist temple and the Confucianist state continued until 844 CE, when everything changed overnight: Emperor Wu Sung mandated all Buddhist temples be destroyed and all monks arrested or executed. Troops seized statues and temple bells, melting them into cannons and for cash. Chinese Buddhism never fully recovered from this onslaught, although, under the rule of Mongol Kublai Khan (1280–1368), monasteries were again free to operate without restriction. The Ming Dynasty (1368–1644) was a period of Buddhist stagnation. The Manchu Court (1644–1911) followed a policy of supporting lamaism in order to build political ties with Buddhist populations in Mongolia and Tibet.

Buddhists sought to convert the Chinese by rendering Buddhist practices more palatable and less foreign. Missionaries were careful to make no overt attack against ancestor worship or the local gods of commoners. While foreign Buddhists sought allegiances in China, they were careful not to impose any power they might have gained. An unstated truce emerged between the political ethics of Confucianism, the philosophies of Taoism, and Buddhist practices (Chinese: *San Jia*).

---

19. Ching, *Chinese Religions*, 126.

Buddhism's entry into China was never a one-way street. As Buddhism began expressing itself in art and literature, it became more accessible to Chinese intellectuals. Taoist doctrines of emptiness and discovery through intuition began appearing in Buddhist teachings. For the most part, Confucian rulers extended patronage to monasteries as a way of bringing them under control. For over a thousand years, the authority of Buddhist monks dominated the religious practices of China. In the final analysis, however, key elements of Buddhism never took root. The Confucian idea that one should take no savior beyond oneself seemed contradictory to the Greater Path's emphasis on bodhisattva intercessors who dispensed merit. Buddhism stressed faith over internal analysis. Miracles ascribed to amulets, relics, and charms were popular in China but probably would have been rejected as superstition by Lord Buddha. For these reasons, Buddhism was never fully integrated into centers of Chinese intellectual life.

GUANYIN

A strong emphasis in Chinese Buddhism was placed on gaining merit toward enlightenment. Buddha was portrayed as a savior while other bodhisattvas (Chinese: *pusa*) came to represent different deities already worshiped within the Chinese pantheon of gods. These deities included Wen-Shu (*Majursi*), the god of wisdom, Amithaba, Lord of the Pure Land in the realms beyond life, and Kshitigarbha, the rescuer from the torments of hellfire.

Guanyin (in Mandarin *Quanying* or *Guan Ying*; in Cantonese, *Goon Yam*) remains China's most revered deity. The "goddess of mercy" uses her powers to release petitioners from trouble and rescue them from poisons, sickness and hungry ghosts. Before the rise of Chinese Marxism, one was able to find Guanyin shrines in almost every hamlet across China. Goddess Guanyin is the "all-sided-one," and is revered for her bounteous compassion. She is a kind guardian who answers prayers. Guanyin, in her infinite compassion, continues to reappear among humanity in many forms, often in our darkest hours of need.

TIAN T'AI

There are four major schools (or types) of the Greater Path in China. Broad categories, however, blur the fact that many other schools emerged, and some of these mixed the teachings of various schools, as well as local beliefs from other religions, into their teachings. Notable Buddhist Chinese schools include Tian T'ai, Hua-Yen, Ch'an (Pure Land), and Ch'ing t-u.

Tian T'ai Buddhism was codified by the monk Zhiyi (*Zhikai* or *Chu Ye*), who lived between 531 and 597 CE. The goal of this school was to unify the diverse strands of Chinese Buddhism into "one house."[20] This school, also called the Lotus School, has gained a wide following worldwide through the teachings of transcendental meditation. Zhiyi taught from his mountain monastery in Zhejiang that wisdom and truth were perfectly summarized in the Lotus Sutra. According to the Lotus School, one gains eternal merit simply by reciting the Lotus Sutra and by venerating Buddha, appealing to his sense of compassion. Tian T'ai teaches that everything is emptiness and, at the same time, one with the Buddha's teachings. One proverb I heard in Yunnan explained that "all of the Buddhas are present in one grain of sand."

HUA YEN AND PURE LAND

Hua-Yen (or Huayan), developed during the Tang Dynasty (618–907 CE), is one of the principal schools of Chinese Buddhism. Based on the "Flower Ornament" (*Hua Yen*) scriptures, this philosophy taught that there was a secret nature of reality—sometimes called the "one-in-all philosophy."[21] Everything in the cosmos springs from one essence—pure mind. One should be filled with "oceanic reflection," the realization of the completely illuminated nature of everything contained within the cosmos.[22] Zealous Hua-Yen missionaries went from China to Japan where their doctrine became known as Nara and for some time was venerated as Japan's official religion.

Another widespread branch of Chinese Buddhism is the "Teaching of the Pure Land" (*Jingtu*). The great masters who advanced these doctrines were Tao-chu (*Tao-ch'o*), who died in 629 CE, and Shan-tao, who passed away in 681. They described the "Celestial Buddha," or Amithaba, who lives in a heavenly realm in the western quarter of the universe. From there, the Celestial Buddha waits to welcome with open arms all who place trust in his power.

Before the Celestial Buddha received the Pure Land, he was a lowly monk who delayed his own salvation to help others. As he studied, the Celestial Buddha was given a revelation of hundreds of thousands of Buddha-lands in worlds-to-come. From an enlightened understanding, he envisioned a "Pure-Land in the West," which was a combination of all that is ideal throughout all the other realms. In Pure-Land teaching, a believer gains merit by constantly reciting Amithaba's name (*Nianfo* in Chinese,

20. Smart, *Buddhism and Christianity*, 31.
21. Simpkins and Simpkins, *Simple Buddhism*, 33.
22. Tsang, "Cultivation of Contemplation," 147.

Nembutsu in Japanese). Common people gravitated to this simple method because it offered an easier access to the heavens. The vigorous disciplines needed to cleanse the soul were replaced by the quick saving mercy of a loving God.

Since the advent of the People's Republic of China (1949), Marxist scholars have criticized Buddhism as a foreign religion that facilitated China's cultural and economic decline. This view, however, can be contested by the fact that missionaries also brought innovative ways of thinking about the world. Further, Buddhist communities often provided needed social cement in societies undergoing a great upheaval. Even the actual structure of Buddhist communities have influenced the ways epochs of Chinese culture have viewed political power. There are countless ways that Buddhism has affected Chinese culture. Art, music, poetry, and dance have many connections to Buddhist influences. Even the language has been affected by Buddhism: "From the proverbs of peasants to the formal language of the intelligentsia, words of Buddhist origin are found in common use by people who are quite unconscious of their origin."[23]

MISSIONARIES IN JAPAN

Greater Path missionaries entered Japan from *Pekche* (Korea) in the sixth century (around 552), and missionaries and adherents increased under Prince Shokotu (574–622) so that Greater Path Buddhism became the religion of the elite. Wave after wave of missionaries arrived, each group finding more success than the last.

Gradually, Buddhism became Japan's national religion. As in China, Buddhism changed dramatically as it entered Japan. Japanese Buddhism is unlike Chinese Buddhism because it has been infused with the latent nationalistic values of the local people. Many Japanese rejected key teachings on death and reincarnation while at the same time embracing Buddhist rituals in hopes that these would pacify evil spirits and bring benefits such as better health and financial wealth. Mission efforts joined with local traditions, and the "Buddhist divinities of India and China and the *kami* of Japan" were considered interchangeable.[24]

The Greater Path mixed with the Shinto traditions of the gods, called *kami*, who oversaw people's daily lives, so that these were rechristened as Buddhas. This syncretism enhanced receptivity to a distinctly Japanese rendering of Buddhism. Some Japanese explain that they are nation-loving

---

23. Wright, *Buddhism in Chinese History*, 108.
24. Earhart, *Religion in the Japanese Experience*, 45.

Shinto in this life and heaven-loving Buddhists in the next life. A watershed event took place in 647 when Emperor Tenno demanded that every house erect an altar to Buddha. Tenno may have intended to use Buddhism as a weapon against the entrenched power of Shinto priests.

Religion and politics have always been intertwined in Japanese life. By the end of the sixteenth century—and throughout the Tokugawa Empire (1603–1867)—Buddhism became subordinate to political forces. At the same time, Buddhists developed huge monasteries replete with warrior-monks who served both as local police and military leaders. This obligated warlords like Oda Nobunaga (1573–1582) and Toytomi Hideyoshi (1782–1798) to attack monasteries in order to weaken their power. Another strategy to monitor religion during the Tokugawa era was to force everyone register with a temple. During the Meiji Dynasty (1867–1877) further controls were enacted—such as the removal of Buddhist emblems from government buildings. Because the Meiji rulers favored nationalistic Shintoism, they forced all Buddhist images to be removed from Shinto shrines.

TENDAI AND SHINGON

Buddhism's main Japanese schools are Tendai, Pure Land, Nichiren, Zen, and various Tantric groups such as Shingon. Zen will be discussed in a later chapter because of the frequent interaction Zen Buddhists and Christians have had in recent decades.

One of the first missionaries from China was Saicho (766–822 CE), "the Luther of Japanese Buddhism," who taught T'ian Tai (or Tendai) as a reformation of previous religious practices. Saicho headquartered on Mount Hei, north of Kyoto and preached that all wisdom truth was based on the Lotus Sutra. Saicho appealed to peasants by incorporating esoteric rituals into rituals that helped them become comfortable with their new faith.

Shingon entered Japan in 806 CE, during the Heian (Kyoto) Period (796–1185). It is a tradition rich in ceremonies, ornate art, monastic orders, and colorful rites such as the fire ritual (*gama*) and an ordination sacrament like baptism (*kanjo*). Even today the founder of Shingon, Kukai (774–835) or Kobo Daishi is honored for blending faith with the distinctives of Heian culture. Kobo Daishi is "credited with being a master of sculpture, poetry, painting, languages (Chinese), and calligraphy."[25] Shingon places ritual above the intellectual benefits of abstract theory. The term *Shingon* means "the true word" or the "mystical mantra." Kobo Daishi had studied the magical side of religion and was taught one had to climb step by step up a

25. Reader et al., *Japanese Religions*, 36.

ladder towards nirvana. The mystical elements of the movement were one of the reasons that Shingon was slow to take root among an uneducated, and skeptical, citizenry. One reason Shingon was popular among the elite was its emphasis on discipline. To enhance spirituality, strict yogic disciplines were emphasized. Shingon gained wider popularity when it introduced rituals for the dead. Priests taught that there were really two forms of Buddhism, one for commoners, and one for those able to embrace secret doctrines of Buddha Mahavairocana, "Buddha of the Sun." The elite were taught secret mantras and gnostic formulae, which opened initiates to the spiritual world.

PURE-LAND

One of the most popular schools of Japanese Buddhism is called the Pure-Land. It took root during the Heian Period, and during the advent of the Kamakura Period (1185–1333), Pure Land schools were launched when Honen (Genko, 1133–1212) brought a revolutionary spiritual teaching from China. Honen had seen his father murdered when he was only eight years old which made him believe that people were evil, and that their only hope for self-power (*jiriki*) was salvation by an outside power (*Tariki*), Amida Buddha. He advocated reciting a simple prayer, *Namu Amida Butsu*, "Praise to Amida Buddha (shortened to Nembutsu)." Whenever he prayed this prayer, he discovered that electric-power and warm-light flowed through his body. Study and adherence to rituals were worthless and there was no benefit in entering a monastery or even living a virtuous life. All of these would not gain the amount of merit we gain when reciting Namu Amida Butsu.

Honen believed that there was a Pure-Land one could reach after death by calling on the Amida Buddha. As we unceasingly pray, "Praise be to the Amida Buddha," we become delivered into enlightenment. Even if we only call on Amida Buddha for one day, we can face death with certainty, confident of eternity in the Pure-Land. Faith comes from *jodo tariki*, the power of an intercessor to deliver the petitioner. We cannot save ourselves, but even the most ignorant devotee can receive grace. Later, the monk Ippen (1239–1289) founded an offshoot of this group that accepted the power of Nembutsu but also taught a series of rituals called *Ji* (occasions) that brought physical healing and daily help. Another monk, Shinran (1173–1262), taught a message called the "Faith School"—that, while popular Shinto gods could help us with mundane requests for daily needs, only the Amida Buddha could offer salvation and entry into nirvana.

NICHIREN

Nichiren (1222–1282), the son of a poor fisherman, was a controversial monk who named himself Nichiren, meaning "sun and lotus." This name attempted to convey his claim that he alone preached the truth, and all other views were false. Believers in the Pure-Land were going to hell, Zen practitioners were demons, and Shingon teachers were ruining Japan. Acting more like an angry prophet than a peaceful monk, Nichiren shouted with irascible intolerance marked by his pugnacious inability to stomach hypocrisy. Eventually, he was arrested for his acerbic demagoguery. Despite his angry diatribes, many people were drawn to his main idea, which was easy to understand: the only true path was found in following *The Lotus Sutra*.

Nichiren's verbose message was infused with passionate nationalism. He was alarmed that his beloved nation had become so decadent, but he offered a solution for their plight. Nichiren believed a terrestrial kingdom would be established in Japan and not in distant realms. It was this bombastic and patriotic zeal that made him so popular with political rulers.

Today, Nichiren followers have kept to their founder's revolutionary, intransigent spirit and have organized several groups to disseminate their truth. *Rissho Kosei-kai* is one of those groups. It is a modern version of Nichiren that focuses more on personal worship than on nationalist ambitions. Members gather in groups on a weekly (or daily) basis in a group-counseling circle (*hoza*) to discuss problems and to meditate together.

Another modern offshoot of the Nichiren message, Soka Gakkai, is more militant and thus more like the founder of Nichiren. Soka Gakkai has been active in politics and zealously asserts that they are Buddha's true messengers who will rescue Japan from destruction. Early followers exhibited a "seeming intolerance of other religions," and this quality, along with "political ambitions of uniting religion and state under its guidance," led to a negative response from most Japanese.[26] In recent years, however, the Soka Gakkai movement has been less confrontative and has stressed its goals for universal peace and brotherhood. Some Buddhists in Japan claim that this group and others like it, are not actually Buddhists.

---

26. Reader et al., *Japanese Religions*, 125.

PART II

Buddhist and Christian Understandings

7

Lord Buddha and Lord Christ

> *A monk asked Yun Men, "What are the teachings of a whole lifetime?" Yun Men said, "An appropriate statement."*
> —Stephen Batchelor, *Buddhism without Beliefs*

> *I came to realize that what really matters is not a set of doctrines called Buddhism but people who live according to the doctrine of Buddha. We are just alike. We are failing to practice what the Buddha or Christ commanded. Comparisons on the level of Buddhist and Christian often produce an embarrassing result.*
> —Kosuke Koyama, *Water Buffalo Theology*

FRAMING THE QUESTIONS

THIS CHAPTER IS DESIGNED to help Buddhists and Christians explore the parallels between Christ in Christianity and Buddha in Buddhism. The very title of this chapter, however, has a decidedly Christian ring, and a more Buddhist rendering of the title might be "the Buddhas and the Christs" because Buddhists believe there are no individual selves.[1] This is expressed

---

1. Hee-Sung Keel describes Jesus as "the single highest incarnation of the Logos but

in the title Buddha used to describe himself, *Tathagata*, meaning both the "thus-come-one" and the "thus-gone-one." In a sense, there is also (so to speak) a Jesus, as there is a Buddha, beyond the limitations of human conceptions—the Buddha or the Christ of direct, personal engagement.

A more accurate way of framing the question might be, How is Buddha viewed among Buddhists, and how is Christ perceived among Christians? At the outset, we can appreciate that there are obvious differences that these founders play within these faiths. For Christians, Christ Jesus is God and the subject of faith, while for Buddhists, Buddha, as a teacher and an example of enlightenment, is the object of contemplation.

CHRIST MEETING BUDDHA

Christians believe Christ Jesus is alive and enters our hearts when we follow him through the agency of the Holy Spirit. Buddhism teaches that Buddha began as a human and pointed us away from himself and toward his teachings, while Christ Jesus who is God incarnate at birth, mandates that we turn to him directly as God, one with the Creator (John 10:30).

Can we draw meaningful parallels between these teachers from such distinct times and with such different messages? Is this even a worthwhile effort? Such considerations open new avenues for interfaith discussions. Is Marcus Borg correct: "If Jesus and Buddha were ever to meet, neither would try to convert the other—not because they would regard the task as hopeless, but because they would recognize each other"?[2] Neither Jesus nor Buddha ever claimed (or perhaps intended) to start new religions. Both Buddha and Jesus had miraculous births where holy men and women wept for joy.[3] Both are born without aid of earthly fathers and to mothers who were chaste.[4] Both Mary and Maya learn of their pregnancies through supernatural revelations. Siddhartha's birth is announced by tremulous earthquakes and gale-force winds. Christians sing of a star guiding the magi to

---

not the only one. Wherever love is at work, wherever there is freedom and self-giving acts of compassion, then the Logos is at work and manifesting itself" (Keel, "Jesus, the Bodhisattva," 184).

2. Borg and Riegert, eds., *Jesus and Buddha*, 79.

3. Asita is a wise man in Buddhism, and Simeon is a wise man in Christianity. Thich Nhât Hanh writes, "Whenever I read the stories of Asita and Simeon, I wish everyone of us could have been visited by a sage when we were born. The birth of every child is important, not less than the birth of a Buddha" (Nhât Hanh, *Living Buddha, Living Christ*, 46).

4. Karentzky cites traditions that state that Siddhartha was born without the "aid of an earthy father" (Karentzky, *The Life of the Buddha*, 10).

an animal-stable. Both Siddhartha and Jesus are announced at birth with ominous signs—from King Herod massacring many innocent children to the foreboding prophecies of priest Asita.

Both Jesus and Siddhartha were child prodigies who showed wisdom from a young age. Jesus taught at the temple as a child (Luke 2:47–49), while the prince entertained scholars at age eight to teach them languages they did not know existed.[5] Both Buddha and Christ become teachers who left their fathers' homes at about the same age to live in solitude before gathering together a group of followers to preach the truth.[6] Both underwent extreme periods of temptation before beginning ministries. They faced desert/forest periods when they confronted external and internal demons and, in triumph, are catalyzed to move into ministry. Did both enter these times of testing with a sense of their mission or eventual goals? After these times of testing, both were comforted by supernatural beings.[7]

At first, their followings were small, beginning with a few selected students. This model of small communities affecting larger contexts has, subsequently, been foundational to the formation of both the Buddhist community and the Christian church. At the outset, their messages would have seemed radical to their first disciples. Buddha's Deer Park Sermon and Christ's Sermon on Mount established notes of confrontation with the status quo. Jesus confronted pharisaic formalism with a declaration of God's kingdom while Buddha challenged Brahmanic formalism with the creation of an egalitarian community.

Both were unafraid to confront many of the social injustices of their times. Both were born during times of major political and social upheaval.[8] Jesus lived under the rule of an autocratic military state while, Siddhartha lived when social tensions increased while standards of ethical behavior diminished.[9] Both advocated for social reforms but focused critiques in very divergent directions.[10] While Jesus focused on the marginalized and poor,

---

5. Thundy, *Buddha and Christ*, 120.

6. The most common age assigned to Siddhartha's going forth is twenty-nine, but some cite age nineteen.

7. Lefebure notes the gods celebrated on the earth for four weeks (Lefebure, *The Buddha and the Christ*, 18).

8. J. Massyngbaerde Ford wrote it was "one of the most turbulent and belligerent centuries of Jewish history. It has been called the seething cauldron of first-century Judaism" (Ford, *My Enemy Is My Guest*, 1).

9. See Chakravarti, *The Social Dimensions of Early Buddhism*.

10. Buddha offered advice for rulers. Christ mostly ignored government's role, saying, "Give to the emperor the things that are the emperor's, and to God the things that are God's" (Mark 12:17).

Buddha attacked the caste system and the centrality of Brahmanism.[11] Buddha also gave a list of guidelines that just rulers should follow, which Jesus did not emulate.[12] Both lived in poverty and owned no possessions. Neither wrote any book. Finally, both men chose the time and place of their deaths and followers carried on their work after they passed into higher realms.

DIFFERENT JOURNEYS

There are obvious differences: Buddha comes as the last link in a long chain of enlightened beings while Christians herald that Jesus had no previous life on earth. Siddhartha was born into wealth as a prince while Jesus was born into obscurity and relative poverty. Jesus learns a worker's trade, while Siddhartha, as a prince, learns how to govern. Siddhartha was married while Jesus never married.[13] Christ dies an inconceivably violent, sadistic death—a humiliating public execution—at a relatively young age after widespread persecution.[14] He is betrayed by followers and abandoned by all. In contrast, Buddha leaves life privately and peacefully at a dignified old age without much opposition. He is surrounded by friends at his passing. Christ's crucifixion is central to Christians while Buddha's passing has no major significance in the ethical teachings of Buddhism. Jesus frequently referred to hell and the end of the world, but neither of these themes have any prominence in Buddha's teachings. Siddhartha is a man clouded in uncertainty, and little about him can be said with any historical confidence. There is no single collection of books like the New Testament that details specifics about his life. What we can say about Buddha goes through the ahistorical filter of

---

11. "Jesus promoted radical egalitarianism in his repudiation of class boundaries, in his anti-hierarchical views, in his skepticism about institutions, and in his empathy with and prioritizing the cause of the poor and the downtrodden of society" (Cabezón, "A God, Not a Savior," 19).

12. According to Chakravarti (*The Social Dimensions of Early Buddhism*, 16–19), these *Dasa Raja dharma*, "Teachings for Just Kings," called for rulers to be nonviolent with subjects. Chakravarti writes that Buddha taught that "the social order rested on property" and called for a social contract between ruler and subject (152).

13. Rahula was born after thirteen years of marriage (Luz and Michaels, *Encountering Jesus and Buddha*, 11).

14. Suzuki (quoted in Lefebure, *The Buddha and the Christ*, 50): "The crucified Christ is a terrible sight and I cannot help associating it with the sadistic impulses of a physically affected brain . . . Buddhism declares that there is from the very beginning no self to crucify. To think that there is a self is the start of all errors and evils. Ignorance is at the root of all things that go wrong. As there is no self, no crucifixion is needed, no sadism is to be practiced, and no shocking sight is to be displayed by the roadside."

centuries of devotional literature. This is also true, to a lesser extent, of the historical facts of the life of Jesus, who lived during a more recent era.

Both Siddhartha and Jesus were born into caring families, and both renounced the security of loving homes to live unmarried lives. Jesus spoke little about family duties and framed many discussions in terms of those that a young person would be concerned with (e.g., leaving your father and mother). He taught that people would have to abandon wives and aged-relatives if they truly wanted to follow him (Luke 9:57–62; 14:25–27; 18:28–30). Karen Armstrong observes, "Gautama took it for granted that family life was incompatible with the highest forms of spirituality. This was a perception shared not only by other ascetics in India but also by Jesus."[15] Both teachers lived outside of the cultural standards that many accept as being normative. Perhaps Jesus was using such emphatic language to emphasize the primacy of the kingdom of God. From a commonly held Buddhist view, one could say that the statements of Jesus show a "certain attitude of unimportance accorded" by Jesus towards "his own mother and brothers and sisters that allows him to share with others a genuine compassion that is free from the limitations of personal bias."[16] Critics of this claim note Jesus announced, "Let the little children come to me, and do not stop them; for it is to such as these that the kingdom of heaven belongs" (Matt 19:14; see also Mark 10:14; Luke 18:16) and recited other parables and teachings that affirm the centrality of family. That Jesus did not leave home until age thirty as well as his relationship with his mother show the value of family relationships in Christ's life.

Even though the blessing of ultimate authority was on each, both Jesus and Buddha experienced lives of tremendous difficulty marked by challenging circumstances. Each rejected a life of comfort for the demanding tasks of itinerant preaching. The Dalai Lama said that "both the lives of Jesus and Buddha teach us that only through hardship, dedication, and commitment, and by standing firm to one's principles that one can grow spiritually and attain liberation."[17]

---

15. Armstrong, *Buddha*, 2. Armstrong continues, "Gautama would not, therefore, have agreed with our current cult of family values. Nor would some of his contemporaries in other parts of the world such as Confucius, and Socrates, who were certainly not family-minded men" (3).

16. Dalai Lama XIV, *The Good Heart*, 73. A monk named Ajahn Amaro states, "As a Buddhist monk living in the West, I am often asked about non-attachment, as people are concerned that it is a kind of callousness or hard-heartedness. Rather than *detachment*, however, one way of translating this Buddhist concept might be more a sense of *non-possessiveness* toward other people and things."

17. Dalai Lama XIV, *Opening the Eye of New Awareness*, 58.

MESSAGES

What helped both Buddha and Jesus to press through hardships was a conviction that they were preaching vital truth. Both Jesus and Buddha dedicated themselves to teach and are described as "doors" into a deeper life. Neither chose an easy path of contentment but shared a message of compassion. Both not only taught their message but lived it and encouraged followers to live with simplicity. Jesus advised us to take nothing for our journey (Matt 10:10; Mark 6:8; Luke 9:3) and to live with of mission-focused humility and contentment.

Although Jesus and Buddha both excelled at public speaking, they also had a personal way about them that invites us into their lives with an authentic transparency. Scriptures in both traditions tell of conversations over meals and a host of other intimate settings. Both teachers spoke in a common language of relevance, clarity, and simplicity. Neither preacher had any interest in opaque sophistry. Sometimes, they used parables and something akin to Socratic questioning.[18] Their focus was not on the intellectual and religious elite but on the uneducated and marginalized: this explains why their messages were taught in the vernacular.

Many of their preaching themes share common ground and were not new but were bold revisions of long-held ideas. Both Buddha and Christ used paradoxes when preaching to drive home a surprising point. Buddha's ideas ran "against the grain of the beliefs current in his time."[19] In the same way, Jesus was viewed as a revolutionary, and followers were seen as those "who have been turning the world upside down" (Acts 17:6). Both teachers realized their messages would not, at least initially, be understood by the poor or readily welcomed by the religious elite.

Both Jesus and Buddha attacked formalized religion and bankrupt spirituality. While some practiced faithful adherence to proper rituals, they were like "white-washed tombs" (Matt 23:27), "blind guides" (Matt 15:14; 23:16, 24), and a "brood of vipers" (Matt 3:7; 12:34; 23:33; Luke 3:7) because they were agents of stale formalism. Jesus taught that many Pharisees were on the side of oppression while claiming to be righteous (Matt 23:23–24). The motives of our actions were central to both Jesus and Buddha. Both confronted those of us who turn rituals into "mere formalities and external elaborations" that lead us towards "bankrupt customs."[20]

---

18. Thundy writes, "The Buddha used Socratic questioning, parables, formulas, and sermons" (Thundy, *Buddha and Christ*, 54).

19. Dhamma, *The First Discourse of the Buddha*, 12.

20. Dalai Lama XIV, *Opening the Eye of New Awareness*, 64–65.

Jesus was divine before he was human (John 1:1). His humanity meant that he was finite and would die, but his divinity reveals that his life has no end. Luke 2:52 says Jesus grew in knowledge and wisdom: The idea of Jesus learning challenges those who would emphasize his full divinity at the cost of his full humanity. Buddhism teaches that every one of us has something inside of us that Christians might call the *Logos* nature, while, according to the Bible, Christ alone is the manifestation of the divine life-giving *Logos*.

How does the eternal die on the cross? How can the "Author of life" be "killed" (Acts 3:15)? How does the son of God learn anything "through what he suffered" (Heb 5:8)? Christ's life defies logic, and like a Zen koan, brings us into a new way of seeing the world. Jesus is a divine koan—the unexplainable divine Word made flesh. God in Christ lays aside the prerogatives of divinity and enters humanity in complete vulnerability. In Buddhism, humanity, as lived by Siddhartha, exists within the finite and enters the infinite by becoming the embodied Buddha. Siddhartha's humanity is perishable while the unfettered Buddha-nature is eternal. For Christians, Christ's fully human nature is resurrected into the divine nature of the eternal God.

It is the physically resurrected, cosmic Christ who calls for a "Great Commission" to go and "make disciples of all nations" (Matt 28:16–20). God's love is expressed in the amazing sacrifice of the cross and is extended in the preaching and baptism of all peoples. The power of God transcends the power of humanity.

Buddha and Christ are called Lord by those who ascribe to them the highest honor. Their lordship is related to ultimate realities. Buddha teaches that each person should open themselves up to divinity as well as to the knowledge that we gain in our humanity. Buddha is awakened and becomes an exemplar of how we can become "thoroughly emancipated by perfect knowledge."[21] Jesus, in contrast, is a divine savior and not only a human teacher. In Buddhism, we rely on the teaching, not on the teacher. One Christian explained, "while Buddha shows us the way, Jesus is the way."[22]

What are some widespread views about Jesus as taught by Buddhists? Christ is honored as one who assumes a bodhisattva-role and is a refuge for followers. In the same way that Buddha is not a singularity, neither is the Christ of God. Free from any need to "rank" Jesus in relation to Buddha, Buddhists see that Jesus has a great ability to influence with "skillful means" those who believe in him.[23] One Japanese monk called Jesus "the person who lives out perfectly the link of into-nothingness and out-of-nothingness,"

---

21. Sparks, "Buddha and Christ," 200.
22. Muck, "Images of the Buddha," 97.
23. Gross, "Meditating on Jesus," 46–47.

while a Thai monk claimed Christ ranked as "an apostle or prophet of truth on par with the Buddha."[24] Buddhists view Jesus as a teacher with a message of prevailing love. Thich Nhât Hanh says that all can learn from Christ because "we are all of the same nature of Jesus," sharing the same potential for awakening.[25] Nhât Hanh also believes Jesus was an enlightened soul and notes that, at baptism, "the heavens were opened to him and he saw the Spirit of God descending like a dove" (Matt 3:16).

Christians have viewed Buddha from many angles, but in this context I will cite only one perspective. Anglican missionary Bishop Stephen Neill remarked about Buddha:

> The first thing that strikes the reader who contemplates the character of the Teacher is graciousness. This is a man filled with real concern for his fellowman, fired with a compassionate sense of mission, always calm, always reasonable, and always gentle, not without a sense of humor.[26]

Neill challenges Christians to shift our predisposition from one dismissive of Buddhism to one of appreciating the kerygmatic heart of Buddha. Neill invites us to be sympathetic toward what is central to the Buddhist community. He calls Christians to see how the mission of Jesus and Buddha are conversant in many regards, not least in the motivation of both to seek and to save the lost. For Bishop Neill, Buddhist and Christian missions are rooted in this passion at the heart of these two faiths. Buddha is a soul who has penetrated the realm of what it means to be human and has seen reality for what it is, not what it should be. Because Buddha teaches the ego of illusion had to be overthrown, his way of helping humanity is simply by telling the truth. Buddha's empathy also explains, for Neill, why the Buddhist community has at times fallen captive to the embrace of civic powers who have used the faith for their own political ends.

For Bishop Neill, what is foundational in any discussion comparing the Buddha and the Christ is that both embody lives of love. For Jesus, it is his oneness with God that undergirds his heart of compassion. For Buddha, compassion arises from surrender to the truth that all beings are interrelated. Love is central to Christianity, revealing that God becomes a human and then ascends to heaven in resurrection, forever changed by Christ's humanity. Jesus has come to "save sinners" and "display the utmost patience" (1 Tim 1:15–16). Jesus is one with God and yet submits to the Father as a full

---

24. Cabezón, "A God, Not a Savior," 16.
25. Cabezón, "A God, Not a Savior," 16.
26. Neill, *Christian Faith and Other Faiths*, 101.

expression of love incarnate (John 5:19-20). For Christians, the revelation of Christ's love provides God's path to our freedom from sin (Rom 5:8-11).

ASCENDED CHRIST, COSMIC BUDDHA

If the ultimate reality is love, then both Jesus and Buddha embody a revelation of that truth. Buddhism declares that emptiness leads us to be full of empathy. It also explains that individuality is a hindrance to the full expression of compassion, whereas individuality is fully embraced within Christianity and is also described to express the fullness.

Both traditions focus on the grandiose task of identifying our suffering and then delivering us from its satanic grip. It is breathtaking to imagine the scope of such spiritual ambitions. It speaks volumes, however, to the breadth of spiritual engagement as practiced by the Buddha and the Christ. Both faiths believe that Buddha and Jesus have the audacious capability to conquer the power of suffering (and even death) with the weapons of divine love. Christians teach that Jesus incarnates God's love for us, and Christians reject all gnostic ideas that disembody God and offer hidden teachings about God's esoteric nature. Each faith offers a path for liberation from the greatest pains of normative human experience.

Buddha teaches that the elimination of the self will lead to an end to suffering. This task rests on each of us, although Greater Path Buddhists claim that power can be granted through the aid of various bodhisattvas. Jesus teaches that the self must also be subsumed but claims that our ego must be surrendered to the perfect will of God. We are unable to achieve these lofty goals through our own efforts. We must throw ourselves on the mercy of a forgiving God and receive as a gift from a loving God the divine work of eternal salvation.

Each faith brims with high idealism. The task of discipleship in both faiths is to actualize these ideals in daily life. Both faiths call their communities to heightened ethical ideals. The agency of the Holy Spirit, or the power of enlightenment, sets us free as we were originally intended to live, in abundant spiritual insight and free from the chains of suffering. Both Buddha and Jesus offer a pathway of light amid the world's suffocating darkness. For Buddhists and Christians, the messages (and lives) of their teachers are very much alive. All that has died is that which is temporary and transient. The eternal Christ will never repeat an earthly life, and his revelation came within the framework of specific history. While Christ died, this emphatically was not temporary, as his physical resurrection proves. Jesus remains in a resurrected body to this very day. Christians proclaim that his nail-scarred hands will remain as the only "imperfection" in heaven. The ascended Christ (Rev 1:17–18) has risen from the dead and is alive through God's Spirit. The cosmic Buddha continues to teach even as the historical Buddha is gone.

For Christians, the resurrection is the ultimate validation of God's salvific work in life (John 20:10–18). It is at the heart of Christ's transforming gospel. Resurrection power over death means that the message bound up in the life of the messenger remains as relevant today as it did when first presented. Saint Paul reminds Christians that if Christ is not raised from the dead then our faith "has been in vain," and "we are of all men most to be pitied" (1 Cor 15:13–19). As he is now ascended, he raises humanity back to God (John 12:32). In the same way, the Buddha is alive because his "consciousness and mind-stream have continued and are ever present." Although his earthly life is completed, he is still present with us as a "state of perfect resourcefulness."[27] Both Jesus and Buddha came from absolute power and returned alive to the eternal homeland of pure love and truth. Resurrection creates the ultimate reintegration of the temporal with the eternal. The ascended Christ and the cosmic Buddha are omnipresent, more accessible in the resurrection than they were in temporal life. Christians believe that Jesus can live in our hearts through the Holy Spirit, in a way that may approximate the way Buddha Nature is now accessible to us through the life of Buddha. The cosmic Buddha and the cosmic Christ—through God's Spirit—are actively working wherever we pray, meditate, or seek to know the way of life and truth.

Both Buddhists and Christians speak about the Lord returning to the earth at the "end of time." The second coming of Christ parallels the eschatology of many Greater Path Buddhists who share that the Buddha Maitreya (Pali: *Metteya*) will return to the world during an epoch of crisis to rescue humanity. Without being infected by a preoccupied millenarian fever, this widely cherished messianic hope illustrates that Buddhists believe that the central force of faith is not a historical figure but a living and dynamic reality—the Buddha.[28]

---

27. Dalai Lama XIV, *Opening the Eye of New Awareness*, 119.

28. One should not forget that Buddhist cosmology is not rooted in a linear metanarrative, which is central to the Judeo-Christian view of a Messiah or of the anticipated Islamic Mahdi.

CHALLENGES

The Greater Path doctrine that there are bodhisattvas who serve as mediators between all of us and the supernatural has obvious parallels to the idea of Jesus as a mediator between God and humanity. Some have conjectured that there might have been some historical connection (especially in China) between Pure-Land Buddhism and a Christianity that focused on the idea that Christ came as a savior to rescue us from suffering. Church tradition teaches that both Saint Thomas and, later, Nestorian missionaries visited India and would have met with Buddhists. There were many trade routes between the Middle East and Asia. The fact that Roman-era Palestinian coins (and other items) have been found in India provides possible proofs of such connections.

If our interfaith goals are focused on a stronger appreciation of what each of our faiths cherishes, then our interactions will move from focusing on the extreme polarities of differences or similarities towards loving acceptance. To quote a Taoist proverb, "To ask a certain question, you have to be a certain kind of person."[29] Asked to make such comparisons, the Dalai Lama replied:

> If you are asking how a practicing Christian should understand the uniqueness of Christ, then my answer is that it is only by relying on the authoritative scriptures of the spiritual fathers of the past that one may understand [Christ]. . . For me, as a Buddhist, my attitude towards Jesus Christ is that he was either a fully enlightened being or a bodhisattva of a very high spiritual revelation.[30]

The question itself says more about the point of reference of the questioner than it does about the issue raised in the question. In *Alice's Adventures in Wonderland*, Alice is asked by the Mad Hatter at a tea-party "why is a raven like a writing-desk?" After Alice thinks about it, she asks the Mad Hatter, who sagely replies, "I haven't the slightest idea."[31] Instead of fixating on artificial correlations, Christians and Buddhists should focus on respectful interrelationships.

---

29. I no longer have the source for this proverb.

30. Dalai Lama XIV, *The Good Heart*, 80–81. The question that he was responding to was posed by the Buddhist monk Ajahn Amaro. The question was: "Your Holiness, I do not know if I dare ask another metaphysical question. But speaking of differences in our traditions, as a Westerner I have always found it hard to accommodate the uniqueness of Jesus Christ, to understand him as a completely unique human being, different from all others that have ever appeared."

31. Carroll, *Alice's Adventures in Wonderland*, 200, 70, 73.

Why do misrepresentations arise in many Buddhist–Christian interactions? For some, the thought that both Jesus and Buddha can exist in God's perfectly ordered cosmos without some interreference seems unthinkable. The complex world must be reduced to the conceivable.[32] The very concept of uniqueness, however, means that more than one person or one message can be unique. While the Bible speaks of Christ's uniqueness, it remains the task of the church to provide an interpretation of that uniqueness that explains how Jesus relates to other faiths. What is the comparative significance of Christ's uniqueness? God is bigger than any limitation.

Both Christ and Buddha lived in distinct times and preached distinct messages. These differences allow us to explore questions about their interrelationships with the rewarding freedom of not being constrained to reach any kind of presumptive or synthetic, synthesizing conclusions. Perhaps there is only one answer to the Mad Hatter's question, but perhaps there are many answers, or even none. What is most relevant to Buddhist and Christian interactions is that we learn all we can about what each of our faiths cherishes, and then work together to live out our beliefs in faithful ways that foster constructive and genuine interactions.

---

32. One is reminded of Captain Barnett in Ray Bradbury's *Fahrenheit 451*, who mandates the burning of all books, not because their ideas are revolutionary, but because they are complicated.

8

Dharma and Gospel

In my own experience, I have found that the most effective method to overcome conflicts is close contact and exchange among those of various beliefs, not only on an intellectual level, but in deeper, spiritual experiences. This is a powerful method to developing mutual understanding and respect. Through this interchange, a strong foundation of genuine harmony can be established.

—The Dalai Lama, *The Good Heart*

BUDDHIST AND CHRISTIAN SCRIPTURES

COMPARING CHRISTIAN SCRIPTURES AND Buddhist writings is like comparing apples with oranges. We should not assume that the way one group views holy books is shared by other groups. Buddhist teachings, for example, are gathered not only from ancient scriptures but also from the examples of other Buddhists, and even from the lessons of the natural world. Buddhist writings aspire to be practical and applicational in scope. Like Christian scriptures, Buddhist scriptures offer followers both "a transcendent path and a practical one."[1]

Religious texts are often examined by non-Buddhists as a starting-point to learn more about Buddhism. Something new emerges through

---

1. Nyanasobhano, *Landscapes of Wonder*, 5.

efforts to launch Buddhist–Christian textual dialogues. Because, according to Christians, God is the author of both changelessness and change, a multireferent hermeneutic of scriptures need not be an obstacle to devotion. The identity of a reader and the significance given to the text affect how texts are understood. When Christians discuss the Bible in the context of learning about Buddhist texts, we can be encouraged to recognize a "symbiotic approach to the reading of texts," which "stresses the living encounter of religions, resulting in a further articulation of implicit meanings which these texts would not reveal unless they are mutually exposed to each other's illuminating discourses."[2]

Shared scripture study might facilitate insights for shared reflection. Even historical narratives of past events may be appreciated considering how they relate to our lives. Origen, in the third century, wrote that the Bible should be read in a figurative, metaphorical way as well as with a literal reading. The Dalai Lama has taught that when we read scriptures, we should remember that what we are reading shows "things that happened in earlier times. In fact, all these things come true to you in a mystical way."[3]

Textual studies are dynamic and fluid readings rooted in specific cultural contexts. Talmudic scholar Aviva Gottlieb Zornberg notes that frequent commands in the Bible for the Jewish people to retell the "story" make it clear that God is as much concerned with the present-tense telling of stories as God is with establishing a memorial narrative about events frozen in the past.[4] A story's significance has a life based on, and not independent of, history.

DIVINITY AND HUMANITY

One of the first questions Gospel readers might ask readers of Buddhist texts is how the Christian concept of God relates to Buddha. If by God you mean the God described in the New Testament, then, of course, Buddhists do not believe in that God. Their texts do not describe a personal, creator God. If, however, you are referencing God in a general sense, then Mahanaya Buddhist texts do speak about an ultimate power source—the Buddha Nature.[5]

---

2. Lee, "Cross-Textual Hermeneutics," 193.

3. Dalai Lama XIV, *Opening the Eye of New Awareness*, 27.

4 See Zornberg, *Moses*.

5. Therevada Buddhists do not speak of each person as inherently having a Buddha nature although they affirm that all beings can reach enlightenment. Recent scholarship, however, has claimed that there was an early esoteric strand in Theravada Buddhism that did involve creating—rather than uncovering—a Buddha inside oneself. I owe these observations to Elizabeth Harris.

Both faiths teach that the absolute is transcendent beyond the limitations of time and space. Terms like *atheism* and *agnosticism* are fraught with problems because they bring to the question their own presuppositions. One teacher explained, "No person who is meditating could possibly say, 'I am an agnostic.' This is tantamount to saying that there is no ocean."[6] Can we say the line between humanity and divinity is blurred in Buddhism? Although this is a very Christian question, the answer is—without apology—yes, in so far as the physical world is not as real as the spiritual world. The clarion potency of reality is the Absolute, and the Absolute is permanent and infinite while all else is impermanent and finite.

A commonly held Buddhist critique of Christianity is that views about God's nature have become the foundation for Christianity's perceived anthropocentrism. This critique reflects the challenges faced by those involved in interfaith interactions where we are forced to think outside the boxes of our own theoretical preconceptions. Guanapala Dharmasiri thought Christianity advocates an "alienated view of [humanity] where man is said to be essentially superior to all other creatures because of being created in the image of God. Because of this, [humanity] is seen as qualitatively different from other creatures . . . This idea inflated and strengthened man's [individual] ego, thus alienating man from the rest of creation."[7] Instead of fostering an inflated sense of ego, the scriptures should "help us understand the world as it really is."[8]

While some Christians think Buddhism is a pessimistic religion, Buddhists challenge Christians to consider views "with eyes-open."[9] Instead of pessimism, "the experience of Buddhism is the experience of joy. Far from being the grim and nihilistic philosophy it has often been mistaken for in the West, it is a supremely optimistic and positive vision."[10] Indeed, what could be more pessimistic than the idea held by many Christians that we are born with a sin nature that can, quite possibly, send us to be tortured in an eternal hell? Even if Buddhist teachings are pessimistic at times, is it not vital to live "without illusion or false consolations"?[11]

---

6. MacInnes, *Zen Contemplation for Christians*, 54.

7. Dharmasiri, *A Buddhist Critique of the Christian Concept of God*, 260. Dharmasiri contrasts this with the Vedic tradition, which calls cow-eaters "mother eaters." In the *Sasa Jakata*, a rabbit, who is always addressed as Pandit Sasa, is a *Bodhisattva* who offers himself as food for a hungry person (261).

8. Batchelor, *Buddhism without Beliefs*, 18.

9. Smart uses the term "eyes-open" for the Buddhist cosmic vision. See Smart, *Buddhism and Christianity*, 51.

10. Corless, *The Vision of Buddhism*, 19.

11. Harvey, foreword, xiv.

A key difference between the two faiths can be seen in two different views of human nature. Bishop Kenneth Cragg writes, "it is clear that Christian faith has a radical quarrel with the Buddhist equation between selfhood and selflessness."[12] Christians believe that there is individual personhood, while Buddhists rejects this assumption. Christian salvation focuses on the transformation of the individual soul (Matt 10:28; Mark 8:36–37), a concept Buddhists reject as unverifiable. Christians claim we are made in God's image, whereas Buddhists believe all beings are interrelated, and no beings are distinct reflections of a being above other beings. Instead of seeing distinctions, Buddhist Charlotte Joko Beck writes in *New Jersey Doesn't Exist* that when you look at the world from the vantage of an airplane, there are no visible boundaries. Boundaries divide places from each other but have no basis within reality. She states:

> We confuse the map with reality itself. Maps are useful; but if we just look at the map, we cannot see the unity that is the United States. There is no Kansas as a separate entity. Like a white blood cell, we're designed to have a certain function within this enormous energy pattern that we are.[13]

Buddhism teaches that when we realize the unity of everything, we will be freed from arbitrary distinctions. A Zen story tells of two monks meeting and exchanging names. In their conversation the one monk asks the other to repeat his name again because he has forgotten:

> Kyozan Ejaku asked Sansho Enen, "What is your name again?"
> Sansho said,
> "Ejaku!"
> "Ejaku!" replied Ejaku Kyozan, "that is my name."
> "Well then," said Sansho Enen, "My name is Enen."
> Ejaku Kyozan roared with laughter.

Because none of us has an individual, distinct ego, we have no reason to feel superior or inferior to one another. Our interconnectivity means that it is only appropriate to show loving compassion to those that we interact with because as we love others, we love ourselves (Mark 12:31). When we are freed from the prison of isolating ego, we experience an exuberant joy. One is reminded of the bold shout of William Wallace in *Braveheart*: "Freedom!" Learning from the scriptures changes our perspectives and serves as a spiritual vacuum cleaner to sweep away false notions in our minds.[14] We

---

12. Cragg, *The Christ and the Faiths*, 254.
13. Beck, *Everyday Zen*, 166.
14. Like our bodies, clothes are useful to keep a person warm or dry only when they

should speak with honest words even when asked to share difficult truths. Insincerity is another form of illusion.

The idea that we cannot fully know ourselves resonates with the words of Saint Paul: "Now I know only in part; then I will know fully, even as I have been fully known" (1 Cor 13:12). Even though the Bible teaches that God is infinite, it also reveals God has become knowable through the incarnation in Jesus Christ. We are made in God's image, with the capacity to relate in intimate communion with the Lord of the world. Christian liberation brings an accurate self-awareness of both our worth as creations of God and our limits as finite beings in temporary bodies. Self-perception in historic Christianity is expressed in the context of a beloved community and in the flow of a right relationship with God. Ulrich Luz writes that the mother tongue Jesus spoke "had no word for the self," so any teaching on self-denial invariably had a corporate sense.[15]

In interfaith dialogue, it is often a question of focus that determines what similarities or differences are emphasized. Christians, for example, often confront the idols of immoral practice, while Buddhists often attack the idols of cognitive ideals that seek to fill the emptiness with the clutter of ignorant delusions. Using these ideas, we might say that a Christian is the purest (leaving aside original sin) when we are newborns because the life of a baby is free from a developed cognitive awareness that relates to our sinfulness.

The terms that we use to describe our culturally rooted religious ideas are often a key factor in promoting a sense of difference instead of fostering an appreciation of what we share. This dynamic leads to a host of obstacles when trying to describe useful parallels between faiths that are exploring distinct questions. Christianity proclaims, for example, the need for repentance from sin, while sin is not as an ontological concept in Buddhism. Christians often view sin to be anything opposed to God's will. Nonadherence to the "will of the Buddha," dharma, or sangha is not a sin but an expression that we are choosing to continue in a state of delusion. Disillusionment, arising from falsity, is attacked by both traditions. Desire is the source of disillusionment within Buddhism. It is the duty of each of us to overcome misconceptions through right-thinking. While Buddhists describe suffering as a problem brought on by false thinking and with no redeeming benefit, many Christians believe that the problem of suffering is

---

are not being used by someone else, when they are empty, and when they are available for our use. See Novak, *The World's Wisdom*, 79.

15. Luz and Michaels, *Encountering Jesus & Buddha*, 59.

rooted in a mortal, sinful nature while also teaching that some suffering can have redemptive value.

LIVING THE MESSAGE

Both Buddhists and Christians seek to gain truth by becoming "born again" into a new life marked by a transformed perspective on reality. Christianity agrees that we are mired in our own desires and need deliverance. True life in both faiths is to be "crucified" of our selfish ego by allowing the Christ-nature to live through daily life (Gal 2:20). While Christians are saved once and for all by Jesus on the cross, Saint Paul in Galatians 5 lists a series of "works of the flesh" that some Christians might continue to fall into when they unwisely feed their selfish ego:

> It is obvious what kind of life develops out of trying to get your own way all the time: repetitive, loveless, cheap sex, a stinking accumulation of mental and emotional garbage; frenzied and joyless grabs for happiness; trinket gods; magic-show religion; paranoid loneliness; cutthroat competition; all-consuming-yet-never-satisfied wants; a brutal temper; an impotence to love or be loved; divided homes and divided lives; small-minded and lopsided pursuits; the vicious habit of depersonalizing everyone into a rival; uncontrolled and uncontrollable addictions; ugly parodies of community. I could go on. (Gal 5:19–21, *The Message*)

Jesus has come to strip us of selfish behaviors (Eph 4:22; Col 3:9) and replace self-centeredness with a newer self (Eph 4:24; Col 3:10), which is embodied in Jesus.

Christians are called to "die" to selfish ego and be "resurrected" into a new reality inside of Christ (Rom 6:3–11; Col 2:12). This "birth from above" (John 3:3) makes us a "new creation" (Gal 6:15; 2 Cor 5:17). When the bondage of death and sin are destroyed within us, a new, inner person can emerge into right relationship with God and in right relation with a community of believers. Christians are called to imitate Christ in death in order to live the Christian life (Rom 6:5; Phil 3:10). Death is no final barrier but only an inevitable starting point in an eternal relationship directed toward right relationship with God.

To use Buddhist language, the full actualization of Christ takes place when ego vanishes and only the ultimate (Christ for the Christian) remains. But the Christian view of this transformed-self remains distinct from the Buddhist belief that the self must be eliminated and will vanish when we become enlightened. Kosuke Koyama explains that Buddha offers followers the truth of "no-self" while Christ offers followers the call for a "new-self."[16]

J. M. Barrie's Peter Pan said that "to die would be an awfully big adventure." Varying views on death in these two traditions spring from distinct views about the nature of existence. Because Christians often hold a linear view of time, death is viewed in a distinct way. Death for a Buddhist does not end the samsara cycle of suffering and does not have the same sense of finality as one would have if they believed in a heaven or a hell. In fact, death might offer a positive step along the path to enlightenment. Death does not touch our soul in Buddhism as it does in Christianity, because we have no distinct soul to be saved or lost. Buddha cannot be a "savior" because there is no distinct being needing to be saved.[17]

The pressing demands of our material world should not be our primary focus for either a Buddhist or a Christian. The distractions of materialism dull awareness and lead to disconnection, disengagement, and ignorance. We should avoid becoming trapped inside an empty, material life. Buddha says, "Those who have not lived a spiritual life and have not laid up spiritual treasures in their youth," will, in old age, "lie around useless like worn-out bows and arrows, sighing after the past."[18] Christianity stridently warns against the dangers of materialism. Jesus told us not to worry about food, drink, clothing, or success (Matt 6:25–34; Luke 12:22–26). Christ says that if we seek to be saved, we will be lost: "those who want to save their life will lose it" (Matt 16:25). The unquenchable cravings of materialism abort meaningful spiritual life.

In language that closely parallels Buddhism, Christians are called to become empty (kenosis) of all individual pride and selfish ego and to follow the example of Jesus who "emptied himself" (Phil 2:7) in obedience to God. Jürgen Moltmann writes that the kenosis of God in Christ is a revelation of God's unselfish *agape* love:

> Everything exists and lives in reciprocal permeation and in dynamic interrelationship. The unselfish empathy of God awakens the sympathy of all creatures for each other. *Perichoresis*

---

16. While Buddhists assert that self-loathing, competitiveness, and insecurity will fall away once a person accepts that they have no soul, such positive traits as self-sufficiency, self-reliance, self-expression, self-motivation would also be lost when one accepts that there is no real self.

17. "When we refute the soul, or atman theory, we are refuting the theory of a substantial person. There is no independent self that exists substantially from its own side" (Dalai Lama XIV, *Buddha Nature*, 38).

18. Muller, *Dhammapada*, 49 (citation, 11.156).

[community in mutual interdependence and interpretation] is the deepest mystery of creation.[19]

Our "emptiness" is to be filled with Jesus in the same way that a Buddhist's emptiness is to be filled with the Buddha Nature. While Christian virtue depends upon a measure of "self-love" given the teaching of Jesus that we are to "love our neighbor as we love ourselves," this self-love is free of the ego that harshly demands its own grasping needs above the needs of others. One Christian observes that in both Christianity and Buddhism, "the egocentric view of one's own ego leads to the result that we get caught in a kind of self-fettering or narcissism."[20]

According to Buddhism, when we are emptied with the disintegration of a separate self, there is no longer any connection to a world of experience. Because experiences are illusionary, any sense that they are substantive must be abandoned. What makes everything interrelated is the emptiness that all things share. When we perceive our own intrinsic emptiness, we see life in its most authentic nature. Because enlightenment can only be actualized through the defeat of desire, we escape suffering by emptying ourselves of ourselves. A vibrant attitude that accepts the reality of human emptiness (*shunyata*) leads to spiritual liberation. When "empty," we are no longer bound by any limitations. When we appreciate our potential for limitlessness, we experience a spontaneous naturalness (Japanese: *jinen*), which includes our embrace of wisdom (*prajna*) and compassion (*karuna*). While many accept the perception of life's "fullness," it is the fundamental "emptiness" of all things we should appreciate. In fact, this central insight about emptiness is "the most powerful weapon against our fundamental ignorance and against all hindrances. It stops the process of erroneous perception, and the overloading of objects (indeed, of all reality) with thick layers of concepts. It eliminates the artificial separation between 'me' and the rest of the world."[21] We must "let go" all notions of self-importance and accept that we are like "leaves in the wind," twirling about by the whims of nature. We are minor in a much larger process of constant change (*samsara*). Those who think otherwise are "wearing out their ingenuity at the impossible and futile task of trying to get the water of life into neat and permanent packages."[22] The force of emptiness (*shunyata*) is that nothing has its own distinct identity or possibility for permanence.

---

19. Moltmann "God Is Unselfish Love," 121.
20. Waldenfels, *Absolute Nothingness*, 81.
21. Dagyab, *Buddhist Symbols in Tibetan Culture*, 5–6.
22. Watts, *The Wisdom of Insecurity*, 14.

For Christians, God is not an impersonal essence that functions as a part of a mechanized universe. God is holy and above us (Hos 11:9). In God's image, we have individual souls (personalities) created with distinct and individual qualities (Rom 12:4–6). The world for Christians is not an entity of factors or random energies or interactions but a place or order and design, invested with the significance of both the ideal and the marred. The suffering that exists arises from the desires of sin. Death has come into the world, and Christ's death will redeem the world. God takes suffering into divinity. In the death of Christ on the cross for humanity, God transforms suffering into an instrument for healing freedom (1 Cor 1:3–7).

The creation has a specific beginning and end point. Gen 1 teaches that just as God created the earth, God also created a beginning. Christianity places God above history and announces that God is the creator of time. The world is not neutral, as is presented in Buddhism. There is both tangible good and intrinsic evil (notwithstanding Augustine's *privatio boni*, the notion that evil, the absence of good, is insubstantial).

We are invested with worth because we are created in God's image and recipients of God's love (John 3:16) expressed in the sacrifice of Christ. God created us for love, and God's love is the reason we are to show love to one another (1 John 4:19). God creates the animals but asks a created being, Adam, to name the animals (Gen 2:19–20). Humans, made in God's image, are eternal beings made for relationship with an eternal God. The natural self, stripped of ego, becomes ennobled by God's glory. The Christ of God knows we are bound in desire but lifts us through divine love. We are not "enlightened beings," but we live within the protective light of the enlightened Christ.

Buddhism is a psychology that stresses personal responsibility above societal forces. Salvation, according to Buddhism, is not relational (as in relating to Lord Buddha) whereas in Christianity, salvation is all about our relationship with Jesus. Christian revelation unfolds within the context of a covenantal community. The church reminds critics that salvation is not rooted in a perverse sense of self-indulgent individuality. For Christians, prayer and meditation are directed toward God and rooted within a covenantal, personal relationship. In Buddhism, right-meditation is directed toward the unmediated experience of reality itself. There is no personification of truth in a salvific-relational sense, whereas for Christians Jesus is the embodiment of truth and the door for believers to experience a personal relationship with God.

For many Buddhists, Christian notions of salvation may be comforting—but they are false. Ou-Yang Ching Wu (1871–1944) generalized the distinction between these traditions when he stated, "Christianity signifies the inequality between the venerated object (God) and the self-humbling (human being). Buddhism, on the contrary, proceeds from the equality of all things, since reality is not dualistic."[23] Some Buddhists claim the Christian doctrine of covenant is an exercise in mysticism based on a faith predicated on its own logic and beyond the scope of any verifiability within the natural realm. A Buddhist might ask why God would create a world that God knew would eventually become a place of suffering. Why did an all-knowing and all-powerful God allow Adam to sin and thus to die? Why should a person filled with cravings worship a God who seems to crave their devotion and seems to have desires, and thus, is not free of samsara? The incarnation of God in Christ, some Greater Path Buddhists note, reveals a being filled with limitation and passionate desires. Why is it logical that the Creator, according to some readings of Genesis, put enmity between animals and humans (and give humanity dominion)? Why is it logical that Christians should rely on an invisible (and historical) savior beyond themselves?

Some Buddhists contend that Christians put trust in our faith because we are looking for the security that such assertive doctrines provide. We convince ourselves that we are eternally secure in Christ, while at the same time admitting that this is an act of faith, not an empirical fact. Such ideas are part of the illusionary nature of samsara and have no grounding in the natural way of things. We turn to myths in hopes of feeling secure. In fact, those who wish to know the "underlying nature of things" must "watch in silence; putting opinions aside."[24] Those afraid to follow the empowering, but demanding, Buddha dharma prefer hollow, optimistic, and mythical misconceptions that assure us we are meaningful instead of an unvarnished truth. Zen Sensei Tony Stultz explained, "You cannot understand life and its mysteries as long as you try to grasp it. Indeed, you cannot grasp it, just as you cannot walk off with a river in a bucket."[25]

THE GOAL

Enlightenment, in Buddhism, is to be experienced in the present moment as we accept what is true about our world and our human experience. Life is neither meaningful nor meaningless—it simply is what it is. Theoretical conjecture about what should or should not be is irrelevant. Any doctrine, as comforting as it may be, is only a construct. Ideas about the world are not synonymous with reality. Theoretical ideas about the nature of reality are

---

23. Quoted in Lai and von Bruck, *Christianity and Buddhism*, 83.
24. Nyanasobhano, *Landscapes of Wonder*, 115–16.
25. Stultz lecture, April 2004.

some of the many questions a Buddhist should respond to with a humble "don't-know-mind."[26] One Chinese proverb reminds us to simply accept: "Mountains are mountains and rivers are rivers."

We should clean our inward motivational filters to avoid suffering arising from desire. Meditation is a form of mental housekeeping. When we live without this orientating sense of rooted purpose and Buddha Wisdom, we become like a hopelessly confused "centipede with a washcloth on each foot."[27] Virtue calls us to renounce all forms of thirst (*tanha*). While it may be our nature to want more, we would be wise to let go our dissatisfactions. Non-Buddhists may think that this is self-contradictory: If we did not care about nirvana, then why would we care about Buddhism? They argue that the fact that a bodhisattva cares so much to help others speaks volumes about our need to make nirvana a goal. The counterargument is the reminder that we will never attain goals if our focus is based on a limiting self-advancement. Buddha calls us to a path of an intentional life marked by calm awareness and free acceptance. Raimundo Panikkar (who calls himself a Buddhist and a Christian) explains that in Buddhism "Salvation cannot be sought. What is sought, what is desired, is transformed by this very act into the object of volition or desire. Such an object cannot be human salvation."[28]

What about the Christian doctrine of an eternal hell of punishment and a heaven of reward? Are these paralleled in Buddhism? There are many ways to answer this based on which school of Buddhism you examine. Jesus spoke of a place where the worm "never dies, and the fire is never quenched" (Mark 9:48); but is this literal or figurative? C. S. Lewis, the Ulster Christian writer, said hell was a "state where everyone is perpetually concerned with his own dignity and advancement, where everyone has a grievance, and where everyone lives the deadly serious passions of envy, self-importance, and resentment."[29] For Lewis, we have to choose hell, which was not created by God for us but "for the devil and his angels" (Matt 25:41).

Visit a temple in China and you will see vast murals of burning levels of hellfire for the wicked. It would seem from these renderings that Buddha agrees with Jesus that "many are called, but few are chosen" (Matt 22:14), and that "the gate is wide and the road is easy that leads to destruction, and there are many who take it" (Matt 7:13). Buddhism teaches that hell is the experience of an unenlightened, grasping mind of ego refusing to accept Buddha's life-giving teachings. Hell is not a punishment as much as it is

---

26. Leong, *The Zen Teachings of Jesus*, 143.
27. Corless, *The Vision of Buddhism*, 86.
28. Panikkar, *The Silence of God*, xxiii.
29. Lewis, *Mere Christianity*, 10.

a consequence of our rejection of wisdom. We create our own hell by not living in the moment and by clinging to our cosmeticized fears or addicting and grasping desires.

Beyond questions of hell and heaven, how do we attain enlightenment or salvation? Many Buddhists and Christians teach that nirvana, or salvation, does not come through effort but through the grace of trusting faith. The apostle James warns that even a devil can know the truth about God (Jas 2:19): "Knowledge about Truth is not Truth itself."[30] We can become a slavish idolater to ideas about truth and miss the path of enlightenment or salvation.[31] For many Buddhists, the realization of enlightenment is rooted in the natural way of things. For many Christians, the ultimate freedom from sin is based on the revelation of God as love expressed in Jesus Christ.

The author of Hebrews explains that "without faith it is impossible to please God" (11:6). The apostle James explains that faith joins with our works to express a vibrant devotion in our daily lives (2:26). True faith is experienced as a life of submission (Jas 4:7) while false faith is marked by insecurity which often leads to the denigration of others. Søren Kierkegaard put the emphasis on faith as the door to accepting God's gifts. In a description reminiscent of Zen *satori* (sudden enlightenment), Jürgen Moltmann says experiencing Christian salvation is becoming "suddenly unselfish and free from fear. When we open ourselves to God's love for all creatures, we gain a new spontaneity" in God's Spirit, which allows us to live no longer in ourselves but in God.[32]

SPIRITUAL PRACTICE

Both Christians and Buddhists emphasize the benefits of meditation and contemplation (prayer) as a path to spiritual clarification. In the article, "How I, as a Christian, Have Learned from Buddhist Practice, or 'The Frog sat on the Lily Pad Not Waiting,'" Frances Adeney recounts, "As a Christian, I intentionally enter God's presence each time I practice silent meditation. Because I believe that God's Spirit meets me in a concentrated spiritual way

---

30. Quoted in Lopez, ed., *Modern Buddhism*, 51.

31. Sensei Anthony Stultz of the Blue Mountain Lotus Society in Harrisburg, PA, told the following story (2004): A monk and a rabbi were entering a temple when the rabbi stopped and said he could not enter because it was a place of idol worship. The monk took a small statue of Buddha out of his vestments and smashed it to the ground and asked if the rabbi would similarly be willing to destroy a copy of the Torah. The point the monk was trying to make is that what we perceive in others to be idolatry might not be as internalized as our own forms of idolatry.

32. Moltmann, "God Is Unselfish Love," 123.

in meditation, my meditative experience is full of presence."[33] Buddhism calls us to be alert, and Christianity reminds us that our errors foster a sense of vulnerability. Indeed, a major motivational force in Christianity is this recognition we are prone to error and evil. Mother Teresa of Calcutta was once asked why she had chosen to give her life to helping the poor. She responded, "Because I realized that I had a Hitler in me."[34] Although many of us think of Mother Teresa as the embodiment of goodness, she recognized her own potential to express evil. This recognition of a darkness potential within us enables us to seek a healthy balance and reminds us, with humility, to be vigilant.

Both Buddhist and Christian tradition established monastic orders to help us learn how to be holy in a difficult world. One of the largest Christian monastic orders was founded by Saint Benedict of Nursia (480–547), who believed pilgrims needed to embark on an inward journey of meditation and prayer. While some Christians pursue monasticism in response to the sinfulness of humanity, Benedict agreed with Buddhism that monasticism is designed "to help human goodness grow" and to "help the experience of God that is already abiding in our hearts to unfold."[35]

LIVING FROM HEART

One of the central themes in both Buddhism and Christianity is the promise of the power of God's or Buddha's love in action. Loving-kindness (*metta*) keeps us from becoming cold and powerless in the face of life's challenges. Charlotte Joko Beck writes, "*Love* is a word not often mentioned in Buddhist texts. It is connected to practice, since the two fruits of our practice are wisdom and compassion."[36] A great enemy of compassion is the "temptation to succumb to fantasies of moral superiority."[37] Christians are called to love others with a humble acceptance of God's nature as loving. One of the boldest statements in Christian theology is the declaration: "God is love" (1 John 4:8)! Christ teaches that "no one is good but God alone" (Mark 10:18; see also Matt 19:17), but that goodness is expressed by seeking to become a loving and compassionate person.

Jesus reduced the myriad legal codes the religious follow to one summation: If we love God and love others, we fulfill all commands of scripture

---

33. Adeney, "How I, as a Christian, Have Learned from Buddhist Practice," 35.
34. Quoted in Unno, *River of Fire River of Water*, 202.
35. Fischer et al., *Benedict's Dharma*, 5.
36. Beck, *Everyday Zen*, 71.
37. Batchelor, *Buddhism without Beliefs*, 89.

(Matt 22:35–40). Jesus linked dogmatic exactitude with the centrality of love when saying that we who declare God's oneness should also love God with all our strength (Mark 12:29). We should follow Christ's example of protecting a woman caught in adultery from public shame with gentle encouragement that she forsake a path of empty sin (John 8:3–8). If a person is righteous but lacks love, that person pleases God less than a tax collector or a prostitute (Matt 21:31). The pathway of love is what Jesus is describing when emphatically explaining that his life was the way of truth and life (John 14:6).

Walking a Buddhist path means we are constantly doing merciful acts of compassion. Kosuke Koyama explains: "Self-denial roots itself in this unity of wisdom and mercy . . . When one is devoted to wisdom and mercy, then one's life will one way or another concretely indicate the dimension of self-denial."[38] The Pali term *metta* (Sanskrit: *maitri*, from *mitra*, or "friend") calls us to a life of loving-kindness that keeps toxicity from overwhelming our hearts. When we practice loving-kindness, we face life with the engaged curiosity and fresh immediacy of a child and the seasoned wisdom of a sage.

Buddhists and Christians are challenged to go beyond "ordinary love" and embrace selfless love, described as *agape* in Christianity. *Agape* love puts others first and is not based on what benefits giving love might bring to the giver. Thinking about the relationship that ego plays on how love is to be viewed also helps some Christians circumvent concerns that Buddhists "cannot love" because they view attachment as central to how suffering arises in the world. Tibetan Thinley Norbu explains: "If we rely on ordinary, dualistic mind, we cannot have deep and lasting love either for our equals or for less fortunate beings, because ordinary, dualistic mind depends on the uncertainty of temporary circumstances."[39]

When we love others without thoughts of personal benefit, we express a nongrasping awareness. Jesus in Gethsemane prayed with such passion that he began to sweat blood (Luke 22:44). Buddhists note that even though Jesus experienced such passion, he did so in a spirit of imperturbability (*passaddhi*) because of having already passed over the dank swamps of desire. Jesus commanded us to be generous and to "give to everyone who begs" and to "not refuse anyone who wants to borrow" (Matt 5:42). As cited earlier, Christ expresses forgiving love as healing justice for a woman trapped in the labyrinthine mazes of adultery (John 8:1–11). In the parable of the good Samaritan (Luke 10:30–36) Jesus links piety with generosity. The Golden Rule (Matt 7:12; Luke 6:31) of loving others as we love ourselves is central

---

38. Koyama, *No Handle on the Cross*, 31.
39. Norbu, *White Sail*, 108.

to faith. Jesus tells us that if we show kindness to the "least of these," we are serving God (Matt 25:40, 45).

Buddhism instructs that our welfare relates to loving others. The Dalai Lama wrote: "It is an observable fact that the more we take the welfare of others to heart and work for their benefit, the more benefit we attain for ourselves."[40] A bodhisattva gives up their own interests to help others. One sutra explains: "If you do not practice compassion toward your enemy then toward whom can you practice it?"[41] Another text calls us to relate to every person as if they were our beloved mother: "Just as with her own life a mother shields from hurt her own, her only child—let all-embracing thoughts for all that lives be thine, and all-embracing love for all the universe in all its heights and depths and breadth—unstinted love, unmarred by hate within, not rousing enmity" (Metta Sutra, 11).[42]

---

40. Dalai Lama XIV, *The Compassionate Life*, 89.
41. Quoted in Dalai Lama XIV, *Opening the Eye of New Awareness*, 48.
42. Quoted in Reilly, "Compassion as Justice," 16.

9

The Zen Teachings of Jesus?

The presence of multiple interpretations is never a problem; it is simply a manifestation of the diversity of life. Many people have completely missed out on the joy, humor, and profundity of Jesus' teachings because they keep holding on to the first interpretation, they were taught in Sunday school.

—Kenneth Leong, *The Zen Teachings of Jesus*

JAPANESE ZEN SCHOOLS

VISIT ANY WELL-STOCKED NORTH American bookstore, and the religion section will offer an array of books on Zen. This is ironic given that teachers of Zen agree that nothing can be written about the nature of truth, and that Zen masters have rarely written anything themselves. Zen has gained popularity because it offers a fresh alternative for a world out of balance. Many Zen teachings offer relevant alternatives to anxious stress, artificiality, and impersonal interactions.

Although it was one of the first forms of Buddha's teaching to enter Japan, Zen is far less popular than other forms of Buddhism. In fact, its very survival may have more to do with the aesthetic and military components of the practice than with the views and monastic rigors that it exemplifies. Zen began as Chan Buddhism in China before gaining disciples in Japan and Korea. The word *Zen* originates from the Chinese word *Ch'an*, which means "meditation."¹ Zen gained popularity during the Kamakura Period (1185–1333), but the first Zen missionary from China (in as early as 526) was a monk with the fitting name Boddhidharma. Zen has been described as a fusion of Taoism and the Greater Path because of a focus on silent meditation and the creative power of emptiness. Another early Zen missionary was Eisai (or Eissi [1144–1215]). In 1187, Eisai, formerly a Tendai monk, returned to Japan after two years in China. His erected a shrine in Hakota and began to teach. Along with his pupil Dogen (1200–1283), Eisai held classes until he was expelled to Kamakura where he established the Rinzai school (Chinese: *Linji*) and came under the patronage of the wealthy Hojo family. Rinzai monks were the first to use koans as teaching tools to shock students. Zen also gained an audience with the Samurai military elite because of its austere tone and stress on pristine simplicity and discipline.

One of the central ideas of Zen is that all knowledge is only a preface for an intuitive (and often instant) discovery of truth. One Zen insight explains that the truest book is simply a finger pointing at the moon. Zen does not emphasize reincarnation, karma, and other doctrines alien to the Japanese worldview. This helped Zen masters win a broad following. Both the simplicity and the complexity of Zen joined with its disciplined monastic organizations to cement its widespread acceptance in medieval Japan.

There are five major schools of Zen. Three of these are predominant in Japan: the Rinzai, Soto, and Obaku schools. Although each claims roots in the same sources, and they share many of the same teachings, differences occur in how teachings are conveyed. Masters warn, however, that to "define Zen in terms of a system is to destroy it—or rather, miss it completely, for what cannot be constructed cannot be destroyed."²

When Dogen (1200–1253) launched the Soto school (in 1223), he was asked how his methods differed from others. He responded, "Anyone who would regard Zen having schools of Buddhism is a devil."³ The Soto school stressed gradual spiritual cultivation and is called the Farmer's Zen" because of its popularity among Japanese laity. Dogen discourages us from focusing on gaining nirvana. Instead, we should practice strict discipline in silence with frequent sessions of silent meditation. Dogen honored hard work and called followers to Shikantaza ("sitting up straight without vain thoughts"). He was a purist who rejected ritualism, although, after his death

---

1. Leong, *The Zen Teachings of Jesus*, 33: "The term *Zen* is the Japanese version of the Chinese word *Ch'an*, which is derived from the Sanskrit word *dhyana*. However, it would be a mistake to define Zen in terms of meditation."

2. Merton, *Zen and the Birds of Appetite*, 3.

3. Merton, *Zen and the Birds of Appetite*, 3.

esoteric rituals entered Soto practice. Although the Soto School is the most widespread in Europe and North America, the Rinzai school was the first to have texts translated into English thanks to the efforts Soyen Shaku, who also sent his most promising disciple, D. T. Suzuki, to the 1893 Parliament of the World's Religions in Chicago to promote Zen.[4]

The last major group to develop, the Obaku school (Chinese: *Huangbo*), gained followers in the seventeenth century and emphasized reliance on the oversight of a master to help attain enlightenment. This is the smallest of the groups, and some scholars even argue that there may not even be any known members.[5] The Obaku school shares much in common with Rinzai and came from China with the missionary Yinyuan (in Japanese, Ingen [1592–1673]). He built a massive temple at Uji, near Kyoto, which focused on the worship of the Amida Buddha, known as the "Buddha-spirit of daily life."[6] Yinyuan taught that the Pure-Land is not an actual place but exists only as a hopeful aspiration in the hearts of noble followers.

NOTHINGNESS

Critics dismiss Zen as a "speculative mysticism" that has meaning only to monks who have practiced for decades.[7] Other critics claim Zen is "utterly absurd and ludicrous, deliberately making itself unintelligible."[8]

According to Zen, a learner must first have a "beginner's mind" willing to accept life on life's terms. Zen stresses that a new perspective of enlightenment will come only when we are committed to meditation (*zazen*), but not through years of effort, as Orthodox (Theravada) Buddhists teach. Enlightenment often comes through a blink of lightning-like illumination (*satori*, "seeing"). Zen training is dynamic: Students invest hours at places of practice (*dojo*) in silent meditation. There are also intensive retreats (often lasting a week) called *sesshin* where every detail of a day (including diet and times to sleep and meditate) is rigidly arranged. Participants chant sutras or meditate on word problems called koans. Sometimes a teacher (*roshi*) will present a teaching (*teisho*) on one of these koans. At the end of a retreat, a student will have a private interview (or *dokusan*) with the *roshi* where concluding insights are shared.

---

4. Goldberg, "Buddhism in the West," 288.
5. Shrobe, *Don't-Know Mind*, 3.
6. Amore and Ching, "The Buddhist Tradition," 287.
7. Suzuki, *An Introduction to Zen Buddhism*, 32.
8. Suzuki, *An Introduction to Zen Buddhism*, 33.

Right-meditation, not study, leads to a mind that is "pure, tranquil, firm, collected, and free of coarse selfishness."[9] During meditation, we should sit still and tall and hold our hands in a specific position (Sanskrit: *mudra*, which means "seal"). Sometimes a Zen master will walk among those meditating and strike drowsy students on the back with a stick in order to "tap every vestige of dormant energy in the retreatant."[10] Beginners should clear their minds by counting breaths to deepen concentration. The goal of meditation is to dissolve our mind (Japanese: *kokoro*) into the breath. When we meditate, we should accept all that is happening within a given moment. To nonadherents, meditation may seem like a waste of time. Why spend hours sitting and doing *nothing*? It is a battle to sit for agonizingly long hours without moving while just staring at a wall for the sake of staring at a wall. But because stability is the base of stillness, the more we remain in this posture, the more we become free from the entanglements of imbalance. Through right-meditation, the conscious mind comes to a standstill, and we develop a "settling power" (*joriki*) rooted in the present moment, stabilizing future responses to an entire life of consecutive moments.

"Zen Buddhists place great emphasis on the importance of attentiveness and patience."[11] We enter nirvana through intuitive discovery instead of through creeds, rituals, or devotion. Meditation in simple forms replaces verbose scholarship. We should accept a path of liberating agnosticism that does not need to understand everything. Everything we need, we already have inside of ourselves. "Zen strives for a homecoming into one's self."[12] All of us are complete; already in full possession of our essential Buddha Nature. The goal of Zen is to strip away any of the external, hindering paraphernalia of religion, which only blurs ability to know truth. We should go with the flow because nirvana will never arrive by going against reality. We should give up a conformist, herd mentality and throw away comforting security blankets that provide suffocating reassurances. Life should become "poeticized" because it is unpredictable and lived with fluidity.[13]

---

9. Thera, *The Vision of Dhamma*, 186–87.

10. This phrase was related to me in a discussion with Xu Qin Sun in Kunming, Yunnan, China.

11. Kennedy, *Zen Gifts to Christians*, 10.

12. Siegmund, *Buddhism and Christianity*, 123.

13. Leong, *The Zen Teachings of Jesus*, 37.

ZEN THINKING

Meditation is vital to becoming aware that all phenomena are empty. Nothing is inherently holy or unholy by itself. Holiness or ungodliness are promoted concepts without any intrinsic meaning. All ideas about the nature of reality are distortions. What is needed is the "discovery of your original face before you were born."[14] Master Shen Hui explained: "The true seeing is when there is no seeing."[15] Life is a journey that must be lived and not simply talked about. Nothing should be categorized based on assumptions.

When you live with the Buddha Mind, you will not get tangled up in your judgments or opinions. Thinking does not set us free and often brings us anguish. Over time, creativity dies in our hearts as proud assertion grows. We choose indoctrination or delivered information instead of fresh learning without preconception. Ideas are not helpful when parroted in rote, institutionalized forms. One of the most frequent ways we get locked into believing that falsehoods are truth is through what is called common sense, but which is nothing more than prejudices acquired through years of social conditioning being repeated endlessly until accepted as fact.

In contrast, Zen masters observe, some cultures strive for an encyclopedic way of looking at the world, while other cultures may be more accepting of nuance and mystery. In response to what she calls as the frenzy of many North Americans to gain knowledge, Elaine MacInnes explains, "In Asia, I discovered we do not need to know everything all the time. Indeed, there are things which are not meant to be known or understood."[16] Years living in Asia, however, lead me to conclude that the idea that Asians are not obsessed with gaining information is far too generalized. While some cultures may valorize more of one virtue than another, such stereotypes about cultures and people groups are easily refuted in our era of ever-increasing globalization.

Zen declares that we should abandon outward concepts about life, and should live in the unfiltered reality of truth. We carry within ourselves the "clock" of our own lives and, perhaps without realizing it, the jewel of nirvana. The Taoist idea that the one who knows is the one who does not speak is accepted. Buddha's greatest sermon, according to Zen, was not his Deer Park Sermon but rather took place when he met disciples and simply held a lotus flower between his hands and smiled. Buddha remained silent because silence alone describes the deepest truths about reality.

---

14. Merton, *Zen and the Birds of Appetite*, 5.
15. Merton, *Zen and the Birds of Appetite*, 5.
16. MacInnes, *Zen Contemplation for Christians*, 15.

The Zen Teachings of Jesus?

Both Christianity and Buddhism agree that all the world's realities first sprang from an initial clay of chaos. A sense of emptiness, according to Buddhism, provides a blank canvas on which we can create a life that is free from falsehood. Clinging to temporal ideas (worthless or valuable) only keeps us from seeing things as they should be perceived. Our imposed constructs about what we think is real are not the same as what is real. Father Thomas Merton postulated, "Zen is not a systematic explanation of life, it is not an ideology, it is not a worldview, it is not a theology of revelation and salvation, it is not a mystique, it is not a way of ascetic perfection, and in fact it fits no convenient category of ours."[17] Indeed, Zen does not seek to systematize the nature of life in the same way as do systemic Christian theologies. According to Zen, all efforts at explanation drive us further from the truths received through meditation. We enter liberation when through not-knowing we become free from both the need to know and the need not to know.[18] Christianity also has a long tradition of accepting mystery with humility in reference to accepting God's will. Even Christ in full humanity, wrestled on the cross with a sense of being abandoned by God (Mark 15:34).

To accept the Zen principle that we do not need to know is the first step towards enlightenment. Worthless efforts at gaining knowledge only scratch at the itching poison-ivy of delusion and make its festering rash spread. Saint Anthony wrote that he attained the aspiration of Greek Stoics, a freeing sense of *apatheia* where we become unconcerned about what happens in life.[19] Thoughts are prisons, and freedom is found by boldly canoeing over the Niagara Falls precipice of nonthinking. We enter a "gateless gate" when, through meditation, we view flashes of insight.[20] Right-meditation is not the same as thinking. It is nonthinking where we empty, and do not refill, our minds. An example of this comes from the Zen sage Bodhidharma, who did nothing but stare at a wall (or look past the wall) for nine years. This wall contemplation is typical of Zen meditation.

KOANS

One of the frequent ways Zen practitioners gain insight is through reflecting on koans (Chinese: *kong-an*)—stories and questions given to students from

17. Merton, *Zen and the Birds of Appetite*, 35.
18. Kennedy, *Zen Gifts to Christians*, 28.
19. Romanian philosopher Emil Cioran also talks about the benefits of an apathetic way of engaging the world. For Saint Anthony, and others, *apatheia* was seen to be a gift from God.
20. Sangharakshita, *Alternative Traditions*, 121.

Zen masters. Koans are often structured as question-and-answer problems (*mondo*) created to reflect "something of the exuberant spirit of enlightenment, a dynamic bursting of restrictive bonds, part of a spontaneous desire to be rid of lifeless religious dogma, to discard empty ritualized formulas and, instead, to be carried by the storm of the spirit."[21] It is not a verbal game, but a way to bring us in touch with our intuition.

Zen practitioners use "paradoxical *koans* to challenge" and "test each other's (as well as their own) ability."[22] The student may study an object or consider a *koan*. Many of these are designed to reject notions of duality or promote a greater depth of awareness.[23] Sometimes they seem abrasive in the same way that the side of a matchbox is rough so that the match can be lit when striking against it. Sometimes we need to be shocked from the familiar into truth. Koans help us see there are no limitations that cannot be overcome if we can move beyond reason.[24] The purpose of a koan (and meditation) is to bridge an artificial divide between thinking and knowing. The goal is to address the problem that many of us overly compartmentalize our lives.

Teaching with a koan is not an anti-intellectual exercise even though koans help us leap beyond conceptual thought into deeper insight. The more we think, the more we become confused. Koans often have no answer. This encourages a paradigm shift, a mind revolution, if you will, from a chaotic so-called monkey mind toward controlling our minds past false feelings of rightness.[25] Every question need not be answered; nor does every question

---

21. Ross, *Buddhism*, 155–56.

22. Kubose, *Zen Koans*, ix.

23. Kubose, *Zen Koans*, 3–5. He also offers these koans: "Unmon said, I did not ask you about 15 days ago; I asked you about 15 days from now. Come say a word about this! Since none of the monks answered, he answered for them: every day is a good day"; "A monk asked Tozan, how can we escape the cold and the heat? Tozan replied, why not go where there is no cold or heat? Is there such a place? the monk asked. When cold, be thoroughly cold and when hot be hot through and through"; "Shuzan held out his short staff and said, if you call this short staff, you oppose its reality. If you do not call it a short staff, you ignore the fact. Now what do you wish to call it?"

24. Kubose, *Zen Koans*, 224–26. Zen koans encourage moving past the limits of reason: "Baso, the great teacher, became ill. A disciple visited him and said, Sir, during these recent days how is your health? Baso replied, Sun-faced Buddhas, moon-faced Buddhas"; "Mokurai said to the novice Toyo, 'you can hear the sound of two hands clapping. Now show me the sound of one hand.'"; "A monk asked Nansen, 'is there a teaching no Master ever preached before? Nansen answered yes. 'What is it?' asked the monk. Nansen replied, 'it is not mind, it is not Buddha, and it is not things.'"

25. Koans with this pattern include, "Bring me a pearl from the bottom of the sea without getting wet," "Show me the sound of one hand clapping," and "What is the straight within the bent?"

merit consideration. It is normal to hold a thought momentarily, but it becomes a problem to hold a thought with rigidity. We clutch question-framed concepts and thus become preoccupied with theoretical fabrications.

We must strive to be free of inward multiplicity. Zen does not want us to become entangled with any one philosophy, but to stand above the need to control through conceptualizations. Some critics think this view assumes an unattainable goal of pure objectivity. But despite possible results, a posture of pure objectivity is an aspiration that merits effort. We must pass beyond systematic thinking. The purpose of a koan exercise is to "subvert all rational attempts to solve it."[26] From the controlling position of habitual thinking and mental gridlock we can find freedom to turn toward the non-rational (intuitive) way to solve problems.

If you find the following koan exercises hard to understand, remember that they were given by specific teachers to specific students in specific contexts that might no longer have any relevance today. Here are a few examples of oft-recited koans:[27]

- How does one get a goose out of a bottle without ruffling the feathers of the goose or breaking the bottle? There it is out!
- What should you do if you meet a Buddha? Kill him!
- Master, if truth is in silence, how can silence be expressed? I will not express it here. Master, where will you express it? Last night, at midnight I lost three pennies beside my bed.

While a koan may work like a plunger against the gritty sludge of the mind to dislodge misconceptions, koans cannot carry us into enlightenment. An infant newly born brims with the purity of the Buddha Nature, and a student of Zen aspires to live a childlike life of immediacy, to see things with a sense of fresh engagement, free from inhibiting filters and exhausting conceptualities. We should not stress about our levels of nonunderstanding.

AID AND ENEMY

Our objective should be to find freedom from delusions. What are some ways that Zen works for this goal? Stories play a major role in sharing truths. Once a student visited a shrine where she watched her teacher bow before a statue of the Buddha only to follow this act of devotion by spitting on the Buddha. When she asked the teacher why she spit at the Buddha, the

---

26. Loy, "Dead Words, Living Words, and Healing Words," 37.
27. Novak, *The World's Wisdom*, 98–99.

teacher replied, "It was I who bowed and you who spit." Still another master on one frosty winter day discovered there was no fuel for the fire. He walked to the altar and threw a treasured, intricately carved wooden Buddha into the fire. His dazed students were stunned. The statue truly embodies the Buddha nature, the master explained, because it had been sacrificed to keep them warm.

There is a beautiful line in Norman Maclean's book *A River Runs Through It*, about the spirituality he acquired from his father while growing up in Montana: "In our family, there was no clear line between religion and fly-fishing."[28] Growing up in Pittsburgh, where there was no clear line between religion and Steelers football, I can appreciate this statement. Even in the ordinary world we can find truths embedded. Jesus taught the Samaritan woman that we need not visit a holy mountain or shrine to worship God. The divine can be experienced anywhere at any time (John 4:21). Even though "salvation is from the Jews" (John 4:22), it was never intended to be exclusive to one group.

Zen warns that we should not think spirituality demands detachment from the world. Actually, it requires engagement with the world. Most of life is filled with mundane, necessary chores. Only the arrogant, burdened by exceptionalism, refuse to value what Hui Neng (636–712) calls the "asceticism of being ordinary."[29] The events of our lives, such as the rising of the sun and the moon, hold life together in what Gandhi called our "blessed monotony." When we are drinking tea, all we should be doing is drinking tea with appropriate concentration. Anything can become a gateway to insight if we open our eyes to appreciate the implicit potential of a given act. Perhaps it will be while we are drinking tea that enlightenment will come. This, however, does not mean that we should "ruin" something as beautiful as tea drinking with an obsession for spiritual insight. Alan Watts warns, "Zen does not confuse spirituality with thinking about God while we are peeling potatoes. Spirituality is just to peel the potatoes."[30] One story tells of a cook making lunch when, over his pot and obstructing his cooking the great bodhisattva Manjushri appeared. The cook took his stirring stick and beat the deity away because he was in the middle of cooking: "Even if old man Sakyamuni came, I would also hit him."[31] Even the divine should not interrupt the mundane.

---

28. Quoted in Leong, *The Zen Teachings of Jesus*, 151.
29. Leong, *The Zen Teachings of Jesus*, 38.
30. Shrobe, *Don't-Know Mind*, 39.
31. Leighton, *Bodhisattva Archetypes*, 109.

The Zen Teachings of Jesus?

There is a simple saying—"drink cold water"—that speaks of the significance of experience.[32] We should resist a "monkey mind" of subjectivity, eager to draw conclusions, as we cultivate a stance of pure objectivity. The infinite generating of expectations clogs the path to accepting truth. Expectations should be swept away to live in the world of "just now and just as it is."[33]

Satori (entering nirvana) can sometimes come unexpectedly, as if we were discovering something long lost. When flexible and open, we often succeed without even trying. One teacher explained, "Zen is the game of insight, the game of discovering who we are underneath the masks and roles we call our personalities."[34] One story tells of a student who meditated for hours: A teacher observed the student's zeal and sat beside him with a brick, which he began to polish with another stone. The perplexed student asked the teacher what he was doing and was told, "I am trying to polish this brick into a mirror. But no amount of polishing will ever make a mirror out of a brick. And no amount of sitting cross-legged will ever make a Buddha out of you."[35]

IMMEDIACY

When we gain enlightenment, our hearts are filled with emptiness and the dynamism of a journey into ongoing discovery. As one Zen teacher explains, ideas are hindrances to be overcome. When a student asked, "Am I right when I have no idea?" "Throw away that idea of yours," replied the teacher. "What idea?"—asked the pupil in perplexity. The teacher responded, "You are free, of course, to carry about that useless idea of no idea."[36]

The aim of Zen is immediacy. We cannot speak about any kind of spirituality that does not both begin and end now. Life and death exist inside every moment. We should have the freedom of a well-prepared archer. When it is time to shoot her arrow, she only needs to pick up her bow and

---

32. Shrobe, *Don't-Know Mind*, 4: "If you attain that, then you attain your true self. If you don't understand, go to the kitchen, and drink cold water . . . The sky never says, 'I am the sky.' The tree never says, 'I am a tree.' The dog only barks, 'Woof, woof.' If you open your mouth, you get thirty blows; if you close your mouth, then you also get thirty blows. What can you do? If you are thirsty, go drink some cold water."

33. Shrobe, *Don't-Know Mind*, 21.

34. Blyth, *Games Zen Masters Play*, 7.

35. Novak, *The World's Wisdom*, 222.

36. The mind must be mastered, which will mean that a person will remove all distracting and "agitating" thoughts (Bodhi, ed., *In the Buddha's Words*, 259). The *Vitakkasanthana Sutta*, I, 118–122, quoted in Bodhi, ed., *In the Buddha's Words*, 275–78.

shoot without aiming or looking. Just as after many years a practiced archer can shoot an arrow without aiming, so with years of training to facilitate the internalization of truth, a student of Zen can express truth with naturalness, without effort. We live in the moment because there is no such reality as an actual past which is forever gone. There is also no such thing as a potential future yet to come but only the experienced present. We can become imprisoned in our past or invent false fantasy hopes about a presumed future. The self is what exists when doing a certain thing. Life is impermanent: There can be no last word or act of finality. Thich Nhât Hanh explains, "Our true home is the present moment. The miracle is not to walk on water. The miracle is to walk on the green earth fully aware in the present moment."[37]

The celebration of pure emptiness has, ironically, created a galaxy of notable art—poetry and culture that has enriched the world. Art can express life and need not be divorced from life through the conceptualizing presses that often exemplify our cluttered, materialistic contexts. Art can empower the warmth of grace, ease, and color that embodies the ethos of truth. A visit to a temple, such as one I visited in Kamakura, Japan, was a revelation of majestic void. A garden of landscaped rock and finely raked sand echoed with the sound of one hand clapping. It was an unforgettable introduction into quiet serendipity and an ancient questioning intuitiveness.

Do the teachings of Jesus call us to live with a Zen-like sense of immediacy and directness? Saint Paul explains, "Now is the day of salvation" (2 Cor 6:2). Jesus announces, the "kingdom of heaven has come near" (Matt 3:2; 4:17). Alive in God, we are alive in all that is eternal. Christians can accept Zen's focus on the potential of emptiness both as it relates to impermanence and as a healthy connection with the physical world. Nothing can (or will) happen twice. Christians are called in the present tense to cling to the living Christ known personally and directly. Emptiness, according to Zen, dethrones a sense of self-importance or a false notion of ego. To be nothing is to make room for everything, including truth: for Christians, the presence of God. The noxious weeds of false preconceptions can be rooted out, for flowers of beauty to blossom in our hearts. One Catholic priest explained his Zen practice: "Emptiness is not a view but the reconstruction of all views."[38]

---

37. Nhât Hanh, *Living Buddha, Living Christ*, 23.
38. Kennedy, *Zen Gifts to Christians*, 86.

WISDOM

Meditation can only carry us so far and then, like every other discipline, should be set aside in order to gain deeper insights. Zen meditation is expressed uniquely and is not "meditation" at all, but the absence of all concentrated efforts to meditate. We become wiser when freed from illusions: "The hours on a meditation cushion soak a practitioner with wisdom and impermanence in an undeniable way."[39] The goal is Buddha Wisdom (*prajna*). Teachings are like the raft, mentioned earlier, that helps us get across a river. Once safely on the other side they can be discarded because they serve no further purpose. This is why we should grip teachings and not allow truth to become calcified into lifeless dogma. Life is best lived with a fresh openness that paddles us ever forward toward new insights. At the heart of each of us is the Buddha Wisdom, experienced through insight. When reached, the wisdom inside of us is released like a trapped bird freed from a cage.

Once a teacher visited the emperor in Nanjing and was asked what merit had accrued from the emperor donating tons of gold to build many temples. The master (*chalan*) answered that no merit would come because the emperor's actions were superficial, like a shadow following an object. The teacher said that if the emperor had not asked such a question, then merit might slowly have arisen within him through an inner discovery of Buddha Wisdom. When the emperor asked him to define wisdom, the teacher replied it was emptiness. When the emperor challenged the teacher to explain what authority he had to make such assertions, he replied, "I don't know."[40]

What happened when Siddhartha was enlightened was not the result of meditation but the bubbling forth of an inner Buddha Wisdom. Just as Buddha discouraged ritual as often distracting, verbosity about knowledge can also become an entangling hindrance that keeps us from releasing inner Buddha Wisdom. When released, it strips-away all that is tangential. These moments of the bubbling forth of our inner Buddha Wisdom are paralleled in the literary descriptions of James Joyce and Albert Camus, both of whom describe heuristic discoveries of captured beatific visions set free.

Enlightenment is not a specific event, nor is nirvana a specific place. It is in every present moment when one is freed through meditation. There is no goal for nirvana beyond the arising of Buddha Wisdom inside our consciousness. Zen students are encouraged to seek *Mu* (which means

---

39. Schneider, *Street Zen*, 188.
40. I no longer have the source for this anecdote.

"nothingness").[41] Any obsessive forms of addiction to an egocentric awareness should be erased. The beating waves of ego may not be stilled because of circumstances, but we can float above the crest of stormy waves and with freedom from anxiety let all thoughts come and go unbound.[42]

Buddha Wisdom leads into a dynamic minimalism that sets everything aside except the Buddha Nature. T. S. Eliot referred to the "still point of the turning world."[43] For Zen, the internalization of enlightenment fosters an inner still point that eliminates falsehoods. Everything around us should be stripped of its deceptively distinct qualities so we can recognize the fundamental unity of all things. When we reach the truth that there is no difference between birth and death, defilement and purity, addition and destruction, we see the world as it is. There is even no difference between ideas of purity and sinfulness. Master Gasan of Tenryuji taught: "I have accomplished everything in Zen. Only one more step remains—ten thousand sins."[44]

In Zen there is no such thing as ignorance because there is no such thing as knowledge. Many are "sunk in the mire of views" unable "to see through the external formulations of the teachings" to arrive at enlightenment.[45] We can become proud, and our ego becomes inflated because "knowledge puffs up" (*scientia inflat*; see 1 Cor 8:1). None of the miseries resulting from either ignorance or knowledge are real. If there is no misery or death, then there can be no such thing as an inner Buddha Wisdom or as attaining Buddha Nature enlightenment.[46]

---

41. This parallels a Christian devotional called the *Cloud of Unknowing* by an anonymous monk. Here's a quote: "You will say, 'Where am I to be?' Nowhere according to you. And you will be quite right. 'Nowhere' is where I want you. And though your natural mind can now find 'nothing' to feed on, do not give up but work vigorously on that nothing" (quoted in Chetwynd, *Zen and the Kingdom of Heaven*, 117–18).

42. The other side of this equation is the discipline of spirituality. Alan Watts warns against a kind of "Western Zen which employs Zen philosophy to justify a very self-defensive Bohemianism." See Lopez, ed., *Modern Buddhism*, 161.

43 Eliot, *The Four Quartets*: "Burnt Norton," line 65.

44. Quoted in Kennedy, *Zen Spirit, Christian Spirit*, 84.

45. Cleary, *Zen and the Art of Insight*, 151.

46. "There are thresholds which thought alone, left to itself, can never permit us to cross. An experience is required—an experience of poverty and sickness" (Merton, *Zen and the Birds of Appetite*, 56).

ZEN CHRISTIANITY

How can we learn from one another and unite to bless a hurting world? What can we share with each other? Pope Benedict (as Joseph Ratzinger) exclaimed, "How interesting it would be if we could compare the ideas of Zen with those of the Bible. If that could be done, it would be a great event, not only for the dialogue between Zen Buddhism and Christianity, but also in respect to the ideological exchange between East and West."[47]

Comparing Zen with Christianity is like "comparing mathematics to tennis."[48] People bring different motivations to any comparative examination: Some Zen practitioners and Christians seek to learn from each other in order to deepen spirituality. Others have reflected upon a host of similarities between these traditions in search of a synthesizing vision. Still others are involved in interfaith work to address specific problems within a given community. Thomas Merton chose to study Zen because he felt that much of modern Christianity had become dryly "activist, secular, and anti-mystical."[49]

An area of common ground between Buddhists and Christians is a focus on contemplation. Adherents of both faiths practice a host of physical disciplines to subdue the body and channel physical experience toward a higher consciousness. There are also differences between how we perceive the nature of that consciousness, which Christians know to be God, and which Buddhists call the Buddha Nature. Zen teaches that enlightenment will be expressed as "the whole body becoming an eye" through mobilizing the power of a person's postures, energies, and breaths.[50] Jesus warned against becoming slaves to pleasures and possessions. Christ fasted and prayed alone in the wilderness for forty days before launching his mission. This example later became the basis for the practice of Christians preparing for Eastertide with meditative Lenten exercises.

Christians are called to meditation as a way to quiet themselves and rest scurrying minds cluttered with preoccupations so that meaning can arise from a "silent emptiness." Silence plays an integral role in both Christian and Buddhist traditions. Meditation practices often include extensive periods of silence because "the state of enlightenment cannot be explained in words" any more than talking about food could replace eating food.[51]

---

47. Quoted in Kadowaki, *Zen and the Bible*, v.
48. Kennedy, *Zen Spirit, Christian Spirit*, 32.
49. Merton *Zen and the Birds of Appetite*, 17.
50. Kadowaki, *Zen and the Bible*, 32.
51. Kadowaki, *Zen and the Bible*, 51.

Christian spirituality also has a rich tradition of silent prayer rooted in Christ's example. Silence in Christianity is not mere "quietism or inner vacuity, nor is it a negation, a blacking out of human reality."[52] There are many examples of Jesus dealing with situations without words. The clearest example is his choice of silence while undergoing mock trials before his execution. In another instance, Jesus encounters a woman caught in adultery and silently ignores her accusers while writing something in the dust (John 8:2–11). Jesus is recorded as speaking only after being centered in a silence that radiates a sense of peaceful composure. Jesus is the *Logos* of God even in a season of nonverbal infancy and even in eons of time before coming to earth.

Spiritual disciplines within Christianity have been taught from teacher to student in the same way that they are conveyed within Zen. For both faiths, true learning is wisdom that is not advanced by theoretical discussions. Teaching is a process of spiritual mentoring in both faiths more than it is about the cognitive, ego-centered transfer of abstract facts. This is what Thomas Merton means when he writes, "Zen does not teach, it points. What it points at is not cognitive content but transformed awareness. The gestures of a Zen teacher are no more 'statements' than is the ringing of an alarm clock."[53] Spiritual mentors, both Christian and Buddhist, invest in students in many ways and with varying methods. Teachers seek to establish an alternative mental culture beyond prevailing views held by the nonspiritual in society. Many times, wisdom-truths are passed on through something like a cross-examination where a teacher, such as Jesus or Buddha, frequently asks questions. Think of these methodologies as ancient spiritual recipes, designed to cook up a delicious soul—filled with the life-giving, healthy ingredients of both wisdom (*prajna*) and compassion (*karuna*).

Mature saints should share what is appropriate or receivable with those beginning a spiritual journey. It is not knowledge that is vital, and often the smartest among us are ignorant of spiritual truth (see John 3:9). Those steeped in the maturity of insight expressed in life are the elders that most merit our respect. In Greek Orthodoxy, for example, a wise teacher is called *gerom* (Greek: "old man") and among Russian Orthodox, *staretz*. Such wisdom teachers are known for both their words and their exemplary lives.

Both Zen and Christianity are pathways that offer a more comprehensive worldview instead of a partial perspective. Saint Paul preached a big-picture story that connected us with the redemptive actions of Christ (Rom

---

52. Merton, *Zen and the Birds of Appetite*, 91.
53. Merton, *Zen and the Birds of Appetite*, 50.

5:12–19; 1 Cor 15:21–22). Jesus preached a gospel for the entire world, beginning with us (John 12:32). A central teaching in Zen is the interrelatedness of all forms of life. As Master Joshu related, "All things come back to one."[54] In Buddhism that one is Buddhist teachings while in Christianity the One is Jesus.

Practices in both traditions aim to purify us. Christianity speak of the need for repentance (*metanoia*), while Zen calls us to embrace emancipation. Some Christians talk about our "sin nature," while Buddhists say our core problem is our stubborn rootedness in delusion. Both traditions teach the primacy of love over fear. Saint John draws this connection when proclaiming, "perfect love casts out fear" (1 John 4:18). Buddha taught that fear is driven away by enlightened reason expressed as compassionate action. There is a story in the Bible about Mary of Bethany, who in a spontaneous act of enthusiasm, pours out expensive oil on the feet of Jesus. The disciples criticize her extravagance because the money could have addressed real needs perceived by real fears (Matt 26:6–13; John 12:5). Jesus looks past the logic of these moralizers and straight into Mary's loving heart: "To [Christ], the act of an ordinary woman pouring out her heart without any consideration of earning praise or moral credit was much more laudable than the piousness of a Pharisee trying to become a moral superhero."[55]

Father Thomas Merton felt that the key difference between Zen and Christianity comes from the fact that Christianity begins in revelation and moves toward experience while Zen flows in the opposite direction. Merton mused, "Christianity has always been profoundly concerned with these [doctrinal] statements," which sometimes makes us forget that "the heart of Catholicism, too, is a living experience of unity in Christ which far transcends all conceptual formulations."[56] While Merton does not make an enemy of doctrine, he warns that when we focus too strongly on doctrine instead of on Christ and the life of the church, then we can lose a right understanding of what it means to be a Christian. We should meet Christ as his first followers did, not only in a secondhand way through books, sermons, or thickets of religious conceptualities, but directly on dusty streets and through the transforming grace of God's Spirit reaching into our hearts. Faith may come through hearing the Bible (Rom 10:17) but is not based on empirical knowledge (Rom 10:2). It is born in an embrace of the person of Christ (Rom 10:8–13).

---

54. Quoted in Kadowaki, *Zen and the Bible*, 63.
55. Leong, *The Zen Teachings of Jesus*, 31.
56. Merton, *Zen and the Birds of Appetite*, 39.

Father Robert E. Kennedy practices Zen meditation while also describing himself fully as part of the Christian church. He feels there is no disruption between such efforts and the core of his faith. Kennedy has not become a heretic, and the church has been supportive of his explorations. He explains that in his experience Zen provides him with a "new way of being Catholic."[57] He observed of his teacher: "this Buddhist might make a Christian of me yet!"[58] Kennedy explains that he and other Christians are "temperamentally inclined toward practicing Zen to enrich their lives" but that such an effort in no way "supplants or criticizes Christianity."[59]

ZEN TEACHING OF JESUS

The Bible is described as a "two-edged sword" (Heb 4:12) because it attacks false ideas about divine revelation. Many hear God's Word but do not comprehend it (Luke 8:9–10) because the gospel is veiled from those who are mired in doubt or filled with corrosive cynicism or negativity.

Jesus attacks misconceptions using paradoxes. These are also widely used in Zen.[60] Sometimes when a truth is expressed in words, it sounds self-contradictory. For example, Jesus says that "for him who has, more will be given" (Mark 4:25). These wisdom-paradoxes challenge our expectations that things are predictable and formulaic. Simone Weil observes, "Contradictions are the criterion of the real."[61] Many parables Jesus tells in the Bible are like stories told by Zen masters. In one story Master Gutei cuts off the finger of one of his followers.[62] This account reminds us of a teaching of Jesus who in one instance figuratively stated that if your hand leads you into evil, cut it off because it is better to eternal life maimed than to mislead those who are weak (Matt 5:30; 18:8; Mark 9:43).

Father Kennedy observes, "The experience of the unity between the absolute and the relative is fundamental to Zen."[63] Similarly, Christianity, according to Saint Thomas Aquinas, calls us to reject simplistic dualities in

---

57. Kennedy, *Zen Spirit, Christian Spirit*, 13.
58. Kennedy, *Zen Spirit, Christian Spirit*, 14.
59. Kennedy, *Zen Gifts to Christians*, 1.
60. To illustrate how widespread paradoxes are in Zen teaching, Kenneth Leong asks the question, "How many Zen Buddhists does it take to change a light bulb? The answer is two—one to change the light bulb and another not to change it." Leong, *The Zen Teachings of Jesus*, 158.
61. Quoted in Leong, *The Zen Teachings of Jesus*, 21.
62. Chetwynd, *Reflections on the Tradition of Meditation*, 85.
63. Kennedy, *Zen Gifts to Christians*, 68.

the ways we view life. The word "diabolical" derives from the Greek word *diaballein*, which means to bring dissention through accusation. The fostering of strident divisions through accusation is seen as the nefarious work of the devil.

Both Christianity and Zen stress life's basic impermanence. Zen warns that when we each come to "the Great Death," we will see our "primal face and the essential nature of the self."[64] Christianity asserts that our deaths reflect the quality of our lives (*quale vita, tale morte*). The apostle James reminds us, life is "a mist that appears for a little while and then vanishes" (4:14). Even our bodies do not belong to us but are temples "of the Holy Spirit" (1 Cor 6:19). We do not even belong to our families (Luke 9:59–62). Jesus says, "Unless a grain of wheat falls into the earth and dies, it remains just a single grain" (John 12:24). One should learn from birds of the air, who live free of stress (Matt 6:26). Even the "Son of Man has nowhere to lay his head" (Matt 8:20).

Jesus also confronted the shortsightedness of egotism. He told a parable of a rich fool who lost everything after he had assumed his security was certain (Luke 12:16–21) Some of us have gained everything but have lost our souls (Matt 16:24–26). In one story from Luke's Gospel, one of Jesus's friends attends to temporal chores while another friend chooses the "better part" of restful worship (10:38–42). Jesus confronted a rich ruler who sought eternal life but could not abandon the false security of wealth (Luke 18:18–23). Ultimately, Jesus is betrayed and monetized for thirty silver coins (Matt 26:14–15). Those who nurture a "what's-in-it-for-me" approach live bound in ego. They are far from the truth of no-self as taught in Buddhism and from selflessness as taught in Christianity. Spiritual transformation is something akin to death, and Zen teaches that we must become "free of the birth-death duality."[65] If a person hopes to save their life, they must first lose it (Matt 10:39). Zen teaches that a wise person will seek freedom from all self-promotion and will become willing to step off a "one-hundred-foot pole and let go with both hands and feet."[66] Christians seek to become transformed into the nature of Jesus, who clung to nothing, but emptied himself. His resurrection came only after a death of unselfish suffering. Similarly, Christians are called to be "crucified with Christ" in sacrifice for others (Gal 2:20).

While God's eternal truths never change, the Bible teaches that truths must often be adjusted to fit varying circumstances. Jesus often reframed

---

64. Kadowaki, *Zen and the Bible*, 32.
65. Kadowaki, *Zen and the Bible*, 155.
66. Kadowaki, *Zen and the Bible*, 131.

biblical teachings, giving them relevance through a fresh rerendering. Jesus said the "truth will make you free" (John 8:32); not calcified into intransigent assertions. Disciples of the Galilean, filled with God's Spirit, will be spontaneous—like the wind, without scripts on how to act in life's changes (John 3:8). We become "born again" and live life without a self-protecting instinct to put grasping egos first.

My eleven children have taught me volumes about living with zest (as I write this, our quadruplets are crying in unison during our 140th day of family quarantine). Every child imagines being a world-maker-wizard. With a common stick they can imagine owning a royal sword. Every child can transform their arms into wings and become airplanes or birds. Sadly, as we grow older, some of us celebrate life less and fall day by day into an ever-increasing measure of dull predictability. Buddhism explains that children have yet to tie themselves into rote habits: "Children are alive, radiant, energetic, carefree, playful, and fun-loving. They live in the moment and are able to let themselves go completely in whatever they are engaged in."[67] Aren't those the same qualities that one needs to live a life of dynamic faith? Jesus told us that we should "change and become like children" (Matt 18:3; Mark 10:13–16). Children do not gain their sense of worth from accomplishments. Adults should be like children and turn away from living from their own self-significance, and when praying to God should use the intimate family term "Daddy" (Aramaic: *Abba*) instead of formal, distant terms of honor (Matt 11:25–26).

Jesus warns that God will remove blessing from the wise and has "revealed them to infants" (Matt 11:25). Some of us think we are "God-like" (Ps 50:21), but God chooses the foolish to confound the wise (1 Cor 1:27–28). When Jesus's disciples rebuked people for bringing children to him, his response to them was that their attitudes were more like those of the Pharisees than his own spirit of love (Mark 2:6–8). One of the most Zen-like verses in the Bible announces, "Do not be too righteous, and do not act too wise" (Eccl 7:16). People need to strip away artificiality and live with humility. Zen teaches that the "mind of a baby is *Mu*."[68] A child is free or empty (Japanese: *mu* = "nothingness" or "no") from the conceptual constraints that make us timid to advance into unchartered waters. Little children are not crippled by their own sense of self-importance. We cannot appreciate life fully by relying on the "monkey mind" of an experience-laden, cynical adult: We should cultivate the immediacy and directness of a child's heart.

---

67. Leong, *The Zen Teachings of Jesus*, 27.
68. Kadowaki, *Zen and the Bible*, 73.

Infants implicitly seem to cherish gentleness. Buddhism and Christianity also place a high value on gentleness. In Chinese culture, gentleness is seen to be what "distinguishes a real artist from a mere craftsman."[69] For Christians, the way of Jesus is easy and his burden light because Jesus is "gentle and humble in heart" (Matt 11:28–30). Life becomes "easy" because we trust Jesus just as a small child trusts their parents. In fact, Jesus was "child-like" in that he was free from the tyranny of the urgent and the choking constraints of time. Sounding like a Zen teacher, Jesus reminded followers that the hour is late, so they should hurry and repent in order to be ready, like bridesmaids preparing for a wedding (see Matt 25:1–13). Jesus lived his life considering eternity and told followers: "Before Abraham was, I AM" (John 8:58). He was linked to the Ultimate Eternal, and he taught that "the kingdom of God has come near" (Mark 1:15; see also Matt 4:17). Because God is present in the eternal Christ, Jesus announced that the "kingdom of God is among you" (Luke 17:20–21) in the right-now. This sounds like the Zen immediacy of truth.

For both Christians and Buddhists, this personal transformation will be expressed in our public actions and in our commitment to being compassionate to all, including even our enemies (Luke 6:35–36). Even death is not an end to love but only a beginning. Saint Paul describes death as a process of "falling asleep" where a person leaves this world only to "wake up" refreshed in the world to come (see 1 Cor 15). As Jesus breathes his last on the cross he cries out, "Father, forgive them" (Luke 23:34), in a direct statement of solidarity with those responsible for his horrific suffering but also as a promise of his eventual resurrection over all forms of evil, suffering and even over death itself.

---

69. Leong, *The Zen Teachings of Jesus*, 55.

10

Sangha and Church

[Jesus's] message focused on the urgency of a radical change in the inner attitude of the people. He recognized fully that out of the heart are the issues of life and that no external force, however great and overwhelming, can long destroy a people if it does not win the victory of the spirit against them. Jesus was the product of the constant working of the creative mind of God.

—Howard Thurman, *Jesus and the Disinherited*

The entire village is mother to the motherless.

—Indian (Tamil) Proverb

AN INTRODUCTION

RITA GROSS OBSERVES: "STUDIES have shown that at both ends of the life cycle, humans more readily survive and flourish if they experience significant contact with other humans; if they experience nurturing, love, and relationship."[1] Community is an ideal context where we can flourish, learn from others, and find support. At their best, communities are places

---

1. Gross, "Some Reflections about Community and Survival," 3.

of nurture that provide the glue of social cohesion. They can be refuges of consolation and mutual edification.

Buddhism takes shape through a community that hosts the continued living presence of Buddha within daily life. The third focus of Buddha's trinity of refuges is the sangha (*"sangham saranam gacchgini"*; "I take refuge in the sangha"). There are three ways Buddhists use the term *sangha*. First, it refers to the historical community, the *"noble sangha"* that gathered around Buddha. Second, the ordinary sangha are communities of monks who have left families to practice Buddhism. Third, Buddhists are part of a universal community where faith is shared with brothers and sisters—"companions on the path of awakening."[2] The Dalai Lama has said: "The *sangha* is like nurses and attendants who are taking care of sick persons. The *sangha* is a group that must work together in realizing the *dharma* in the world . . . Without a *sangha* there is no Buddhist teaching."[3]

MONASTICISM

Sangha is a term that also refers to any monastic community. Buddhist monasteries, dedicated to teaching and promoting acts of kindness, flourish worldwide.

Buddha taught that monks should pursue a middle way between the two extremes of austerity and hedonistic comfort. There is no benefit in sensuous pleasures because they provide false comforts, will hinder spiritual concentration (*samadhi*), and harm the moral life (*sila*). In many countries, nuns and monks are highly visible for their austere lifestyle, shaved heads, and flowing gowns. Except for Japan (and in diaspora), monks and nuns are traditionally celibate, although celibacy is not expected for laypeople. Nuns and monks are also forbidden to use alcohol (except in Japan where liquor is sometimes called "wisdom water") or other intoxicants because they can cloud the mind.[4]

Early Buddhist nuns and monks in India found their yellow robes in garbage dumps. This was a statement about priorities and not an expression of asceticism. Their hope had given them a new way to overcome sensual and mortal preoccupations by purifying their minds. A monk or nun has renounced all common duties: One scripture explains, "Full of hindrance is a household life; it is a path of grime and of passion. Free as the air is a monk

---

2. Habito, *Experiencing Buddhism*, 68.
3. Mitchell and Wiseman, eds., *The Gethsemani Encounter*, 201.
4. Nakamura, *Buddhism in Comparative Light*, 91.

or nun who has renounced all worldly things."[5] Wealth and family matters are of no concern to monastics. Theirs is not a negation of something good but an affirmation of something much better.

Nuns and monks follow a strict communal discipline and place themselves under the oversight of a teacher. Admission to the first orders is open to all men over twenty years (dated from conception)[6] : they take on new robes and are given new names. One of the first acts upon entry is to have one's head shaved. This reminds the novitiate they are being born into a community in the same way a newborn comes into the world. This practice has the additional benefit of removing one more distraction. Sister Kristine explains, "Now, I don't have to worry about having a bad hair day. Also, food is no longer a big concern. I must be more mindful now about eating. I can't just open my refrigerator any time that I am hungry."[7]

All Buddhist monks and nuns observe at least 227 different precepts in daily life.[8] Some groups have even more rules: Many Orthodox novitiates, for example, follow such strict guidelines as not being allowed to handle money, to eat anything after noon, to attend stage performances, or even to live in the same building as a member of the opposite sex. The lives of many nuns and monks are upheld by the alms round, *pindapata*: they are dependent on the laity for food; in return, laypeople's generosity provides them merit for the next life. Orthodox Buddhist monks—constituting the world's most numerous clergy—spend much of their lives in the study of scripture and in meditation.

ETHICS

Right-morality is vital for the coherence of any community. Buddhists are commanded not to destroy life, steal, lie, drink alcohol, or engage in sexual immorality. Two prized ethical values of Buddhism are wisdom—where moral life begins—and compassion, where it reaches its zenith. Apart from Christianity, there is no tradition which places such an emphasis on loving others. Love (*karuna*) is a prelude to, and a consequence of, wisdom (*prajna*). To empathize with the sufferings of others is to begin the path to enlightenment. We do not love because we are ignorant and, in ignorance, lack the wisdom of perspective. Ignorance is the root cause of all evil. Once

---

5. Nakamura, *Buddhism in Comparative Light*, 79.

6. For more information on women and Theravada Buddhism, see Sundara, "Women in Theravada Buddhism."

7. Sister Kristine (Thich Nu Pho-Chau), "Life as a Vietnamese Nun," 57.

8. Mitchell and Wiseman, eds., *The Gethsemani Encounter*, 104.

freed from ignorance, we become filled with sympathetic friendliness (*maitri*). Harmony in any society is enhanced through mindfulness and compassionate kindness, one toward another.

Buddhism teaches not to love enemies but simply not to hate them, because hatred is a hindrance to inner peace.[9] Love is a part of self-perception and is the emphasis on compassion that gives the dharma its appeal to the unenlightened. Buddha once met a monk who was about to go as a missionary to a hostile tribe. His advice was that even if bandits carved the monk limb from limb with a two-handed saw, even then the monk should not become angry. Love is the guiding motive of right conduct—the fourth step in the Eightfold Path. All merit that can be gained for doing right is worth a tiny fraction of the emancipation of the heart through love.

Ethical excellence is an indispensable quality of an enlightened life. Certainly the lofty ethics of the sangha speak well in comparison to the violent histories of other religions.[10] The aim of right-conduct is not personal transformation but abolishing all traces of individuality. Especially in acts of charity we should stay on the middle path and not seek merit for ourselves. It would be better to be dispassionate than to do deeds to seek merit. In Tibet, for example, it is taught that Milarepa forbade charity if motives were rooted in self-benefit and created any pride. Nonetheless, moral virtue remains the visible proof of progress along the path toward nirvana. Ethical action promotes social cohesion and lessens the pains of those who suffer.

SHARED HEALING

The first sangha and the first church in our lives is found within a family that shares faith and devotion. Both Jesus and Siddhartha had lives brimming with "family affairs."[11] There are many family issues addressed in both religions because families are at the heart of fostering healthy civic society. Critics have inaccurately argued that "Buddhist values are anti-family."[12] For a Buddhist, family ties aid steps toward liberation because "in a family there is no room for pretense and no place to hide. Families are an ideal

---

9. Traditional meditations on loving-kindness in Therevada Buddhism include surrounding enemies with loving-kindness.

10. Some contest, as a remnant of orientalist reduction, that all Buddhist societies are pacifistic.

11. Strong, "A Family Quest," 122.

12. Carmody, *Serene Compassion*, 49: "Buddhism, like Hinduism, ideally did not disparage family life."

context to nurture virtue and learning."[13] Families eliminate loneliness and promote open-mindedness and sharing by necessity with myriad domestic challenges. Intimacy within our families allows us to "work on letting go of a fixed sense of self."[14]

Monastic traditions are a significant way the sangha and the church have advanced the faith. Monasteries become embedded in local cultures and unite communities while expressing both cultural and religious values. At the same time, neither community teaches that those who are not in monasteries are second-class believers or less part of the sangha and the church. Buddha, like Jesus, lived a life of celibacy marked by many ascetic qualities. However, neither Jesus nor Buddha demanded that followers become monks and nuns. A monk or nun is not automatically a "better Buddhist than a layperson and both need each other for mutual growth."[15] The monastic life holds both advantages and disadvantages for spiritual progression.

Jesus said, whenever "two or three are gathered in my name, I am there among them" (Matt 18:20). Jesus is present in acts of charity to the poor (Matt 25:31–46), whom he calls us to see as "brothers and sisters." Christians are bound with Jesus and bound with each other ("the body of Christ") in the same way that a vine relates to its branches (John 15:1–5). Across all differences and in every age, Jesus is the center of all Christian communities. In the same way, Buddhist teaching is central to any sangha. The first *sangha* was born at the Deer Park in Varanasi when the Buddha first taught, while the church was born on the Day of Pentecost when the Holy Spirit first appeared after the resurrection. Church and sangha are vitalized by a shared commitment among members to honor one another in love. Thich Nhât Hanh writes, "A church or community that is not filled with the Holy Spirit is not alive. A Sangha that is not pervaded by the energy of mindfulness is not authentic."[16] It is through community that humility expresses itself with the greatest joy. Both Jesus and Buddha called us to build communities around others and not around self-interested ego-demands. In healthy community, everyone has something to teach us. When we are in right relationships with others, we are free from the slippery slopes of icy pride and no longer bound by unhealthy fears that we will be rejected because of any whim or situation.

---

13. See Sure, "Filial Respect and Buddhist Meditation," 64.
14. Hoebrichts, "Bringing Zen Practice Home," 208.
15. Corless, *The Vision of Buddhism*, 75.
16. Nhât Hanh, *Living Buddha, Living Christ*, 67.

RITUAL POWER

The sangha and the church are contexts where ritual is integrated into daily life. Both faiths warn against separating faith from practice: "Living faith requires practice, and practice is the way in which religious human beings express their faith."[17] The poetry of faith is vividly expressed through rituals. Sometimes rituals are elaborate and sometimes they are simple, but they often change.[18] Rituals also educate the next generation with tangible expressions of beloved teachings.

Critics dismiss faith-based rituals as pompous expressions of glorified child play. Rituals are dismissed as magic-generation that serves no utilitarian function. Some mock Tibetans who insist that the strange liturgies of the Vajrayana are theurgic and, probably, invocations to demons. Some find absurd the care given by Catholic priests, who celebrate the miracle of transubstantiation in the bread and the wine, as a farcical charade. Critics dismiss such rituals as ringing a bell at a communion altar to herald the coming of Jesus or a Tibetan invocation to summon the divine among the living. Skeptics, bereft of visionary empathy, see rituals as contrived and superstitious activities. For critics, rituals are exclusion-making distractions and entertainments. For the faithful, ritual is miraculous as its re-visions the mundane and affirms faith. The believer is touched through ritual's consecrating potential. Ritual is a language that does not try to rationalize or justify faith. The expressions of various rituals point us to what is meaningful midstream in the pressing preoccupations of life.

Ritual provides intriguing paths for interfaith-dialogue. Some, however, wonder if it is possible for prayer to be shared between people of different religions.[19] Some view interfaith prayer as a form of spiritual "infidelity."[20] Others see it as a "loving risk" where we meet others in devotion and not in argumentation. Catholics note that Pope John Paul II participated in a wide number of multifaith prayer services and taught that "every authentic prayer is called forth by the Holy Spirit, who is mysteriously present in the heart of every person."[21]

---

17. Ingram, *The Modern Buddhist–Christian Dialogue*, 165.

18. Smart, *Buddhism and Christianity*, 71: In modern Christendom, "the trend has been overwhelmingly towards the simplification of rituals, and to their being more direct and expressive in their impact."

19. Ruland, *Imagining the Sacred*, 93.

20. D'Costa, *The Meeting of Religions and the Trinity*, 145.

21. Quoted in D'Costa, *The Meeting of Religions and the Trinity*, 151.

TEACHING COMMUNITIES

Faith communities often appoint and recognize elders as authoritative voices for mentorship. The teacher lives for others and surrenders personal life for the greater corporate good. While people of faith cherish books in abundance, many find solace in relating to teachers who model the truth in daily life. Teaching is relational: A teacher only becomes a teacher with permission of a student. A teacher without students is not a teacher but a thinker. In many cultures, a student chooses a teacher and, because of this, has the most leverage in the exchange of learning. One should carefully choose one's teacher or teachers with reflection because who you become may accrue, in large measure, based on whom you invite to be your teachers. A teacher is only one part of the learning equation. A good teacher seeks to uncover a higher and internal teacher in each student, what some call the "inner guru," who teaches us through "subtle consciousness (Tibetan: *rig pa*)."[22]

Teaching can be a practice where spiritual and social transformations can be released, even without words. The Buddhist notion of "thought-transference" asserts that simply being in the presence of someone will cause us to be affected, either positively or negatively, by those with whom we spend time. The student needs only to be with her teacher. Whether the teacher speaks verbally is not as important as simply being beside a wise soul. A noted example of thought-transference happens between Buddha and his disciple Kashapa who received truth from Buddha without hearing any words from his lips.

Thought-transferences are when a student immerses their minds in antirational constructs. These are intended to tear down misconceptions. The "monkey mind" of constant agitation is clogged with thousands of racing preoccupations, all of which are held up by the teetering, ramshackle scaffolding of false assumptions. Once incorrect notions are knocked away—often dramatically—the mind becomes an empty vacuum able to become filled with the pure air of enlightenment. Whenever we think, what we are doing is trying to order our delusions, which give ourselves a sense of false security, by imposing upon our cluttered minds a set pattern of words.

According to some Buddhists, the impartation of insight does not come through Buddha (as, for Christians, it does through the Holy Spirit) or through the community, but through our inward and outward teacher, the Buddha-nature. This explains why teachers are sometimes referred to as "dharma-friends." Truths are passed through teachers and across generations

---

22. Dalai Lama XIV, *Answers*, 58.

and cultures. Teachers are artisans, craftspeople, or scholar-warriors who should continually refine their techniques and adapt their methods. Teaching can never be formulaic because a teacher, like a doctor, deals with the ills of each student on a case-by-case basis. Teachers are "soul-doctors" who provide healing cures for souls and work to keep away mind-sickness from our lives.

Teaching is an exercise of "skillful means" (*upaya-kaushalya*) or, in Chinese, "appropriate method" (*fang-pien*). Another term Chinese Buddhists use to describe teaching is *chiao-hua* or "teaching that brings transformation." Roger Corless notes, "What appears to be philosophy in Buddhism is more like pedagogy. The non-liberated being is regarded as a child or a fool (*bala*). Because we cannot teach children everything adults know, we tell them stories—even white lies—until pliable minds are mature enough to understand more."[23] In a parable from the Lotus Sutra a woman lures her children out of a burning house with enticements of new toys that she is not actually able to provide. What she can provide is a refuge, and those who accept her skillful deceptions will later appreciate the salvific reasons for her methods. Just as Saint Paul said that now we know in part, a time will come when the partiality of knowledge will be swept aside by a forceful tsunami of transformative insight, we will know even as we are known (1 Cor 13:12).

Teaching is strong medicine for those ensnared in mundane assumptions and misguided expectations. Truths taught confront those who blindly cherish the status quo. Enlightenment is an agent for change that can lead to an inner revolution. Truths taught destroy unhealthy thought patterns or actions that accommodate a life of selfishness and indolent comfort. The truth taught confronts obsessive and false hopes. A teacher is a "dangerous friend," who challenges us to move beyond "mindless obedience" toward the "infinite possibilities of enlightenment."[24]

SEXUAL ETHICS

Faith communities remind us how forces of human sexuality relate to the formation of cohesive social ethics. Sadly, countless examples of paternal sexism have trumped mutual respect across the history of both sangha and church when it comes to the promotion of healthy, committed, and empowering, equality-based sexual values.

Christianity historically defines sexual ethics in terms of the bonds of marriage, which foster loyal, faithful commitments instead of immediate

---

23. Corless, *The Vision of Buddhism*, 217.
24. Dorje, *Dangerous Friend*, xv.

pleasure and gratification. The Catholic Church, for example, values marriage as one of the seven sacraments of faith. Unchanging principles must be readapted to changing communitarian practices and paradigmatic assumptions about sexuality, and social cohesion also must be reexamined. The shared sins of lustful lechery and adultery have long been attacked because they erode the fabric of social cohesion and counter integrity, trust, and relational stewardship. Similarly, pedophilia, rape, and other dehumanizing, violent, dominating, and abusive, nonconsensual sexual practices have been confronted by many people of goodwill.

Buddhism teaches that the foundational principle of any sexual ethic must be to "do no harm." Harm is that which oppresses and fosters relational disrespect. People should avoid any mechanistic or "boorish misuse of sex" rooted in "sexually exploitative activities."[25] When we betray the trust of others, we betray our own values and hopes for relational integrity. Thousands of years of faith commentaries are filled with discussions on how healthy sexuality relates to social cohesion as well as spiritual advancement. Domination is also a key concern because "from a Buddhist perspective, working with sexuality is working with attachment."[26]

Discussions about homosexuality should take into account the larger context of dharma insight because Buddha has no implicit focus on same-sex relationships and is neutral on how homosexuality and heterosexuality might be interrelated.[27] Historically, same-sex relationships have been common and accepted in many Asian cultures (such as among the Samurai in Japan).[28] At the same time, the European and North American preponderance of ontologically identifying human-nature in terms of sexual preference is a newer development. For Buddhists, same-sex relationships are fundamentally "neither good nor bad" generally but could be either good or bad depending on interpersonal, relational dynamics.[29] What is of consequence is how any experience of sexual activity is either beneficial or abusive.

A larger focus of most widely taught Buddhist social thought is that tolerance and flexibility are essential to addressing changing sexual values. One Buddhist teacher explained, "To my knowledge, no North American Buddhist organization has never marginalized its lay homosexual constituency,

---

25. Jones, *The New Social Face of Buddhism*, 131.

26. Kaza, "Finding Safe Harbor," 23.

27. A source for reflection on this topic comes from the Gay Buddhist Fellowship (GBF) of San Francisco.

28. Corless, *The Vision of Buddhism*, 79.

29. Warner, "What Do Lesbians Do in the Daytime?," 112.

nor have any ever impeded the full participation of lay homosexual men and women by, for example, requiring their abstinence. To my knowledge, no gay Westerner has ever been denied Buddhist ordination because of his or her sexual orientation."[30] For the sangha there is an unequivocal rejection of any expression of homophobia. Both religions teach that any assertions rooted in an arrogant dismissal of the other can never be healthy or healing. All of us should be acknowledged and respected free of any nondivine judgement about choices made.

Celibacy is another issue of sexual ethics where both faiths share a legacy of promoting it as a path to insight. Saint Paul advised that a single person has greater freedom to serve God than a married person, who faces extra responsibilities (1 Cor 7:27-35). Jesus taught God has "given" to some the power to "renounce marriage" for the sake of the kingdom of heaven (Matt 19:11-12). Celibacy can help one keep a focus on the eternal and keep one from temporal attachment. Leaders of the sangha have forbidden all sexual practices among monks. Culturally, some Asian religious groups forbid even masturbation because the "intentional emission of semen," is seen as a "weakening of vital life-energies [Chinese: *qi*]."[31] In Christianity, Jesus lived a celibate life, and Saint Paul taught that the physical body was a battleground in a spiritual warfare (e.g., Rom 7:24). In contrast, celibate Buddhists are not told to combat urges but to accept, "sexual feelings without either acting on them or repressing them, but just letting them pass through."[32] Both traditions see celibacy as a way to find more time for spiritual devotion. Both traditions see celibacy as an additional resource to promote deep friendships among members of our faith communities.

EMBODYING FAITH

Faith communities share values through acts of service to those outside their walls. Temples and churches have served as places of hospitality, as healing centers, and even at times as feeding stations. Even when silent, the sangha and the church exist as a witness to neighbors about the centrality of eternal values.

---

30. Cabezón, "Homosexuality and Buddhism," 94.

31. Corless, *The Vision of Buddhism*, 79.

32. Ryan, "Buddhist and Catholic Monks Talk about Celibacy," 144: Father Peterson of the Blue Cloud Abbey in South Dakota related, "When college kids ask me—how can you live without sex? My answer is—'God's a better kisser.' In celibacy I transfer my desire for fulfillment to God."

Is the authority of the sangha equal to that of the Christian church, the "body of Christ" on the earth (1 Cor 12:12–13)? In Buddhism, the sangha is also essential to the experience of faith. The dharma is understood through community. The three jewels relate to one another other and depend equally on one another for support. For Christians, the church is not only a place of nurture but embodies the presence of Jesus on earth. One cannot be a Christian apart from the body of Christ (Rom 12:46). The church is a dynamic priesthood of believers (1 Pet 2:9) and the bride of Christ (Rev 19:7; 21:2, 9), animated by the Holy Spirit. In a real sense, salvation is found only inside the church in the same way that a marriage relies on a partnership of two people. Similarly, one cannot be a Buddhist apart from participation in a community.

One should not separate Buddhist teachings from communities any more than one should separate Christian teachings from churches. Buddha's first preaching coincided with the creation of a community while Acts 2 shows that the visitation of the Holy Spirit marks the birthday of the church. A church is a gathering of pilgrim people passing through life. In the same way, the sangha is an outpost of truth in a world of delusion. Christian and Buddhist communities are not only united in shared beliefs, but also function through shared commitments and covenants.

REORIENTATION

While both Christians and Buddhists undertake personal faith journeys, both traditions teach that they are tied into a transgenerational and international community. Communities serve as centers where we share a collective awareness of all we aspire to and cherish.

Interdependence or "dependent co-arising" is at the core of Buddhist dharma. We can be compassionate (*karuna*) with all because we exist in webs of interrelationships with one another. Nuns and monks do not build fellowships only to enhance their spiritual lives. Faith communities exist to serve as centers of welcoming hospitality and to provide respite, social provision, relational healing, and shared learning. Communities of faith stand midstream in turbulent waters and offer alternative visions. Communities that take a "prophetic vow of poverty" and seek to live simply characterize many most monastic orders.[33] Buddhist monks and nuns, for example,

---

33. Although the specifics would obviously vary from order to order and time and place, it was frequently the case that Buddhist monks were allowed only the following possessions: a piece of cloth, one change of clothing, an alms basin of iron or clay (but not of valuable metal), a razor, a belt, and sometimes also sandals and an umbrella. See

often take no food after midday, vow not to watch entertainments, never to use perfume or ornaments, not to use a high couch or bed for sleeping, and never to handle gold or silver.[34] Benedictine monk Mayeul de Dreuille teaches that monasteries are "signs" that remind humanity that "the aim of life is not the possession of perishable goods but rather, to become one day, citizens of heaven, a privilege that all can begin to enjoy here and now, through intimate contact with the divine Presence."[35]

Recently, a group of Russian Orthodox and Buddhist monks met to discuss meditation. From these experiences, Ulrich Luz noted, "Buddhist meditation is not prayer" because right-meditation is an internal tool for reorienting one's worldview and not about responding in relationship to an ultimate being outside of one's self.[36] Speaking of the psychological effects of prayer, another participant noted that the "resemblance between the Buddhist sense of mindfulness and the various ways the Orthodox *Philokalia* addresses the idea of guarding the heart."[37]

The goal of any fellowship of faith is to lay aside personal agendas and work to support one another. For Christians, there is a contrast between the "share-community of the Kingdom of God" with the "greed-community" of ancient Roman oppressors.[38] Christ's vision of the kingdom of God stands in direct confrontation with worldly empires based on greed, power, and control. Christians are called to change societies as "salt and light" (Matt 5:13–14), with lives of loving presence. It is through a caring mother sangha that Buddhism breathes. It is through the vibrancy of an engaged mother-church that Jesus works towards healing a broken humanity.

Luz and Michaels, *Encountering Jesus & Buddha*, 163.

34. Corless, *The Vision of Buddhism*, 102.
35. De Deuille, *From East to West*, 127.
36. Luz and Michaels, *Encountering Jesus & Buddha*, 151.
37. Garvey, *Seeds of the Word*, 122.
38. Crossan, *God and Empire*, 117.

11

Partnerships for Social Justice

According to Buddhism, compassion is an aspiration, a state of mind, wanting others to be free from suffering. It's not passive—it's not empathy alone—but rather an empathetic altruism that actively strives to free others from suffering.

—The Dalai Lama (2005)

SOCIAL ENGAGEMENT

FAITH COMMUNITIES SHOULD REACH beyond liturgical and devotional practices to change a world overflowing with tragedy. Injustices should move us to tears, a tender heart, and shared action for social justice. A lack of tears relates to a lack of devotion. Franz Metcalf encourages us to ask, in every situation, "What would Buddha do?"[1] One teacher challenged fellow Buddhists to "get all of our Buddhist boats rotting in the harbor out to social action!"[2]

Both faiths preach a social vision that promotes love for neighbors. The Ten Commandments provide the ethical foundation for the way that Jesus calls followers to live within the world (Matt 5:21–37; Mark 10:19).[3]

---

1. Metcalf, *What Would Buddha Do?*, 1.
2. Jones, *The New Social Face of Buddhism*, 229.
3. Axel Michaels notes that the "ten actions" cited in Buddhist scriptures closely

Both faiths deepen cords of connections in order to address injustices such as the (contested evil of the) death penalty.[4] Sangha and church lift us to see the bigger picture and the social-justice implications of our dynamic interrelatedness. Faith communities vie with non-faith-based communities (such as globalized economies), which exist to promote their own aims—such as corporate-generated consumerism and rampant market greed that privatizes profits. Paul Knitter warns that apart from an appreciation of our "common context," religion will remain as an "elitist enterprise with little relevance to the lives of oppressed persons."[5] Working together on such issues will make us more appreciative of our fundamental need to be mutually supportive. We have less reason to isolate ourselves from others when we are securely based within mature communities that emphasize a high degree of mutual interdependence.

How can faith communities confront injustice? Christianity sprang from a prophetic tradition where God calls for the establishment of just communities, with the litmus test of success being how the poorest, the weakest, or the loneliest are treated. Christ promoted a middle path that attacked the idolatry of wealth while also reminding followers that humanity does not live by bread alone (Luke 4:4) and that faithfulness would be defined by those who fed the hungry (Matt 25:37), and who consider oppressed people with respect as brothers and sisters.

Gustavo Gutierrez was born in the Montserrat barrio of Lima, Peru, in 1926. He studied theology in Chile, Belgium, and France and then returned to a Lima slum (Rimac). Gutierrez soon realized his education had not prepared him for dealing with the ravaging economic oppression of his homeland. This led him to write *A Theology of Liberation* (1971), which was the opening salvo in a movement now known as *liberation theology*. Gutierrez taught that Jesus lived and worshiped among the poor and today suffers in the middle of brokenness, calling the church to leave sidelines of comfort to serve those in need.[6] Some have embraced an idolatrous religion *about*

---

parallel the Ten Commandments. See Luz and Michaels, *Encountering Jesus & Buddha*, 79.

4. Nhât Hanh, *Living Buddha, Living Christ*, 75: "The death penalty is a sign of weakness, an expression of our fear and inability to know what to do to help the situation. Killing a person does not help him or us."

5. Ingram, *Buddhist-Christian Dialogue*, 12–13.

6. Pope John Paul II proclaimed, "In light of Christ's words, this poor South will judge the rich North. And the poor peoples and poor nations—poor in different ways, not only lacking in food but deprived of freedom and other human rights—will judge those people who take goods away from them, amassing to themselves the imperialistic monopoly of economic and political supremacy at the expense of others" (quoted in Lefebure, *The Buddha and the Christ*, 187).

Jesus and have abandoned the ethical religion *of* Jesus.[7] Gutierrez was not forging a new theology but was rearticulating an original message of Jesus, warrior for justice.

Some Buddhists have begun to call their practice Congregational Buddhism or Engaged Buddhism to emphasize a commitment to social justice.[8] These communities are dedicated to an activist ethic and often out of principle (like some Christian groups such as the Quakers) have sought to be less authoritarian in structure, based on their vision for social equality. Buddhists should work for justice (*rita*) where morality (*sila*) is expressed with liberality, impartiality, and generosity toward others. One teacher explains: "Buddhism is the religion that is freest from prejudice or exclusiveness, or even from bigotry."[9] In fact, the only thing any Buddhist should be intolerant of is intolerance. This sense of impartiality (*samena*) encourages all Buddhists to be liberal-hearted in giving aid to the sick, poor, traveling, vulnerable, elderly, oppressed, and needy.

Buddha taught that through compassionate moral values, a spiritual path can emerge to confront social injustices. We should not even speak harshly, because angry speech can undergird violence which can beget more violence in a never-ending cycle of destruction. Buddha advised rulers to give gifts to their enemies instead of warfare because it would be cheaper in the long run. Like Buddha, we are called to resolve tensions by stepping between combatants and offering our lives, if need be, for the cause of peace. A Buddhist liberation theology has emerged, which works to establish "the best of social and economic theory and practice, focusing on issues like globalization with the full lens of Buddhist teaching."[10]

REJECTING VIOLENCE

Ours is a violent and inequitable world. Citizens of the United States live in the most militarized country in history—a nation that spends over a billion dollars a day on weapons.[11] Many of these expenditures are justified for

---

7. Patterson, *Rituals of Blood*, cites Rev. King's teacher Howard Thurman, who suggests that the religion "about" Jesus was more a construction of Paul than of Jesus.

8. Thich Nhât Hanh wrote a play, *The Path of Return Continues the Journey* (1967), about five monks who were taken from Binh Phuoc and shot beside the Saigon River on July 5, 1967. Four of the five died, and the play talks about how these four had met Mai, a woman who set herself on fire on May 16, 1967.

9. Tachibana, *The Ethics of Buddhism*, 237.

10. Simmer-Brown, "Remedying Globalization and Consumerism," 43.

11. Loy, "Dead Words, Living Words, and Healing Words," 37. In 2000, the United States spent more on weapons than the next fifteen largest nations. Loy states: "The

use as being "peacekeeping" initiatives. At the same time the percentage of Americans in prison is higher than the percentage of incarcerated citizens in any other nation-state worldwide. In the United States, large numbers of women and children have been physically and sexually abused while a booming pornography trade promotes the objectification of women. The clawing reaches of snarling violence extend into our forms of entertainment: movies, television, and even graphic games for children. Pope John Paul II dreamed of turning a grim "culture of war" into a noble "civilization of love."[12] A clear similarity between Christianity and Buddhism is the rejection of violence to resolve problems. Buddha thought using violence created more problems than it solved: "Victory breeds enmity, the defeated one sleeps badly while the peaceful one sleeps at ease having abandoned victory and defeat."[13]

Some Christians reject violence while not opposing governments that sanction its use. Yet, Christ called us to "turn the other cheek" (Matt 5:39) and said that peacemakers would be blessed (Matt 5:9). Pacifism is often dismissed as untenable, but it was the vision of Jesus (Matt 4:43–45). Jesus offered a revolutionary way to engage the world, but is it even possible? How can we love enemies while seeking to kill them? How can we confront evil without protecting ourselves with the option of limited, necessary force?

According to Christianity, God has a "preferential option for the poor."[14] This is expressed because the poor are most often the victims of injustice. When the powerful use strength unjustly against those of us who are oppressed, then the immorality of the promoters of evil will be judged. Christians are assured that God will use human weakness to perfect strength (2 Cor 12:7–9). Perhaps this is what Alcoholics Anonymous means when it says that a person must gain moral power by being willing to be socially powerless.[15]

Because ours is a violent world, our faces will be slapped, and we will be persecuted. What matters is how we respond. Christians who allow for the occasional use of violence note that Jesus cleared the temple of businessmen with a whip (John 2:15). The focus of his message, however, stands against the use of violence. Jesus was the victim of the harsh violence of the cross. While both Jesus and Buddha rejected violence, neither called for toleration

---

violence of secretive terrorist groups is minor compared to the large-scale terrorism that modern states use to enforce their control and extend their influence" (37).

12. Phan, *Being Religious Interreligiously*, 187.
13. Bhikku Bodhi, trans., *The Connected Discourses of the Buddha*, 177.
14. Phan, *Being Religious Interreligiously* 193.
15. Alcoholics Anonymous, *Twelve Steps and Twelve Traditions*, 21.

of evil. One should be "spiritually violent" against evil, which is what Jesus meant when using the term "violence" (Matt 11:12). In contrast, Buddhism explains that in cases of self-defense or in the protection of many, an act of killing might become necessary.[16] Pacifism is ideal, but not always possible. The Dalai Lama explains that if one lives in a situation where violence is rampant, a person should "make the appropriate response . . . tolerance and patience, but this does not imply submission or giving in to injustice."[17]

A stark example of violent protests against military violence includes the accounts of both Buddhist and Christian Vietnam War protestors, who committed sometimes fatal acts of self-immolation. During the 1960s, some Buddhist clerics, including Thich Qung Duc and Nhat Chi Mai, set themselves on fire.[18] On November 2, 1965, Robert McNamara recalled that a "young Quaker named Norman R. Morrison, father of three . . . , burned himself to death within forty feet of my Pentagon window."[19] Another

---

16. Buddhism makes room for what is called "compassionate killing." The Dalai Lama tells the story of a previous birth of Buddha as a sea captain: "One of his crew of 500 intended to kill all 499 of his shipmates in order to make off with their goods. The bodhisattva was unable to convince the potential murderer not to do the deed and figured 'it would be better to take upon himself the karmic burden of killing one person in order to spare that person the *karma* of killing 499, so he killed the would-be murderer" (Florida, *The Buddhist Tradition*, 45).

17. Dalai Lama XIV, *Opening the Eye of New Awareness*, 108.

18. King, "They Who Burned Themselves for Peace." Nhat Chi Mai died outside the Tu Nghiem Temple nunnery on May 16, 1967, on Vesek, the Buddha's birthday. Her letter addressed to the US government read, "I offer my body as a torch to dissipate the dark/to waken love among men/to give peace to Vietnam/the one that burns herself for peace" (128). Two days before her death she appeared to her friends at the nunnery wearing a "beautiful violet *ao dai* with gold embroidery . . . Mai's hair was arranged beautifully, and her new dress made her look as if she were about to attend a ceremony. Right away, she began slicing the banana cake she had baked especially for us" (129). Friends joked with her that maybe she was about to get married, "but Mai just smiled silently" (129).

19. King, "They Who Burned Themselves for Peace," 137–38. Morrison's death may have "played the critical role in igniting McNamara's doubts about the war and developing in him the sensitivity that finally led him to cease prosecuting the war" (138). McNamara received a letter from Morrison's widow, Anne Morrison Welsh, that he often cited in lectures. Of the letter, McNamara wrote, "She is a noble woman. That anyone could have gone through what she did and then write the person, who in the mind of her husband, was responsible for the actions that resulted in his killing himself. . . I was deeply moved" (138). Norman Morrison's act was celebrated in artwork throughout North Vietnam. Morrison had three children and even had his youngest daughter Emily accompany him to the Pentagon that day. Christina, Norman Morrison's oldest daughter, wrote: "I have often felt that, in a sense my father sacrificed all five of us in hopes of saving the people of another country. As a child, I wondered if they were more important to him than we were. I still wonder if he had any idea how much his action would hurt us and would he have done it if he had known" (139).

Quaker woman, Alice Hertz, also set herself on fire.[20] Thich Nhât Hanh, responding to these self-immolations in Vietnam, refused to say that these acts were unethical.[21] In contrast, most Christians have condemned such actions because Christians must "do no harm," including not harming themselves.[22] It takes more courage to live to fight for justice than to fight violence with further violence. These acts continue: Beginning in 2012, some Tibetan Buddhists have set themselves on fire to protest Chinese rule.[23]

When Buddha rejected the sacrificial offering system of Vedic rituals, he was not only promoting humaneness to animals but also putting the sangha on a course that emphasized that all forms of violence are harmful. Not even violent sacrifices in the name of truth are acceptable. Rene Girard writes that the historic focus on the violent death of Jesus has made Christian history an unending parade of ruthless violence.[24] In contrast, Christians argue that as soldiers arrested Jesus, he told Peter to put away his sword (John 18:10). Jesus went to the cross "like a lamb that is led to the slaughter," and many see the entire life of Jesus as an expression of nonviolent action. On the cross, Jesus is participant in humanity's suffering.

Father Laurence Freeman claimed that the cross and resurrection were signs of blessings for Tibetans: "The cross and resurrection are human realities that belong to all people, and not to one people alone. We have seen Tibet crucified, but we have also seen the resurrection of Tibetan wisdom."[25]

20. King says, "In America, to my knowledge eight people burned themselves to death during the war. Two were Quakers: Norman Morrison and Alice Herz. Roger LaPorte, a former Trappist seminarian who had become a Catholic worker, immolated himself one week after Morrison. The others were: Hiroko Hayasaki, a Japanese-American Buddhist; Erik Thoen, a student of Zen Buddhism; another university student, George Winne; a high school student, Ronald Brazee; and Florence Baumont, described as a 'housewife.' A number of others attempted self-immolation but survived" (King, "They Who Burned Themselves for Peace," 128).

21. Martin Luther King Jr. was moved by reading this book and gave it to his friend Andrew Young.

22. The acts of these self-immolators brought pain, not only to themselves but also to their families and friends. Therefore, they must never be encouraged. King writes, "While there is some ambivalence among both Quakers and Buddhists regarding these acts, the Quaker community has come out more clearly opposed to the act of self- immolation than the Buddhist" ("They Who Burned Themselves for Peace," 141). King, however, does note that the Dalai Lama described the self-immolation of Tibetan Buddhist monk Thupten Ngodup (on April 28, 1998) as an act of violence ("They Who Burned Themselves for Peace," 146).

23. US Congressional-Executive Commission on China, *Special Report*.

24. Girard writes that by submitting to violence without protest, Jesus "reveals and uproots the structural matrix of all religions" (*Things Hidden Since the Foundation of the World*, 178–79).

25. Dalai Lama XIV, *Opening the Eye of New Awareness*, 37.

For Christians, as we go into all the world to preach (Matt 28:20), we go in peace. The invitation to Christianity is to a life of faith, hope, and love (1 Cor 13:13), free from coercive violence. Christians are called, not only to live at peace with God, but also with all humanity.

OPPRESSING RELIGION

Faith is often co-opted to work against hopes for social justice. Is it true that many of the social problems of Europe and North America "grew up in and, in many ways remains tied up with Christianity"?[26] Paulo Freire states that faith has often been a vehicle to advance oppression. American southern evangelical churches, for example, often supported the terrorism of the Ku Klux Klan throughout the Jim Crow era. Native Americans, women, and others have often, sadly, been oppressed by Christians in the name of a poor peasant teacher from Galilee.

Such affronts continue today: Evangelical Pat Robertson once warned listeners that the promotion of equal rights for women would result in the "weaker sex" being encouraged to "leave their husbands, kill their children, practice witchcraft, destroy capitalism, and become lesbians."[27] It is hard to argue with Rosemary Radford Ruether: "For me, the oppressive force of Christianity for women and other subjugated people comes, not primarily from this or that specific doctrine, but from a patriarchic reading of the whole system of Christian scriptures."[28]

Buddhist–Christian relations have sometimes seen horrific attacks against each other in the name of twisted versions of holiness. In Japan, for example, twenty-six Jesuits were crucified by authorities who planned to rid Japan of Christianity. On the other hand, one of the first Protestant missionaries to China, Carl Schurz, distributed Bibles on the very opium ships working to bring the scourge of addiction on the Chinese people. Although Saint Paul had determined he would only "proclaim Christ crucified" (1 Cor 1:23), it has often been the case that Asians have "experienced Jesus Christ as bulldozing and crucifying them."[29]

When Buddha's message becomes perverted, it also becomes an instrument for oppression. In Japan, Zen teachings became a "particularly pernicious variation" of the "nation-protecting Buddhism" that empowered

---

26. Waldenfels, *Absolute Nothingness*, 59.

27. Quoted in Gross and Ruether, *Religious Feminism and the Future of the Planet*, 101.

28. Gross and Ruether, *Religious Feminism and the Future of the Planet*, 88.

29. Koyama, *No Handle on the Cross*, 109.

Showa military leaders before World War II.[30] Even noted Zen scholar Daisetz Suzuki claimed justifications for militarism with co-opted teachings about "Imperial Way Buddhism."[31] Horror stories abound of ways that Japanese nationalists dehumanized Chinese in Nanjing, the Nazis (97 percent of whom claimed to be Christians) murdered six million Jews, or how American Christians massacred Native Americans at Sand Creek and Wounded Knee. People of faith have often sacrificed moral codes on altars of political power.

Religious communities have often remained silent when tides of economic injustice have swept over the poor. Some clerics have even blessed profligate economic injustice that offers wealth for the few at the expense of the many. People of faith have stood by as economic injustices have dislodged time-honored social patterns. Faith communities have been both victims and victimizers in these trends. Of the support of parasitic capitalism, Buddhist Ken Jones claims:

> Capitalism makes public the ancient Buddhist [and Christian] fires of acquisitiveness and aggressiveness by maximizing the freedom of individuals and groups to aggressively pursue wealth as an ultimate social virtue and by legitimizing the immense power this wealth has vested in the few over the many.[32]

Paulo Freire, in *The Pedagogy of the Oppressed*, argued that one should not assume that economic injustices take place because global economies are malfunctioning. These systems are performing smoothly—just as they were created to function, which is exactly why there is such widespread poverty. The world's wealthy directly benefit from the economic destitution of others. Indeed, poverty is "*conceptually* necessary if the world is to be completely commoditized and monetarized . . . The poverty of others is also necessary

---

30. Victoria, *Zen at War*, 228.

31. Shaku Soen, in Chicago in 1893, spoke on behalf of Japanese military force. Zen scholar Reiho Masunaga told kamikaze fighters that what they were doing was "the perfection of selflessness and as such, the achievement of complete enlightenment" (Schmidt-Leukel, "War and Peace in Buddhism," 34). During the Vietnam War the Thai Buddhist monk Kittivuddho declared that "killing of Communists is not demeritous because Communists should not be regarded as 'real persons' but as *maras*, that is, manifestations of evil forces who strive to destroy nation, religion, and monarchy. To kill them would not be the same as killing human persons but would be ridding the world of devils and should be regarded as the 'duty of all Thai'" (Schmidt-Leukel, "War and Peace in Buddhism," 35). Schmidt-Leukel cites one of the most egregious instances of violence advocated in the name of Buddhism in the acts of the Japanese Tantric Buddhist sect Aum Shinrikyo, led by Shoko Asahara, which carried out a poison-gas attack at a Tokyo subway station in 1995.

32. Jones, *The New Social Face of Buddhism*, 69.

because it is the benchmark by which we measure our own achievements."[33] The answer to the question of how to end poverty should be the focus of faith communities worldwide. The problem is that we "lack a collective will to overcome the simple fact that those who have the most control over the earth's resources" care less about justice than profit.[34] Economic injustices originate from the self-interests of those unwilling to confront their ethical obligations to those less fortunate. Genuine solutions to structural economic problems can be pushed by faith communities. Instead, many have used religious teachings to justify ongoing oppressive forces; for example, some use biblical passages to promote violence.[35] The history of religion is filled with violence, but the greater issue is whether or not "religion as such, in its historical emergence and, by its very nature, is intrinsically an institution of violence.[36]

AUTHENTIC JUSTICE

During many sordid historical events, Buddhists and Christians were present as agents for justice. There are many examples: In Europe, Dietrich Bonhoeffer, Father Maximilian Kolbe, and Andre Trocme of Le Chambon, France, stood against Hitler. In Japan, Nichidatsu Fujii (called Guruji by Gandhi) staged protests before the war. Afterwards, students of Guruji built "peace pagodas" to remember the victims of the atomic bombs that immolated many innocent people in Nagasaki and Hiroshima.

Others confront compromises within their own faith communities. Peace activists such as Dorothy Day and Peter Marin of the Catholic Worker Movement, Archbishop Desmond Tutu, and Father Daniel Berrigan

---

33. Loy, *The Great Awakening*, 63 (italics original).

34. Loy, *The Great Awakening*, 71.

35. Phan, *Being Religious Interreligiously*, 199. He states, "Girard has ignored or played down the many 'texts of terror' of both the Old and New Testaments whose embarrassing violence later theologians will attempt to attenuate by an allegorical interpretation. Raymond Schwager points out there are six hundred passages of explicit violence in the Hebrew Bible, one thousand verses where God's own violent actions of punishment are described, one hundred verses where Yahweh expressly commands others to kill, and several stories where God kills or tries to kill for no apparent reason. Michael Desjardins [cited by Phan, *Being Religious Interreligiously*, 199] notes that while there is a call to peace in the New Testament, there are many aspects, especially the apocalyptic notion of a cosmic war that cannot easily be reconciled with a call to peace. It must be acknowledged that in the Hebrew-Christian imagination the Crucified God stands side by side with God the Warrior" (Phan, quoting from Schwager, *Must There Be Scapegoats?* and Desjardins, *Peace, Violence, and the New Testament*).

36. Phan, *Being Religious Interreligiously*,190.

confronted those who overlooked injustices. In South Africa, Desmond Tutu won the Nobel Peace Prize when joining with Buddhist and Christian groups to end apartheid.[37] Another Nobel Prize winner, Aung San Suu Kyi, fought corrupt Burmese dictators, before, sadly, making ethical compromises once coming to political power. Behind bars, groups such as the Christian Prison Fellowship and the Buddhist Prison Ashram are fighting for change.[38] Mennonites and Quakers, not to mention groups such as Baptist Peacemakers and Buddhist Peace Fellowship, have nurtured peacemakers. Thich Nhât Hanh used the term "social engagement" to discuss how Buddhist values of nonviolence affect societies.[39] The first step in bringing peace is to bring peace inside ourselves.[40]

One visible context of oppression is Tibet—now entombed within the People's Republic of China. Tibet was invaded by the People's Liberation Army (PLA) in 1959. Thousands of Tibetans who fought against the Chinese were brutally slaughtered. Thousands of women were raped while many others died of starvation. On March 31, 1959, the Dalai Lama entered India at the Chuthangmo Checkpoint and began a life of exile. Today the Tibetan Youth Congress and the Tibetan People's Freedom Movement works to raise awareness of Tibetan grievances. As Tibet's de facto leader, the Dalai Lama has called for dialogue with all people of goodwill. He stated, "I do feel that dialogue could promote a better understanding and mutual respect in the areas of ethics, conduct, and metaphysics—in other words, in the areas in which there are many parallels and compatibilities, as well as the areas in which there are many diversities and differences."[41]

People of faith should also unite to educate, advocate, and work for environmental justice. Christians often claim to be God-ordained stewards who are "above" nature, and have responded to ecological questions with a "fundamental dualism" that separates humanity from the environment.[42] On a positive note, both Buddhist and Christian artists have celebrated nature's power to foster spiritual insight.[43] Buddhists, led by Joanna Macy,

---

37. The first Buddhist society in South Africa was the Overport Skaya Buddhist Society, opened in Durban, 1917. The first Zen Buddhist center, the Dojo Marisan Nariji, was founded in 1979.

38. The Prison Dharma Network was founded in 1985 by Fleet Maull. Other prison groups include the Engaged Zen Foundation (EZF) and the National Buddhist Prison Sangha (NBPS).

39. Ingram, *Buddhist–Christian Dialogue*, 11.

40. King, *Being Benevolence*, 175.

41. Dalai Lama XIV, *The Good Heart*, 79.

42. Kjellberg, *Urban Ecotheology*, 151.

43. A story told of a novitiate to a monastery who, upon his arrival, said to his

have protested the disposal of nuclear waste at Arizona's Yucca Mountain. The Green Gulch Zen Center (in Marin County, California) calls itself an *ecosattva* while prioritizing environmental initiatives.

Early Buddhist teachings explain that all animate beings can attain the enlightenment of Buddhahood, which explains why it is incumbent on all of us to protect every form of life. Jay McDaniel, author of *Of God and Pelicans: A Theology of Reverence for Life*, encourages Christians to "feel the world as God feels it with sensitivity to the intrinsic value of each and every life and with delight in the sheer diversity of forms of life."[44] Brian Brown asserts that Buddhist environmentalism advocates against all forms of "distorted arrogance," which fail to recognize that all things are interrelated in a worldview that is "grounded in universal Emptiness."[45]

Another context for interfaith justice partnerships is the confrontation of the modern slave trade and sex-trafficking trade in Christian-majority nations (such as the Philippines) and in Buddhist-majority nations (such as Thailand). The pain that women and children experience in lives of constant rape and slavery sometimes also ends with HIV/AIDS.[46] Tragically, some families have chosen to sell their own family for economic gain. Sadly, many of the women imprisoned in (Hindu-majority) India's brothels were taken from Buddhist homes in Nepal. Sex trafficking in Thailand and Cambodia is tolerated because it is a major income source for local economies. Tourists who claim to be Christians and Buddhists have been major income providers in human trafficking. Christians and Buddhists must unite to confront these problems.[47]

---

teacher, "I have just arrived and found the gate to the monastery. Now, help me to find the gate into the Way." The teacher asked if the student could hear the stream in the valley below. When the student said he could, the teacher said, "Enter here." The sound of a valley stream can be our link from the world of our minds, filled with delusions, to the world that is true. From MacInnes, *Zen Contemplation for Christians*, 173.

44. McDaniel, "The Garden of Eden, the Fall, and the Life of Christ," 81.

45. Brown, "Toward a Buddhist Ecological Cosmology," 136.

46. Khandu Lama estimates as many as 60 percent of the women in brothels on the Indian subcontinent are infected with HIV/AIDS (Khandu Lama, "Trafficking," 169). She cites that 75 percent of the women in brothels in India are Buddhist. Khandu Lama, "Trafficking in Buddhist Girls," 165–72.

47. Buddhists such as Dr. L. P. N. Perera claim that "there is no justification in Buddhist philosophy for slavery in any form" (Florida, *The Buddhist Tradition*, 130). Florida (111–31) cites three references to slavery in the Buddhist scriptures. Monasteries in India relied on slaves to clean their properties. In Sri Lanka, people even sold themselves into slavery and gave gifts of their wives and children to gain merit. Slaves, "human goods," were central to the economic life of monasteries in China and central Asia as well. Sometimes Chinese leaders made gifts of slaves to monasteries of criminals, debtors, and those condemned to death. In Thailand, King Chulalongkorn (Rama

Women worldwide often encounter horrific oppression. Buddhist congregations in North America, often led by women, have raised concerns about oppressed Buddhist women. This activism is vital because many feel alone in their plight. It is transformative when women come together to support one another.[48] Gender-based violence traumatizes millions caught in webs of physical and sexual abuse. According to the United Nations, women and children make up 7 percent of the world's poor and 80 percent of all refugees.[49] Women of color; women with disabilities; women in poverty; and women in the sexual, religious, or cultural minority sometimes face a multiplicity of oppressing forces.

While there are always hypocrites who use religion to abuse people, Buddhist and Christian tradition offers rich resources for the promotion of social justice.[50] One Burmese social justice activist observed, "it was a perversion of Buddhist thought and values for authoritarian governments like Burma's military regime to denounce human rights as antithetical to indigenous values."[51] There is a widespread misconception that religion invariably has discouraged a "primordial hope for progress and serves as a threatening bar toward swift modernization."[52] In the same way, a devout Buddhist cannot support any glorification of the military. Because of this a Buddhist should not "watch military maneuvers or parades or stay without need in a military camp. People are not allowed to earn their livelihood by trading in arms," and Buddha taught that any "soldier who dies in battle will go to hell because at the moment of his death, his mind is governed by the intention to kill."[53]

Throughout history, some Christians have "awakened to the revolutionary spirit of early Christianity" by working for social justice.[54] Buddhists, such as Thich Nhât Hanh, have also called for a revolutionary spirit

---

V, r. 1868–1919) issued an order for the gradual abolition of all forms of slavery. The practice was finally abolished in 1905.

48. In 1975, a five-day festival sponsored by *WomanSpirit* magazine included participant Hallie Mountain Wing (Inglehart), who wrote, "In the openness, support, and love that we created, we were able to be who we really are—full, free women." This quote is from Christ, *Diving Deep and Surfacing* (3rd ed.), 127.

49. Chhabra, "Redefining and Expanding the Self in Conflict Resolution," 98.

50. Many Buddhists have been nominated for the Nobel Peace Prize, including Cambodia's Maha-Ghosananda, Vietnam's Thich Nhât Hanh, and Sri Lankan A. T. Ariyaratne, who focused on Tamil-Sinhalese healing.

51. Quoted in Florida, *The Buddhist Tradition*, 104.

52. Haynes, *Religion in Third World Politics*, 23.

53. Schmidt-Leukel, "War and Peace in Buddhism," 41.

54. Palihawadana, "A Buddhist Response," 42.

dedicated to social justice.[55] Social justice in Buddhism springs from the Buddha-nature, and Christianity roots the idea of justice in God's character (Isa 45:8). Those who are indifferent to the needy will experience God's judgement (Ezek 16:49–50). Jesus taught that decisions made on the Day of Judgment will be based on how we help those who are oppressed (Matt 25:31–46). Moses commanded people to love their neighbor as they love themselves (Lev 19:18). If we claim to love God but hate our neighbors, we are liars (1 John 4:20).

In our fragile world, those who are victimized often need someone to speak for them and help them from their chains. Distinguished Baylor University scholar Ralph Wood calls for Christians to serve others with humility as "little ones, the hobbits of the world."[56] Cistercian monk M. Basil Pennington believes that "peace can only be built on justice, a just sharing of the divine Goodness which gives gratuitously to us all so that every human person can live a human life."[57B]

---

55. "To prepare for war, to give millions of men and women the opportunity to practice killing day and night in their hearts, is to plant millions of seeds of violence, anger, frustration, and fear that will be passed on for generations to come" (Nhât Hanh, *Living Buddha, Living Christ*, 77).

56. Wood, *Preaching and Professing*, 92.

57. Pennington, "A Source of Hope, an Instrument of Peace," 211.

12

Creative Interfaith Engagement

Imagine ourselves meeting each other, / bringing gifts, bringing news.
—Denise Levertov, from "The Cutting-beam," in *The Freeing of the Dusts*

CREATIVITY

PSYCHOANALYST ERICH FROMM THOUGHT creative people were more able to deal with life's puzzles because they are born-again every day, "feeling a new sense of the self."[1]

Creativity, and the creation of shared artistic spaces, is a delightful path to forge new relational pathways. An artist, with zest and attentiveness, often provides nuanced perspectives on what had been commonplace. Although the arts are interpretive, they can move us beyond the superficial and leave room for new interpretations. "Art is about seeing and being sensitive to reality. It is right-brained... Art is not about thoughts. Rather, it is seeing, listening, feeling, and touching."[2] George Santayana wrote, "'Art critics talk about art. Artists talk about where you can buy good turpentine.'"[3]

---

1. Eric Fromm (1900–1980) also mused, "Education makes machines which act like men and produces men who act like machines." I no longer have sources for these statements, but they can be found here: http://thinkexist.com/quotes/erich-fromm/.
2. Leong, *The Zen Teachings of Jesus*, 67.
3. Quoted in Leong, *The Zen Teachings of Jesus*, 67.

Artistic people of faith can contribute to a zestful engagement of multifaith dialogue. Both Buddhism and Christianity teach that creativity is an expression of the image of God/Buddha within our lives. Sharing art, music, poetry, and dance may generate unexplored pathways for appreciation. The magic of creative expression is integral to what it means to be a fully flourishing person.

Kosuke Koyama writes, "God-talk belongs in the realm of poetry."[4] Buddhist John Daido Loori explains, "The creative process like a spiritual journey is intuitive, non-linear, and experiential. It points us toward our essential nature, which reflects the boundless creativity of the Universe."[5] Buoyant creativity in a multifaith context implies a willingness to go in unchartered directions. Interfaith interactions fail when they are inflexible. They should be marked by the "absence of formula and the need for improvisation and originality."[6] Interfaith conversations are a form of art as they move, with fluency, away from long-held fortresses of preconceptions. A needed first step is often to lower self-defensiveness. What does a guarded posture say about our willingness to relate with people of other faiths? All of us should embrace interfaith dialogues, in the words of the World Council of Churches, as "common adventures in unchartered waters."[7]

The depths of human imagination seems endless, and art can serve as another way to communicate with supernatural powers. Tibetan Chogyam Trungpa relates the creation of art to spirituality: "Creating art is like meditating. You work with one technique for a long time and finally the technique falls away."[8] God is described by some Christians as an artist who uses nature as a painter's palette. Interfaith dialogues that honor the creativity of God or Buddha may often best be expressed in the aesthetics of celebratory appreciation and artistic and creative exploration.

---

4. Koyama, *Water Buffalo Theology*, xi.

5. Loori, *The Zen of Creativity*, 1.

6. Leong, *The Zen Teachings of Jesus*, 39. Leong explains: "Jesus' teachings are poetic and not pedantic, simple and not laborious . . . Picasso showed his understanding of this when he said, 'I used to draw like Raphael, but it has taken me my whole life to draw like a child'" (41).

7. Sheard, *Interreligious Dialogue in the Catholic Church since Vatican II*, 274.

8. Trungpa, *Dharma Art*, 115.

HEALING FRIENDSHIPS

Zen offers a simple definition of who an outsider is: anyone who is outside![9] Hearty laughter, warm food, lifting music, playful simplicity, and the poetic sensuality of everyday life should find their places within interfaith encounters as encounters shift more towards friendships of mutual respect. In the same ways that jazz music flows during an improv gathering, so also interfaith discussions should invite participants to be artists, musicians, poets, or storytellers.

Healing interfaith encounters begin with the relational and the personal. Jesus on the cross was not an abstract object but a bleeding person. Hans Waldenfels notes, "The kind of death that Jesus dies—the death of a criminal and hence a death in solidarity with the most abject of creatures in this world," is a revelation of God's love for humanity.[10] The Buddha was not a theoretical concept but a striving, hungry being who was actively involved in our human story. The dharma and Gospels unfold as messages of loving engagement. Buddhists who suffer and Christians worldwide being persecuted bleed countless liters of actual blood, not pious analogies and metaphors. Both faiths' incarnate truth is expressed in lived experience. Kosuke Koyama served as a Christian missionary among Thai Buddhists. He reflected that as his friendships deepened and his language skills improved, he realized that "what really mattered is not a set of doctrines called Buddhism, but *people* who live according to the doctrine of the Buddha. Accordingly, my interest shifted from Buddhism to Buddhist people."[11] Koyama asks if Christians see Buddhists as individuals with unique expressions of God's image, or are they seen through simplistic categories? Is the "other" in our hearts or in our heads? One Catholic priest asked:

> Do we perceive the murdered Israeli soldier or Palestinian demonstrator as a Jew or an Arab, or as a human being who happens also to be a Jew or an Arab? How do the figures strike us—as

---

9. Kennedy, *Zen Spirit, Christian Spirit*, 127.

10. Waldenfels, *Absolute Nothingness*, 159.

11. Koyama, *Water Buffalo Theology*, 93: "Thanks to some knowledge about library-Buddhism [today's equivalent would be internet-Buddhism], I began to say a few sensible words about Buddhism. But when I realized the difference between library-Buddhism and street-Buddhism, my library-Buddhism was paralyzed . . . Yet, it is the street-Buddhists who are the brothers and the sisters that I see, with whom I speak, and with whom I love. To love them as they are in all their complexities and not just to love anthropological, sociological, theological formulations of brothers and sisters is the command of God whom we have not seen" (151).

individual tragedies or as statistics that are being used as political weapons?[12]

A compelling spiritual force, rarely appreciated, is the power of friendships. Friendships offer ordinary invitations to share a cooked meal or cups of coffee instead of a dramatic interfaith dialogue. When Jesus rose from the dead, he first visited friends, huddled beside the chilly Sea of Galilee one morning asking for something warm to eat (John 21). Jesus met friends in day-to-day ways and exemplified the connections between friendship and wisdom-sharing. Trust and vulnerability without preconditions grow in the loamy soils of kind, openhearted friendships.

Elie Wiesel writes, "Friendship marks a life even more deeply than love. Love risks degenerating into obsession; friendship is never anything but sharing."[13] The friendly among us are at ease, nourishing and protecting us with acceptance. Friends do not usually worry about status enhancement or how friendships promote their own egos. For the philosopher Cicero, for Saint Augustine, and for others, friendship was not a starting point but the goal of transformative interactions. Education prepares us for meaningful, lasting friendships.

What should friendships between Buddhists and Christians look like? Genuine friendships express a shared willingness to listen to each other with respect—the foundation for empathetic appreciation. Saint Aelred of Rievaulx, a thirteenth-century monk wrote (in *Spiritual Friendship*) that friendships cannot be based on "exploitative desire or hatred of others because these negative qualities betray human nature."[14] Saint Aelred claimed, "The perfection of human friendship is an epiphany of the real presence of Christ. Christ makes the third person between us."[15]

Healing Buddhist and Christian interfaith encounters are relational before they are informational. Friendships are rooted in shared experiences of those willing to set barriers aside in order to create a shared space of respect. Geri Larkin, in *Tap Dancing in Zen*, states: "The Buddha taught that friendship is a summary statement of a good life because it draws on equanimity, joy, and compassion."[16] Buddha and Jesus cherished many friends.

12. Dalai Lama XIV, *The Good Heart*, 9.

13. See Wiesel, *The Gates of the Forest*, 1, 26–27. Henry David Thoreau wrote, "The most I can do for my friend is simply to be his friend. I have no wealth to bestow on him. If he knows that I am happy in loving him, he will want no other reward." I no longer can track down the source of the Thoreau quotation, but both Wiesel and Thoreau quotations can be found here: http: thinkexist.com/friendship/.

14. Quoted in Dalai Lama XIV, *The Good Heart*, 8.

15. Quoted in Dalai Lama XIV, *The Good Heart*, 8.

16. Larkin, *Tap Dancing in Zen*, 82.

Once, when discussing this, a friend wondered out loud if Jesus and Buddha would be friends on WeChat, Facebook, and Instagram!

The Buddhist word translated "compassion" (Pali: *metta*), is linked to the word for "friendship" because compassionate people are friendly people. Buddhist texts teach that being a friend means you will consistently help others who "serve as a refuge to you when you are afraid."[17] One of Buddha's students asked if it was not true that "friendship was not half of all that matters." The Buddha said that, actually, "friendship is everything."[18] It is a force that flows from the heart and is rarely defeated by changing circumstances. It is a gift, not always serene, that is a shared responsibility between us. Supportive friendships often shed advantages to gain harmony.

Think of friendship as a shared room where Christians and Buddhists can be comfortable together. We need to be in each other's presence and be present together. The initial question when we gather is, Are we among enemies or among friends? Benedictine Father Laurence Freeman explains: "Presence in dialogue is nonverbal and nonconceptual, it might sound vague or platitudinous; but is nonetheless a fact. It is difficult to describe but it is the first thing we experience in dialogue. How are we perceived by each other?"[19] The willingness to enter friendships calls for a spirit of confident flexibility. The Bible states, "Perfect love casts out fear" (1 John 4:18), and fear characterizes many who are unable to forge friendships across faiths. Sharing faiths should be the friendship-sharing of encouragement, edification, and empowerment

INTERFAITH SPARRING

When structured interfaith dialogues become wrestling-matches around conflicting ideas, little progress results. For some, relying on words—essentially the only knowledge they can share about their faith—is not incarnational or relational but analogical, doctrinal, and categorical. Gandhi observed, "The very attempt to clothe thought in word or action limits it."[20]

Interfaith engagements eventually should transcend the obvious limitations of language. Wittgenstein parallels this idea when he notes that life's problems vanish once they are divorced from the theoretical. Of course, Wittgenstein also thought that language developed to overcome life's

---

17. Senauke, "Personal Notes," 101: True friends are not "bottle-friends," who only love you until the wine is gone.
18. Larkin, *Tap Dancing in Zen*, 82.
19. Dalai Lama XIV, *The Good Heart*, 5.
20. Quoted in Kinahan, *A Deep but Dazzling Darkness*, 11.

problems. In any event, theology is a process of clarification in response to specific questions rooted in specific cultures. Those who are Buddhists or Christians create an entirely distinct, unfamiliar set of questions that require fresh clarifications. Disagreements can only take place once two people agree to speak the same language. The Buddha-nature and the God of Christianity—the creator of the world's confusing Babel (Gen 11:1–9)—are far above the limitations of assertions.

We sometimes over-rely on language to assess meaning. While language "casts a spell" which leads to "the bewitchment of our intelligence," to quote Wittgenstein, language is not the truth itself.[21] Truths must be experienced, and words and thoughts about the truth can shackle just as easily as they can liberate. Many of us become preoccupied in thoughts and intellectualize our lives so much that we hypnotically "eat the menu instead of the meal."[22] For Christians, God became Christ incarnate and alive in our hearts—not a remote ideal. Alan Watts notes that most problems vanish when we embrace a "non-verbal dimension of consciousness. Theology, philosophy, and metaphysics as we ordinarily talk about them cease to be urgent problems."[23]

When the conversation becomes more fluid, and language is freed from intransigence, Christians and Buddhists can meet each other with a greater sense of immediacy. Cardinal Francis Arinze, head of the Pontifical Council for Interreligious Dialogue, said that people from various religions should work and live together in constructive ways and "leave aside speculative discussion."[24] Cardinal Arinze advocated that people of faith should be open to untested possibilities as the worlds around them are in need of new solutions. Dialogue can be a series of reinvigorated reconsiderations of previously assumed differences. Horizons may appear at sunrise that we could not have envisioned as possible at midnight. Interfaith dialogues should create spacious contexts for constructive interactions instead of rounds of tiresome interfaith sparring.

Often, studies of "others" are theoretical and generate problems instead of empowering mutuality. Father Aloysius Pieris claims that some people "study" religion instead of "practicing" faith: "Religion is a department in many a Western university just as it has become a "department" in life."[25] Interfaith interactions are an optional project for some in more

---

21. Quoted in Keithley, *Into Every Life a Little Zen Must Fall*, 58.
22. Keithley, *Into Every Life a Little Zen Must Fall*, 118.
23. Quoted in Keithley, *Into Every Life a Little Zen Must Fall*, 102.
24. Quoted in Kennedy, *Zen Gifts to Christians*, 55.
25. Pieris, *Love Meets Wisdom*, 3.

homogenous religious-cultural contexts, while in much of the world the skills of interfaith interactions are basic to daily civic life. The goal is not to air "pompous resolutions made in comfortable circumstances" but to invent usable relational strategies to sustain our shared mutuality.[26]

Interfaith partnerships are built on trust, and a lack of trust reveals a lack of love and respect. Some assert that differences between Buddhism and Christianity are so vast that there is no common ground. While I disagree, I think that what we share in common is not nearly as vital or interesting as sharing our differences—the unique dynamisms of our personal experiences. We do not live our faiths "simply from a position of notional assent lacking experiential, personal verification."[27] An early biblical lesson is that knowing facts about God, a form of abstracting idolatry, is not the same as having a warm, direct, and personal encounter with the living God.

Buddhists and Christians both claim to have discovered the unfamiliar within the familiar. Interfaith engagement can be an adventure in sharing life instead of defending codified theories and ideas. Experiencing the unfamiliar in faith reminds us that we have more to learn. There are significant differences between the two traditions, but these are opportunities to learn how our subjectivity relates to objectivity. The "objectivity of truth does not reject the subjective" but can integrate the "particular and the universal" into a present-tense interfaith engagement.[28]

As Jesus comes to Cambodia and Buddha comes to Canada, unconsidered ways of appreciating cherished beliefs can make adherents of both traditions richer. Interfaith discussions carry the potential for mutual conversion or change. Each faith has the opportunity to re-express cherished stories when set in new interfaith contexts. Some see the very notion of seeking common ground as dangerous. In fact, both common ground and difference provide the yin and the yang, the night and the day, of healthy Buddhist and Christian encounters. Father Robert E. Kennedy writes: "Our reach must always extend beyond our grasp. The mandate of the church to promote truths other than our own must be followed, for the goal is one of peace finally among religions."[29]

Interfaith challenges need not be feared by those secure in their faith. Depth of conviction need never be challenged, and the surety of conviction allows us to be more authentically bold, confidently open, and refreshingly creative. A center core of a sustaining spirituality allows us to be secure

---

26. Pieris, *Love Meets Wisdom*, 3.
27. Dalai Lama XIV, *The Good Heart*, 5.
28. Dalai Lama XIV, *The Good Heart*, 9.
29. Kennedy, *Zen Spirit, Christian Spirit*, 124.

enough to avoid simplistic dismissals of other faiths. Sturdy foundations allow us to explore other points of reference beyond our own traditions and experiences. Instead of a Pavlovian fear-response to difference—and instead of a suspicious view of the other—we can celebrate our differences as heuristic resources. Deep foundations of faith are not built through shrill assertiveness and insecure criticisms. They are rooted in lived experiences and expressed through loving desires to reach out to others.

Interfaith dialogue raises a host of questions: Why is it hard for some to listen to those of other faiths with a sense of openness? Why is it necessary for some to claim to hold a unique revelation of truth more true than the central truths of other faiths? What holds us back from a willingness to engage others without fearful insularity? Is the basis of doubt an external threat or an internal uncertainty? Does an unwillingness to face tough questions reflect spiritual immaturity? Why is it hard for some to listen to adherents of other faiths without feeling obligated to compare these views with what they find familiar? Why do we find solace in the familiar by attacking the unfamiliar?

For some, such questions amount to mere sophistry. Some feel obligated to sabotage intimacy with others when the first glimmers of mutuality begin to fleck the horizon. For some, a willingness to listen to the other seems disquieting. Why is that? I am genuine in asking because I have deep roots in faith, and these roots are not challenged when I learn from, and listen to, others. Jesus calls followers to be witnesses (Matt 28:20) and not crass marketing representatives or feisty pit bulls in a battlefield of snide, competing religious assertions.

Cultivating the art of creative listening across faith traditions may be, as in the case of other art forms, a lifelong process toward greater maturation. As Buddhism teaches, the people we were at age twenty are entirely different from the people that we will be at age forty or eighty. None of us thinks the same as we once did. We may have to be patient with others as they try to do something that they have never been asked to do before—namely, to listen to another's point of view without jumping to conclusions. For Catholics, the mandate of Vatican II to share our faith with other springs from a mandate to appreciate what others cherish within their own faith and cultural backgrounds. Listening is the center point of interrelationships and often leads us to new insights. Father Robert E. Kennedy affirms this viewpoint: "I have come to understand what matters most is that we listen to one another, not as adversaries, but as compassionate people bringing gifts to one another to help us each discover our still unrecognized possibilities."[30]

---

30. Kennedy, *Zen Gifts to Christians*, 6.

FREIGHTED EXPECTATIONS

Creative interfaith meetings are mandated for both so-called Great Commission Christians and so-called All World Buddhists. Buddhism calls this "whole-body-and-mind seeing," which calls for an all-accepting perspective for those enlightened. Jesus called followers to lift up their eyes to fields ripe for harvest (John 4:33). Some assume that we cannot even have a dialogue with others without first hunkering into shark-cage, steel-frames of assertion (the kind that protect ocean divers from menacing sharks!). Interfaith discussions should encourage supple heart-to-heart engagements between people of different faiths. Chinese theologian C. S. Song wrote,

> The Christian phobia of other faiths will continue to frustrate our own vision of a united human community with many conversations between Christians and Buddhists taking on a defensive tone . . . We have been in the habit of always being on the lookout for "Christian questions" in order to give "Christian answers."[31]

Song is challenging Christians who have been negative toward Buddhists to have a more open posture. Christians should never become freighted down with fear, which is really a lack of love.

Those who assume that there is no neutral ground between people of differing faiths rarely find any. They see the other as a rival with a competing agenda and may venture into the realm of pseudodialogue only to convince others of the errors of their ways. When we study another faith, we have to develop levels of "verbal quarantine" to avoid "terms from one religio-cultural context," which stifle our "intellectual commerce" by a "black economy, where contraband meanings will soon bankrupt what we want to say."[32] The beauty of the vague—which fills God's natural world from morning fogs to evening sounds—is sometimes squashed by desires to erase any trace of ambiguity with the fabricated assertiveness of self-validation. Those who think they know never realize how much they do not know. With the gift of participating with another faith tradition, comes with the responsibility to be humble and to listen with openness and respect.

---

31. Song, *Tell Us Our Names*, 55–56.
32. Arthur, "Maitreya, the Buddhist Messiah?," 54.

HARDENING OF THE SPIRITUAL ARTERIES

We are beset on all sides by layers of self-induced stress: Our lives—often centered on our cell phones instead of our spirits—seem complex beyond all measures from living a dog-eat-dog societal drive for success called progress. Premodern social cultures with deeply embedded religious values have been replaced by new, rootless social networks. In our era, meaning and ritual have been buried under clutter for people from traditional societies who have streamed from the countryside into bustling cities. New myths wait to be born as old ones die or are forgotten, lost-in-translation. On small screens, media viewers watch mythical families live pristine lives. Others watch documentaries with envy about holy people who live apart from the overstuffed, multitasking hustle and bustle of our preoccupied, exhausted world.

Many in contexts of privilege are literally drowning in a sea of opportunities while still embracing confusion and accepting deep levels of debt-filled discontent. A modern tsunami of apparent choices is rooted in cultures of distracted wealth and unfair entitlement. Choices are not only about cereals and clothing brands or car models, but also about competing worldviews. Many feel that their only choice is to plunge into an unbounded sea of infinite openness and to flee from any notion of adherence to one specific faith tradition. To do so, however, leaves us without the benefit of our own spiritual legacies. Buddhism and Christianity both offer relief for today's captives. As we embrace our own faiths, we can also learn from the rich wisdom legacies of others.

Privileged people are often those most likely to jettison their life vests or parachutes of tradition and religious heritage. Critics argue that religions have often been forces for evil. They should also acknowledge that faith communities have also often been at the forefront of social-justice causes and have confronted the unjust excesses of many societies. In North America and Europe, for example, many Buddhists and Christians have offered new pathways of simplicity that confront the poverty of materialism and cynical disengagement. One such faith-based observer of North American culture was Mother Teresa of Calcutta. When she visited America and was asked by a reporter how she felt coming from a poor country like India to a rich country, she responded that she had never visited a poorer country in her life than the United States.[33]

Buddhism and Christianity teach that the highest wealth we can enjoy is spiritual contentment. Jesus taught we should not focus on wealth, which

---

33. I no longer have the source for this anecdote.

"moth and rust consume" (Matt 6:19–20), but on the inner qualities of spiritual wealth and emotional health. Even while we admire those embracing simple lives, many of us strive to become increasingly hyperconnected and hypercommunicative. We clog our phone lines and our arteries with excess. Fast food and junk food match our frenzied, fast-paced lifestyles. Many live on treadmills of constant distraction, with minds overactive but exhausted from gathering and processing information. Thich Nhât Hanh notes that because Buddhism forbids us from using things that cloud our minds, such as intoxicants, we should also stay away from the "never-enough consumerism" that compels us to waste hours in front of media, on cell phones, on the internet, and many other addictive technologies that keep our lives cluttered.[34] When Jesus invites us to come to him to find rest for our souls (Matt 11:28–30), we also find freedom from all of the other barricades erected in our hearts that keep us discontented. Because they are handicapped by their own self-obsessions, unhappy people also try to make others unhappy. Some of us bring out the worst in others because we have not yet learned to listen to others. Much of the stress we bring on ourselves comes from bad habits. If we have a problem at work, maybe it is because we are trying to control what should not be controlled. In fact, "the more we try to tell people exactly how to do their work, the less they will bring their creativity to it. The more we try to control, the less influence we will have. The wise know that nothing good can be compelled from people; it can only be elicited from them."[35]

Jon Kabat-Zinn, founder of the Center for Mindfulness in Worcester, Massachusetts, warns that stress should not be unceasingly shoveled into the coal-furnaces of our lives with reckless abandon. Life should be lived with a cultivated appreciation of how fragile the gift of every moment really is to us.[36] We need to pause. Radhakrishnan explains, "The soul in solitude is the birthplace of faith" and points to the examples of Moses, Jesus, Buddha, and Muhammad.[37]

Mindfulness is the best medicine. Many of us have minds so preoccupied that we are literally lost within our own thoughts. Paul Ingram writes, "Interior dialogue concentrates on participating in Christian and Buddhist spiritual practices and techniques and reflecting on the resulting

---

34. Quoted in Loy, *The Great Awakening*, 38.

35. Autry and Mitchell, "Giving Up Control," 113.

36. Jon Kabat-Zinn notes this in multiple books, courses, and talks. One of his best-known works is *Wherever You Go, There You Are*.

37. Quoted in Nakamura, *Buddhism in Comparative Light*, 87.

experiences."[38] When we live with greater simplicity, we become able to live with greater freedom, immediacy, and clarity.

FAITH MEETING THE FAITHS

Interfaith encounters benefit us in surprising ways. Sometimes what we learn will take us out of our comfort-zones and leave us silent when we do not have all the answers. The story is told of a student who went to Zen Master Hakuin and asked him what would happen after death. Hakuin said that he did not know and asked the student why he had asked him such a question. The student said, simply, because he was a Zen master. "Yes," said Hakuin, "but not a dead one!"[39]

Humble people are also usually more approachable than those of us who claim to have all the answers. Humility puts the needs of others in front of personal needs. Many poets write about how their mothers, for example, were role-models of selflessness because they put love for their children before their own needs. In the same way, both Christ and Buddha, out of infinite love, put humanity's needs at the forefront in lives of humble service. In Buddhism, humility (*kshanti*) is the best way to engage society for change. Those who are humble use humility as a source of forceful energy (*virya*). The Korean monk Wonhyo (617–686) serves as a vivid example of someone who overturned arrogant enemies with powerful humility. Jesus modeled the transforming power of humility and said that those who were proud were like old wineskins unable to receive the "new wine" of God's grace (Matt 9:17; Mark 2:32; Luke 5:37).

One of the greatest benefits of interfaith engagement is the splendid opportunity to reflect on—and reframe—our own traditions.[40] Those in dialogue with people of other faiths describe how dialogue experiences often enhance their spiritual growth by providing a "mirror" to see what they cherish most in their own faith.[41] One example of this happened when a group

---

38. Ingram, *Buddhist–Christian Dialogue*, 13.

39. Jones, *The New Social Face of Buddhism*, 115.

40. British Methodist Kenneth Cracknell noted that John Wesley wrote from his mission trip to North America that "my chief motive, to which all the rest are subordinate are the hopes of saving my own soul but I also hope to learn the true sense of the Gospel by preaching it to the heathen." Cracknell said that Wesley thought the act of preaching encourages us to be "as little children, humble, willing to learn, and eager to do the will of God." Cracknell, *Towards a New Relationship*, 13.

41. This is Paul Knitter's argument for expanding the teaching of world religions in Christian seminaries: "Although we cannot realistically expect either students or professors to be proficient in all the major religious traditions of the world, we can

of Christians and Buddhists met to discuss the life of Saint Francis of Assisi: "Empty of all cravings and desires, Francis opened up to his Lord and discovered God in all creation in some mysterious, ineffable way."[42] Evangelical Gerald McDermott wrote that Buddhists often remind Christians to "guard against the presumption that our thoughts can capture God's being" and can "refresh our sense of awe before the mystery of every moment."[43] Even though what we hear may already be familiar, hearing a similar view voiced within another tradition can empower insight. Paul Knitter explains that when we appreciate the faith of others "more deeply," we actually "preserve" the relevance (praxis) and staying power of our own faith.[44] James Fredrick thinks that one of the main benefits of interfaith interactions is to "gain a better understanding of the meaning of Christianity."[45]

There is a story in the Bible where Joseph "seeks his brothers" (Gen 37:16) even though they were responsible for many of his problems. C. S. Song calls the reconciling work of interfaith bridge-building a "struggle for wholeness" because when we experience the love of God we are reminded that "if there is no love, there is no church" because the God of Love is the author of the church.[46] Those who have been thirsty may enjoy a cold glass of water more than anyone, and those who live atop an icy mountain may appreciate a tropical beach resort. Each tradition has its own gifts to contribute, and the sharing of these gifts is at the heart of healthy interfaith discussions.

MYSTERY

Another dimension of interfaith interactions is learning to embrace the mysterious. Mysteries of faith can just as easily drive us towards a deeper faith as away from faith. Theologian Jacques Maritain spoke of the "supreme incommunicable wisdom" of Christianity, which claims that God somehow entered humanity in Jesus Christ.[47] Jean-Paul Sartre stated that "faith, even

---

entertain more modest yet nonetheless helpful ideals . . . The goal would be for students to become so at home in another religious tradition that it would become a conversation partner for the students as they go about their study of Christian theology" (Knitter, *Jesus and the Other Names*, 162–63).

42. Camps, *Partners in Dialogue*, 102.
43. McDermott, *Can Evangelicals Learn from World Religions?*, 155.
44. Knitter, *Jesus and the Other Names*, 9.
45. Fredericks, *Faith among Faiths*, 169.
46. Song, *Tell Us Our Names*, 154–55.
47. Waldenfels, *Absolute Nothingness*, 133.

when profound, is never complete."[48] The acknowledgment of the mysterious facilitates a spaciousness of spirit. Karl Rahner describes Christ as an "uncomprehended and intractable mystery."[49] Each of us knows in part and understand in part (1 Cor 13:9).

The mysteries of the divine nature mean that we cannot put God in a box that imagines God as a "great big controlling micro-chip in the sky or in any other image that makes God as static as a wooden idol."[50] Living in the acceptance of mystery is not the same as living in doubt. One Buddhist teacher said that doubt can lead to "openness and unknowing. It is a willingness not to be in charge, not to know what is going to happen next. A state of doubt allows us to explore things in an open and fresh way."[51] Another Zen teacher explained that "uncertainty is readiness" because it is "pregnant with constant possibility."[52] This "pregnancy" need not devolve into a paralysis of indecision or noncommitment to a given creed. While doubt can arise from a lack of knowledge, it can also facilitate insight.[53]

Living with freedom empowers the security we need to see things from multivalent directions. When we have safely put down our roots within our own faith, we are most able to learn from others with a sense of open engagement. The souls of those comfortable with uncertainty are not troubled as much as they are supple, engaged, and awake to ever-revitalizing possibilities. The world is full of incongruities, and "good from one perspective has the potential of being evil from another."[54] John Daido Loori claims, "Mystery abhors naked exposure and explanation . . . Zen art is open-ended. The *enso*, or Zen circle, a symbol of enlightenment, for example, is left open. The missing piece is supplied by the viewer."[55]

Because all of us are only glimpsing at God's mysterious truths our adherence to faith reveals that, while we may not always know how a situation will conclude, we can live with the assurance that God's Holy Spirit (or the Buddha-nature) will guide us forward. We can enjoy the freedom that comes from childlike, trusting humility. Insecure egos and prideful assertions can be set aside. Jesus told the cautious empiricist Nicodemus, looking

48. Kinahan, *A Deep but Dazzling Darkness*, 21.
49. Rahner, quoted in Waldenfels, *Absolute Nothingness*, 138.
50. Kinahan, *A Deep but Dazzling Darkness*, 94–95.
51. Queen, "Glassman Roshi and the Peacemaker Order," 101.
52. Quoted in Fischer, "On Questioning," 13.
53. See Berger and Zijderveld, *In Praise of Doubt*. In the chapter "Certainty and Doubt" the authors quote Robert Musil's claim that "the voice of truth has a suspicious undertone" (89).
54. Crosby, *Living with Ambiguity*, 75–76.
55. Loori, *The Zen of Creativity*, 197, 199.

to find a world of predictable certainties, that the wind blows wherever it wills, and so is everyone who is born of the Spirit (John 3:8). Jesus is trying to teach Nicodemus that life is more than a scripted predictability. Situations are often improvisational and demand from us open flexuosity and childlike simplicity. Life is always happening, and it often feels somehow out of reach or beyond our ability to control results. When we accept the rootedness of our own place within a tradition then the authority of those contexts, and not a Ouija board, a "Dear Abby" column, or any other source can upend the pilgrim in our acceptance of mystery with humility.

Jesus told followers to "search, and you will find; knock, and the door will be opened for you" (Matt 7:7; Luke 11:9). Saint Gregory of Nyssa claimed, "To seek God is to find God and to find God is to seek God."[56] The truths of faith will continue to unfold in the lives of those who are listening, learning, open, and humble. Our capacity for insight cannot be contained by anything but our own self-imposed limitations.

---

56. Quoted in Dalai Lama XIV, *The Good Heart*, 12.

Conclusion

The Truth is half of any argument.
—Indian proverb

Our unique cultures, geographies, and histories shape the way in which we develop our systems of being in the world. But we do not all need to believe in the same God to live without fear, gracefully, and in peace with one another. What we can agree on is compassion.
—Angel Kyodo Williams, *Being Black*

QUESTIONS OF ULTIMACY

BUDDHISM AND CHRISTIANITY DRAW strength from the truths of the Dharma and the Gospels, the sangha and the church, the Christ, and the Buddha—which are also truths about our shared humanity. Are these truths contradictory or complimentary? Both faiths promise refuge for the quarter of the world's population who are Buddhists and for the third of the world's population who are Christians. One of my students mused that her church was a "one-way-to-heaven-only bunch."[1] It is often this deeply rooted, exclusivist claim about the true nature of God that drives Buddhists away from wanting to learn from some Christians.[2] It is often sheer ignorance about

---

1. Alicia Tye used this phrase in 2008 during a Topics in Asian Religions course at Baylor University.

2. The Council of Florence (in the fifteenth century) proclaimed, "No one outside

Buddhism that keeps some Christians from wanting to learn and listen to Buddhists.

The problem may not be with the theological assertion of exclusivism, per se. In varying degrees, all religions maintain an inherent sense of exclusivism in that they hold to the conviction that they have a message of ultimate truth. The Dalai Lama, for example, believes his way "makes final sense," and that "all religions and all forms of Buddhism will eventually come to the insight of the truth held by and practiced by the *Gelugs*" (Tibetan Buddhist teachers).[3] He asserts that only Buddhism teaches the truth that can bring liberation and that "*nirvana*, is only explained in the Buddhist scriptures, and is achieved only through Buddhist practice."[4]

The exclusivity of Buddhism, however, does not exactly parallel the exclusivity of other traditions for a few reasons. Buddhists acknowledge that the world has many religions, and that each of these meets different needs in distinct cultures. Because of the central conviction that everything is interrelated, Buddhists assume that there exists a fundamental interrelationship among all faiths, religious traditions, searches, and experiences. There is no real competition but only perceived differences. It is assumed that everyone benefits from a diversity of spirituality traditions because of the doctrine that everything is changing (*pratityasamutpada*) and the best doctrine is only a portion of a much more vast, ultimate truth.

A more static (often) European notion of exclusivity, as it is often described in some Christian theological assertions, is about the truth that does not change. Foundational Buddhist teachings make it easier, perhaps, for Buddhists to think of the agreements or disagreements of various dharmas as something like a conversation. Each community has their own perspectives on religion. As different individuals in a group speak, they share their varying views. In the same way, the ocean holds both menacing sharks that threaten to attack and harmless fish that provides a livelihood for fishers. The ocean is many things depending on our point of view or location. Ronald Nakasone explains: "Shifting centers and perspectives illustrate the openness and fluidity of the principle of *pratityasamutpada* to include everyone at every point of view."[5] This view invites humility, openness, and tolerance and precludes the embrace of exclusivity or a sense of an ultimate truth as often presented in some categorical Christian assertions.

---

the Catholic Church, not only pagans, but also Jews and heretics and schismatics, can share in eternal life, but will perish in an eternal fire prepared for the devil and his angels" (quoted in Wiles, *Christian Theology and Inter-religious Dialogue*, 9).

3. D'Costa, *The Meeting of Religions and the Trinity*, 83.

4. Dalai Lama XIV, *Answers*, 28.

5. Nakasone, ed., *The Transforming Spiritual Landscape*, 35.

Relationship dynamics can also include a sense of exclusivity (or superiority) even if these are unintentional. It is this relational exclusivism which is the issue that exclusivists need to explore as they consider why their beliefs often alienate themselves from followers of other traditions. Everyone should cherish an appropriate sense of loyalty (affinity) to the teachings of their respective Mother-communities. This sense of identity, however, need not devolve into a form of judgmental exclusivism. Why cannot there be cherished loyalty without didactic judgmentalism? Wesley Arirajah argues that while his daughter says that he is the best father in the world, she is speaking the truth based on her love-filled experience. In the house next door, however, it should not be surprising if another child thinks that her parents are the best on the planet. It is this effusive language of adoration, according to Arirajah, that explains Acts 4:12 ("There is salvation in no one else, for there is no other name under heaven given among mortals by which we must be saved"), which is rooted in the language of devoted love; not in any specific reference to another (Greek or Roman) religion.[6] Loving loyalty animates the declarations of Acts 4:12 while the text comes from a specific context and should be viewed in light of the way that God mandated that Peter would have to change his unaccepting perspective toward non-Jews (see Acts 10:34–43).

Another way to think about this question is to describe the misuse of an exclusivist conviction as being an expression of sectarianism. This is belief without wisdom and free of relational concerns. Sectarian exclusivists feel the need to reject other views and to enforce an accept-or-reject, true-or-false, right-or-wrong, realm of simple dualities and clear polarities. For them, biblical texts (such as John 4:22; 14:6; or Acts 4:12) cannot be interpreted in any other way but as such sectarians demand that they be read. To invite conversation is to incite compromise or needless confusion. Discussion is viewed as implicit criticism, and questions are framed as insults against divine truths. At the same time, the dogmatist is not only on the defensive but often seems driven by a blinding need to devalue others, and in so doing creates something that approaches hatred (or, indeed, becomes hatred) and intolerance. How would this promotion of hatred be justified, for example, by the lives and messages of the Buddha or the Christ? Fundamentalist sectarians often express a need, either intentionally or unintentionally, to feel superior to others. They know that they are in the light

---

6. Shenk, *Who Do Men Say That I Am?*, 39. One might also say that their beloved is the most handsome/beautiful person in the world, which is true for that person. Shenk also talks about this issue (39): "Acts 4:12 is reinterpreted to be an affirmation for Jesus without ruling out the possibility of other saviors. Exclusive statements are said to reflect the way people spoke."

while others are lost in a benighted darkness waiting to be freed by those holding the keys of truth. They alone have the divine truth and, as a result, see no need to learn anything from, or about, others.

When these religious demagogues become teachers or pastors, their students or congregants pass on this toxic gene of nonrelational and myopic dualism and all the negative energy that comes with such assertiveness. In fact, exclusivists, while claiming to be voices of tradition, are innovators who carve-out conceptual fiefdoms of their own design where they can rule supreme. They create "limited-access-code" religions because they assume the authority to reduce and essentialize both their own faith and the faith of others.

Buddhist Thinley Norbu Rinpoche believes that such sectarians "are only disguising dualistic mind's ruminations with a spiritual veneer."[7] In contrast, all interfaith learning is, to varying degrees, committed to the advance of mutual respect between peoples and cultures. A sense of openness will move us beyond sectarian constraints into a genuine interest to learn about others on their own terms (without such learning becoming an opportunity for anyone's self-aggrandizement). Some of the most uninteresting and inaccurate (so-called) scholarship in the study of religions has been generated by sectarian exclusivists in the service of their cause. Examples abound: Jean Danielou dismissed Buddhism as a "natural religion" while describing Judaism and Christianity as "supernatural religions."[8] Pope Benedict XVI once claimed (and I hope I am not taking his words out of context) that Buddhism "seduces" because it promotes an "auto-erotic spirituality."[9] It was unfortunate when Pope John Paul II made sweeping generalizations about the "atheism" of Buddhism, which he argued held an "almost exclusively negative" worldview.[10] Fairly or unfairly, Pope John Paul II's further generalizations about how God responds to the prayers of non-Christians resulted in some Sri Lankan Buddhists boycotting the pope's 1995 visit to their country.[11]

Some Christians have a long history of dismissing Buddhism at the expense of working to forge any sort of mutuality with Buddhists. The faiths of others are all too often caricatured. Those in other traditions live in the outlying provinces of difference, beyond the embrace of fellowship and the warmth of truth. Other faiths are rejected as invalid based on the

---

7. Norbu, *White Sail*, 44.
8. Danielou, quoted in Fredericks, *Buddhists and Christians*, 3.
9. See Ruland, *Imagining the Sacred*, 93.
10. See Ruland, *Imagining the Sacred*, 92.
11. Cowell, "Pope, in Sri Lanka."

assumptions imposed upon them from the outside. I am not suggesting that to dislike some idea is the same thing as misrepresenting the idea. This has certainly been the case for me as I have studied the perverse nature of religiously supported racist oppression in North American Christianity. As dialogue partners gain a more accurate understanding of a given idea, it does not automatically mean that we will come to agree with each other. My question is this: How can one gain a clearer picture of the worldview of others while assuming all along that such views are mired in inaccuracies or falsehoods? The act of biased interpretation inevitably thwarts the potential for an observer to enter into the distinct logic or at the starting point for the views of others. In the face of dismissal, the subtle, immensely nuanced, and multivalent Buddhist philosophical arguments are often ignored by those Christians who have made a career out dismissing the validity of Buddhism. Their simplistic reductions bring assuring conclusions. Invariably, those who paint with a broad-brush are rarely sympathetic with those they really do not want to understand.

KNOWING IN ORDER TO REFUTE

Asbury Theological Seminary professor Dennis Kinlaw explained, "Bad theology is a hard taskmaster."[12] Evangelical Sir Norman Anderson writes that Buddhism teaches that "man is working out his own salvation."[13] It would seem that Sir Norman Anderson has a very glib assessment of the faith of a billion people. Anderson claims that while Buddhism is rich with wisdom, it is a religion that includes "some elements" that are "definitely false and which, I, for one, believe comes from the 'father of lies'—whose primary purpose is not so much to entice men into sensual sin as to keep them back, by any means in his power, from the only Savior."[14] Anderson views Buddhism as an empty religion and a crafty fabrication of Lord Satan intending to deceive a childlike humanity. How can constructive dialogue proceed from such a starting point of dismissal?

Along these same lines, Emil Brunner argues that Christianity alone presents the truth and, because of that, "Christianity is not one of the religions of the world."[15] Gerald McDermott sets Christianity apart from all other religions, explaining that "God permitted these [all other] religions

---

12. From class notes in spring 1983 on Dennis Kinlaw's lecture course called Christian Theology at Asbury Seminary.

13. Anderson, *Christianity and World Religions*, 102.

14. Anderson, *Christianity and World Religions*, 172.

15. Brunner, "Revelation and Reason," 49.

because of his grace and forbearance toward human hardness of heart."[16] Sri Lankan pastor Tissa Weerasingha warns, "Since the serpent promulgated the false wisdom," countless errors have arisen which lead him to "vehemently disagree with the Buddhist view" of the world.[17] For him, Buddhist enlightenment is actually "escapism" while Christianity offers the only truth about the nature of the world.[18] Pastor Weerasingha studies his misled neighbors in order to "tactfully dismantle the central presuppositions of Buddhism."[19] Such reassuring black-and-white exceptionalism springs from the certainty that Christians alone possess the truth, which makes respecting other faiths only a polite exercise in courtesy and mission—in the same way a death-row inmate is treated with the respect of the last meal before execution. Those who are self-assuredly free from the need to learn from others are bolstered by the intellectually violent denigration of what others consider to be sacred. Fundamentalist dogmatists are like seal hunters who quietly creep ashore to club unsuspecting baby-seals who cannot begin to imagine the intentions of those drawing closer to them from behind with menacing, bloodstained bludgeons.

Timothy C. Tennent warns against other Christians who fail to "affirm the historic Christian confessions"; he continues, "yet curiously they continue to identify themselves as Christians."[20] Tennent asserts that interfaith dialogue is often carried out by specialists who "stand outside the boundaries of historic Christianity," and yet presume to represent the faith with the "tragic result that many readers assume that the positions taken by these scholars reflect a broad consensus among Christians around the world."[21] Tennent notes that the foundations of Christianity are unchanging, but the preaching of the faith must constantly adapt in ever-present intercultural engagements. Because the risen Jesus is active in the world seeking to save, our witness to God's present-tense initiatives should be missiological and relational instead of abstract and categorical. Even though Jesus lived in an intensely multireligious environment, he never advanced his message by denigrating Samaritan, Greek, Roman, or Syro-Phoenician faith. In fact, Saint Paul said nothing to attack the pagan beliefs of the Greeks on Mars Hill, because his goal was to share the living Christ and not to argue about historic dogmas (Acts 17:16–31). While Tennent claims that all interfaith

16. McDermott, *God's Rivals*, 161.
17. Weerasingha, "Buddhism through Christian Eyes," 157–58.
18. Weerasingha, "Buddhism through Christian Eyes," 145–46.
19. Weerasingha, "Buddhism through Christian Eyes," 145.
20. Tennent, *Christianity at the Religious Roundtable*, 10.
21. Tennent, *Christianity at the Religious Roundtable*, 10.

Conclusion

dialogue is a test between "truth and falsehood," he also makes clear that the first priority for Christians in witness is relational: "To be, first and foremost, a faithful witness to an unchanging Christ in response to an ever-changing world and in ever-changing contexts."[22]

Hendrik Vroom is another evangelical scholar who refuses to dismiss Buddhism with limiting—and invariably inaccurate—straitjacket. Vroom writes, "Dialogue between Christians and Buddhists is exceptionally exciting; there is an affinity on many points. Christians and Buddhists share many insights, although it is not easy to penetrate to the core of correspondence and difference of views."[23] It should be enough to acknowledge differences, as Vroom does, without fabricating contrived resolutions to unsolvable (and often unasked) questions and problems. Vroom works to represent the views of Buddhists with accuracy and in an appropriate historical and cultural context. One can be committed to the task of persuading others, Vroom notes, only to the degree that one is fair with the content of their views. Vroom reminds his audience, "Not everybody understands salvation to mean the same thing. Not every religious school is directed toward salvation on earth . . . The only way to deal with differences is to discuss them, study them, think about them, pose critical questions, give answers to questions, and learn from one another."[24]

INTERFAITH CONTEXTS

One of the first encounters between Christians and Buddhists took place during the seventh century (around 631) when Nestorian Christians arrived at the ancient city of Xi'an, China. One interesting source for learning when Christians might have first arrived in China is a roadside stele that mentions Christians and dates from the year 781. What is significant about the inscription on this monument is how friendly the people of these two faiths seemed to be in their recorded interactions. Warm collaborations seemed to characterize these first efforts at interfaith dialogue in China: We are far removed from that world.

Ethnicity has always been tightly woven into the fabric of what it means for people to call themselves religious in various communities. Today, the church worldwide and the global sangha are interacting with followers of different faiths as never before. The everyday experience of Christians and Buddhists in multireligious settings (particularly in Asia) means that they

22. Tennent, *Christianity at the Religious Roundtable*, 243.
23. Vroom, *No Other Gods*, 42.
24. Vroom, *No Other Gods*, 172–73.

have no choice but to develop theological paradigms that address issues of religious pluralism. While this does not mean, according to Jacques Dupuis, that Christian (or Buddhist) mission will be "reduced to dialogue," it does mean that people of faith worldwide will no longer be able to communicate their ideas with clarity from a starting point of smug ignorance and theological insularity.[25]

Lamin Sanneh observed that the Bible is a multicultural book filled with stories of Christianity that both "revitalized its Jewish roots and destigmatized Gentile cultures."[26] Sanneh's observation might serve as an interesting pattern for future interfaith dialogues.

Christian mission history brims with intriguing stories of missionaries such as Francis Xavier in Japan and Mateo Ricci in China, who felt that their reason for traveling halfway around the world was to preach Jesus, and that this mandate required that they develop creative ways of sharing the gospel to those they met. Saint Francis Xavier, for example, arrived in Kagoshima, a port city on the southern island of Kyushu. One of the first things he did was to visit a Zen temple. Later, Xavier wrote about his interactions with the abbot (Ninshitsu), whom he befriended. The accounts of this meeting reveal two people struggling to relate to each with an authentic desire to learn from each other. Xavier concluded from this meeting by asking for future interactions and expressing hope that such meetings would be mutually encouraging. Xavier's open approach seems to contrast with the more confrontative efforts of the Portuguese Jesuit Cosme de Torres, who visited a Zen shrine (in Yamaguchi) where, it seems, both sides dug in their heels with little result. Finally, early Christian mission efforts in Japan were smashed by the rise of the tyrant Toytomi Hideyoshi (1535–1598), who decreed the crucifixion of nineteen Japanese Christians and seven European Franciscans on February 5, 1597, in the city of Nagasaki.[27]

In China, missionaries such as Mateo Ricci and his companions believed that working for unity instead of underlining differences, and fostering brotherhood instead of promoting the exiled status of others brought the greatest glory to God. Their motive in relating to Buddhists was to share the gospel in a way that was relevant and accessible. This attitude may help explain some of their actions. Ricci and his companions were celibate, based themselves in (or near) Buddhist monasteries, and took the robes worn by

25. Valkenberg, "Jacques Dupuis," 154.
26. Shenk, *Who Do Men Say That I Am?*, 187.
27. One Zen priest became a Jesuit and was given the name Fabian Fucan (1583). Fucan later renounced his faith (1608) and wrote an anti-Christian tract (1620). This polemic, called *Ha Daisu* ("Against the Christian God") was a popular anti-Christian polemic for over three hundred years. See Nasu, "Fabian Fucan."

local monks (*seng*).²⁸ They did not believe that the gospel needed to be a destroyer of culture, although sometimes that is what happened. When word of Father Ricci's efforts reached Rome, he was removed from his mission because he was viewed as being excessively tolerant toward Buddhism. Ricci's humble intentionality was misread by those in distant Europe, who thought he was being unsupportive of the historical claims of Christianity even though these claims were made in very distinct cultural contexts. Those who judged from a distance and for political reasons concluded that Ricci's genial attitudes were not consistent with their notions that Christianity was vastly superior to any false, benighted superstitions that originated in Asia and could not possibly contain the truth.

Since Ricci and Xavier, many missionaries have dismissed Buddhism as a worthless falsehood that is essentially bankrupt. Some have taught other Christians that it is dangerous to try to learn from Buddhism except when listening serves as an evangelistic stratagem to gain a foothold within enemy territories. Because conversion, not appreciation (or a commitment to faithful witness), was often the central motivating force for these missionaries to meet with Buddhists in the first place, there were ample opportunities for people to become suspicious and guarded with one another. Katsumi Takizawa complained that most Christians completely miss the essence of Buddhism: "In discussions with them I often had the feeling as if I were a poor child misunderstood by grown-ups who could not explain himself to their scoldings but yet knew all along that in reality things were not as they thought."²⁹ Many Christians thought that their mission was to preach and convert and not to lovingly learn and respectfully listen. Or, to say this another way, they felt the only reason that they should learn and listen was so that they could preach and convert. A focus on the didactic instead of the relational, often handicapped any hope of gaining an audience or being a faithful, loving, winsome witness to the life of Jesus. These missionaries failed to see that the Bible mandated Christians to be faithful witnesses to Christ both in their words and temperament. Instead, they chose a result-oriented, bottom-line approach—a form of evangelistic capitalism—that only alienated people and made them more defensive. It seems the question What would Jesus do among Buddhists? was rarely considered. Few followed the example of Jesus, who spent thirty to thirty-three of the years of his earthly sojourn as a silent witness and faithful member of the local Jewish faith community. When faithful Christian witnesses do begin to share,

---

28. Ricci argued with monks and presented a simplistic view of Buddhism in his attacks against the faith. See Lai and von Bruck, *Christianity and Buddhism*, 71.

29. Waldenfels, *Absolute Nothingness*, 121.

their teaching should remain relational and adaptable to the distinct views and needs of their neighbors. Some have forgotten that Christianity is first about who we are and whose we are. This should mean that our call to be witnesses for Jesus should express the dynamic heart of the Christian faith, not just the factual ideas and systematic doctrines of Christianity in order to gain numerically verifiable results. While we teach the gospel with words, we should not undermine our efforts with arrogant and dismissive attitudes uncharacteristic of Jesus.

The early history of Buddhist–Christian relations must also be considered. Asian resistance to culturally dressed European Christianity has often had to do with the facts that missionaries arrived in Japan alongside the military forces of Commodore Perry's American gunships (1859), and that missionaries arrived in China alongside the military forces of British gunships during the Opium Wars (1839–1842 and 1856–1860). These horrible correlations make it hard to distinguish Christ from white European Christianity and hard to accept that "Christianity is not identical with Jesus Christ."[30] Considering this negative starting-point, it is vital to recognize that, colonial theology rooted in European assumptions, has often expressed the ideological violence of an extremely sordid colonial history.

Given an awareness of this historical foundation, is there any hope for progress? The first step for both Christians and Buddhists is to admit that while we share many common religious experiences, we filter these experiences through the different lenses of our own cultural contexts. All of us rely on our worldviews to give meaning to our experiences. This should be appreciated when we examine the experiences of others. An appreciation of this complexity should replace the desire for a categorical, simplistic way of evaluating the worldviews of others. Despite certain claims to the opposite, every religious assertion has emerged out of the mud of cultural contexts and specific historical realities. While all religions share various teachings in common, such teachings occur in radically distinct cultural contexts. What is most vital to understand is not what is being said—but how a given idea functions in "shaping the faith and practice of the community."[31]

MERCY AND HUMILITY

My motivation for interfaith work is rooted in my faith. God calls the faithful, "to do justice, and to love kindness, and to walk humbly with your God" (Mic 6:8 NIV). How does this relate to interfaith dialogue? Striving "to do

---

30. Koyama, *No Handle on the Cross*, 108.
31. Phan, *Being Religious Interreligiously*, 103.

justice" among those of other faiths means that we will accurately portray their ideas in gentle complexity and not as caricatures drawn in the worst light imaginable. The call "to love kindness" means we will not throw others into categorical dungeons but will relate to them with empathy and respect. The command "to walk humbly with your God" means that we will relate to those of other faiths in the same way Jesus related to others—with gracious humility. When we are humble, we come alongside others in meek mutuality. Kosuke Koyama writes, "Our lack of love comes from our lack of exercise and not just of love, but also our appreciation of the greatness and the goodness of God. We cannot in honesty dismiss someone else's experience of God since our own attempts can never even begin to do justice to the infinite God we claim to worship and serve."[32]

While Jesus attacks money changers (Matt 21:12–17; Mark 11:15–19; Luke 19:45–48; John 2:13–22) and rebukes hypocrites for being "whitewashed tombs" (Matt 23:27), we should leave such judgments to God. While Jesus cursed fig trees (Matt 21:18–21; Mark 11:12–13, 20–21), we are called to discern the nature of a tree by its fruit (Matt 7:15–20; 12:33–37; Luke 6:43–45). The axiom "Do to others as you would have them do to you" (Matt 7:12; Luke 6:31) is a clear guidepost that applies to all interfaith meetings. Jesus showed a high degree of empathy with those he encountered. He shed tears when friends were suffering (John 13:13), and every interaction with others was expressed through his humble self-understanding. Christians teach it is only Jesus who will be the final judge. Relationally, this means that we have no grounds to usurp Christ's divine role and plop ourselves down uninvited on his heavenly Great White Throne of Judgment.

Christians need to seek forgiveness for centuries of dismissiveness toward people of other faiths. Too many people have been marginalized, misunderstood, categorized, dismissed, and avoided. When Christians among those of other faiths seek that forgiveness, we are relationally placing ourselves below (and at the mercy of) those whose forgiveness we seek to gain. One should not seek the forgiveness of others to gain a tactical advantage. A mindset of repentance, however, will often foster a fresh beginning in a damaged relationship. Fortunately, both Buddhist and Christian spirituality traditions have historically recognized the power of relational healing through forgiveness. When we look at each other asking for forgiveness, new pathways of trust have the potential to be carved out of the dense underbrush of labyrinthine conceptual differences. The need for forgiveness "is familiar to both Buddhists and Christians. Jesus' characteristic declaration is 'Your sins are forgiven.' This can mean that from God's point of view,

---

32. Kinahan, *A Deep but Dazzling Darkness*, 47.

they were always forgiven . . . Failure to forgive one's self can be paralyzing, and the words of release, 'Your sins are forgiven,' mean you don't have to hang on any more."[33] Jesus calls us to accept forgiveness (Matt 9:22; Mark 2:5; Luke 18:42, etc.) and extend to others the same commitment to forgive others as we ourselves have been forgiven.

Christians who have relied upon simplistic caricatures of the beliefs and practices of other faiths also need to seek forgiveness. Any faith tradition is a sprawling house of cultural and religious differences and experienced in many ways rooted in many assumptions and aspirations. No person of faith should attack those of another faith with static dismissals based on monolithic generalizations. Instead of meeting people from other faiths as critics and judges, we should come as fellow pilgrims and open friends. We should embrace the truth of the ancient Irish proverb that "there is plenty of sky for plenty of birds" and not assume that our solutions can solve other people's problems. It is good to remember that any, and every, faith tradition is constantly in a state of transition—adapting to new forms in new situations. This fact came to me clearly when, once attending a dharma talk in the southern US, I heard some children singing a little song: "Buddha loves me. / This I know, for the Sutras tell me so; / little ones to him belong: / they are weak, but he is strong!" As traditions adapt, everything is possible and nothing should surprise us!

People of different faiths can begin with the same objective: to appreciate one an other with trustworthy respect. On a positive note, people of other faiths could learn much from the example of many Christians who have initiated a series of interfaith dialogues. Of course, this can also be two-sides to this sword: C. S. Song observes that because some programs originate from a Christian initiative, there is a sense that "Christians are the hosts and Buddhists are the guests. This sets the pattern of interhuman relationships in a dialogue."[34] This leads to a form of "one-way traffic," which often is seen as aggressive instead of amicable.[35] Given these tendencies, it is more vital than ever for Christians to "go the second mile" on the Buddhist path of relational investment.

Christians are capable of adapting to new challenges with unchanging values. Past patterns of seeing interfaith dialogues only as word-centered programs can be replaced by more informal times that share devotions, reflections, meditations, discussions, and experiences. Those who insist on traditional dogmatic a priori approaches may discover that their efforts are

---

33. Fischer et al., *Benedict's Dharma*, 25.
34. Song, *Tell Us Our Names*, 134.
35. Song, *Tell Us Our Names*, 134.

like the attempts of a man who tried to fish for trout in his bathtub! Jacques Dupuis notes, "The documents connected to the central teaching authority find it hard to admit in theory what for others is lived experience."[36] In response to one criticism, C. S. Song concluded, "All in all, what Buddhists are saying to Christians is that we have not understood them. We have belittled faith as life and life as faith. We have always wanted to isolate faith from life and culture and are not content until we have put them in a clean, neat, manageable, separate compartment."[37]

Do Christians appreciate why Buddhists are sometimes hesitant to initiate interfaith interactions? The answer to that question may come from Buddhists reflecting on meetings with Christians. Lama Anagarika Govinda explained how as a Buddhist, he had trouble with Christian assumptions about the world. He responded to one Christian who claimed that all religions were deficient by saying, "Just as the beauty of a garden consists precisely in the extent and variety of its trees and flowers, so too the garden of the spirit derives its beauty and life from the multiplicity and variety of its forms of experience and expression . . . That is what we have in common."[38]

Interfaith encounters will change us in ways we cannot predict. We may have to surrender a sense of control, which may seem frightening. An emphasis on the relational over the theoretical, however, mandates fluidity. Confidence is required as people of faith learn to truly accept "others" without anxieties that such meetings will weaken their convictions. Reliance on past categories should be set aside in ongoing efforts to listen and learn. Instead of relying on tired assumptions that confine others, we should enjoy dialogues that flourish in the idiosyncratic expressions of individuals experiencing unique circumstances and expressing often surprising perspectives.

ENDING AND STARTING POINTS

The first question, then, is why and how Buddhists and Christians should talk—not what we should talk about. Questions need to be asked with honesty about our ignorance. Christians among Buddhists can begin dialogues by admitting what they don't understand about Buddhism and then express a willingness to become a participant in learning in a posture of engagement. This is a first step needed for dialogue to move from intransigent differences to a desire to learn together.

---

36. Dupuis, *Christianity and the Religions*, 185.
37. Song, *Tell Us Our Names*, 135.
38. Govinda, *A Living Buddhism for the West*, 1.

The next step, already mentioned, will be to discard sweeping generalizations. Instead of blanket assertions, people of faith should consider what it is that others cherish and how they perceive faith directly—without wide filters of dismissal. Language-based dialogue can also seek the phantoms of what Song describes as "scientific clarity and technological precision," which are concerns more rooted in didactic scholarship than in ethical priorities or lived experiences.[39]

Faith communities help adherents navigate through the demands of social changes within society. This is done through local communities, whether a sangha or church, in committed interrelationships rooted in shared assumptions and historical values. If people of one faith enter as guests into another's community, that should foster a common language of mutuality. From there we can affirm together shared values that are neither disruptive nor insensitive—the proverbial "least-common-denominator" in early interfaith equations. The focus on difference in initial discussions, in contrast, often torpedoes long-term prospects for mutual respect. Our unfamiliar beliefs, when not yet grasped, should not threaten the fledgling foundations of future interactions. When we begin the process of engagement by embracing shared goals, we shore up common-ground under our feet. Committed adherents should exchange island-like paradisiacal geographies of isolation for shared spaces for mutual learning.

There is no need for Christians or Buddhists to worry about compromise or syncretism. Although we are sisters and brothers, we share different perspectives and pursue distinct objectives. All that should be jettisoned between us is arrogance and insularity, and not cherished convictions or ancient beliefs. Indeed, there cannot be substantive multifaith interactions when those representing both their own personal views and those of their faith communities try to reshape their religious traditions as if they were theirs to independently reform.

TRANSPARENCY

Transparency is at the heart of all healing interfaith engagements. Christianity and Buddhism should have faithful representatives, not disingenuous compromisers. Sadly, some Christians have used "dialogue as a tactic to soften up non-Christians" to make them more receptive to Christianity.[40] While

---

39. Song, *Theology from the Womb of Asia*, 135.

40. "Dialogue with other believers is in no way understood as a mere 'softening up' tactic to make the proclamation of Christian truth more acceptable; it is not merely a patient, courteous letting the other side have it say so that we can deliver our own

Christians are committed to evangelism rooted in faithful witness(which the Bible says leads to "joy in the presence of the angels of God" [Luke 15:10]), there is no place for deceptive efforts that conceal the true intentions of those claiming to represent Jesus. Wesley Arirajah was told that efforts by the World Council of Churches to have Hindu-Christian dialogue programs had "no credibility at all," because some had been using such initiatives to advance evangelistic agendas.[41] This fear is shared by many—and with good reason—based on past experiences. Passion need not denigrate into insularity but has the positive potential to flourish into question and curiosity. Indeed, it is only those who truly love their faith who can best share with others. One Spanish proverb says, "When a man loves one woman, he loves all women but when he loves all women he loves no woman."[42] In the same way, the faithful, because they are rooted, are those freest to explore their faith as well as the faiths of others without fear of losing equilibrium.

When Jesus says the road of life is narrow and few there are who find it (Matt 7:13–14), he is not promoting dogmatic exclusion but is calling us to be intensely God-focused. We should be single-minded in the inclusion of sympathetic inclusivity, which promotes mutuality, and in the exclusion of judgmental exclusivity, which seeks to alienate and marginalize. Intense singularity of focus on the work of compassionate engagement promotes interfaith tolerance because it keeps what is relationally vital constantly at the forefront.

UNIQUENESS

For Christians, Jesus is a singularity who expresses a plurality of revelations about the nature of God. Christ's church is a consistent singularity expressed in the tremendous plurality of blinding cultural diversity. The same is true of the sangha. Buddha presents a specific revelation of the truth, which is expressed in a plurality of forms and expressions. The sangha is also both plural and singular in the ways that it expresses the truths of their traditions. In addition, some consider themselves both Buddhist and Christian at the same time and note that the early Christians, originating from a Jewish background, thought of themselves as belonging to both Christian and Jewish communities.[43] Ninian Smart observes, "I sometimes count

---

message" (Knitter, *Jesus and the Other Names*, 139).

41. Ariarajah, *Not Without My Neighbour*, 79.

42. Quoted in Meider, ed., *Prentice-Hall Encyclopedia of World Proverbs*, n.p.

43. "More and more individuals confess to being partly Jewish and partly Buddhist, or partly Christian and partly Hindu, or fully Christian and fully Buddhist" (Cornille,

myself as a Buddhist Episcopalian when I'm not worrying too much about contradictions."[44]

Although some argue that particularity should lead toward a sense of essentializing reductionism, others claim that their distinctives are valid because they embrace all that is inside of their known world. Traditions, in their very distinctiveness, provide unique perspectives beneficial to those outside of those traditions. Some Christians need to be reminded that God is a God of impartiality (Rom 2:9–11) who loves the entire world (John 3:16). God is not partial to us or to our specific community. Other Christians note that Jesus frequently offended people by speaking of "sheep and goats" and "wheat and chaff" and did so on categorically theological, and not on ethical, grounds. Christians who are most convinced that there is an actual heaven or a hell (John 3:36) should be the first to build bridges of relational trust instead of promoting shrill diatribes about how others will be damned to an eternal hellfire while they enjoy a land of perpetual bliss. Clearly, there seem to be as many interpretations among Christians about such issues as there are denominations of Christians. While some are inclusivistic, others conclude that when Jesus spoke of "many dwelling places" (John 14:2—just before John 14:6), he was referring to the reward that "other sheep" (who view the Absolute from other perspectives) would enjoy (John 10:6).

The inclusivist-exclusivist debate is an exhausted, beaten mule—a clearly demarcated dead-end street. It is a paradigm rooted in a categorical and nonrelational ambition to assert truth in a vacuum. Modern globalizing trends have left long-cherished assertions bankrupt in their irrelevance. The book of Amos, written in a dramatically shifting era of multicultural engagement, called those who felt that they were chosen to reconsider their sense of spiritual entitlement. God tells humanity that divinity does not show favoritism (Amos 9:7): "Are you not like the Ethiopians to me, / O people of Israel? says the Lord. / Did I not bring Israel up from the land of Egypt, / and the Philistines from Caphtor and the Arameans from Kir?" There is no space for arrogant exceptionalism for those who claim God sends rain on both the righteous and errant (Matt 5:45).

Narrowing towards absolutist—and nonrelational reductionisms—limits the fulcrum of truth to express its fullest potential to embrace relational circles of spiritual fellowship. God's ways are far beyond human assumptions. "God is spirit, and those who worship him must worship in spirit and truth" (John 4:24) instead of through rigidity and bluster. Kosuke Koyama reminds Christians that because John 14:6 says that Christ is the

---

"Dynamics of Multiple Belonging," 1).

44. Smart, *Buddhism and Christianity*, 3.

"Way," we should walk alongside Jesus in a progressive and unfolding ministry of his patient work among neighbors. It is only in the walking alongside God's Spirit that we experience the reality of truths we need to understand.

Those who promote differing views should be listened to before being castigated as heretics. José Míguez Bonino advocates refocusing questions from a shopworn exclusive-inclusive paradigm to discussions about how Jesus is One with the Father.[45] Schubert Ogden suggests that Christianity, along with all other faiths, claims to have the truth, which means that Christians should relate to followers of other views with a goal of communicating truth.[46] When a person becomes fluent in another language, they do not need to abandon their own language. In the same way, Christians who learn to step into the accurate usage of the language of another faith and can speak that language with fluency are not betraying their mother-tongue. John Cobb Jr. calls this mindset a journey of "crossing over and coming back."[47] With students, I use an acronym to describe the "common raft" between people of different faiths: R-A-F-T; *respectful* in tone, *accepting*, *faithful* to our own faiths, and *thoughtful*—measured by the depth of our intellectual curiosity. Believers in dialogue need not cease being Christians or Buddhists. Hopefully, however, they may become a little wiser and little more compassionate.

All that we can share is our own story in the context of how that story relates to the sangha and church, the Buddha and the Christ, the dharma and the Gospels. The Christian message was incarnational from its inception and is throughout its clearest, most faithful articulations. Christians are called to be witnesses of what God has done. This is a generalized mandate with a personalized context. There is no room for abusive, dismissive interfaith intimidation when the nearness of immediate and personal experience directs the ways we live with each other.

---

45. Míguez Bonino writes, "I wonder to what extent the problem of the Christian's relation to people of different faiths is primarily a Christological question, or a theological question. Christians must try to clarify for themselves the theological issues that arise out of their dealings with peoples of other faiths" ("The Uniqueness of Christ," 41–42).

46. Ogden, "Christian Identity and Genuine Openness," 23. Ogden adds: "That exclusivism and inclusivism both presuppose a constructivist type of Christology is evident from their both affirming that salvation becomes a possibility only because of the event of Christ. But for just this reason, a Christian monist of either kind cannot consistently claim formal truth for his or her Christian beliefs without thereby implicitly disallowing even the possible formal truth of the religious beliefs of others" (26).

47. Quoted in Jones, *The View from Mars Hill*, 169.

"LISTEN-OLOGY"

Saint Paul encourages Christians to be living letters read by all (2 Cor 3:2–3). A letter is something that in Paul's time was never as widely copied or as quickly distributed as books and other documents can be today. Each of us has a unique contribution to share with the lived experiences of others. If you have been touched by Buddha or by Jesus, then you already have more than you could ever need when it comes to sharing with those who do not yet know your story. Your experience of a transformed life is the richest story you can share. As you listen to others, you will find that others will also listen to you. Geri Larkin exhorts, "Be the best listeners ever. Let's be the ones who don't interrupt anyone who is talking to us, and let's be the ones who really care about the words being said."[48] The greatest gift we can give, simply, is to listen.

Dialogue is a fluid process brimming with potential. Listening to others might best be expressed by entering a shared silence. "For Buddhists, the deepest expression of wisdom is silence . . . Absolute truth or ultimate reality cannot be expressed in words."[49] When Isaiah cried out to God, the divine responded by cleansing his lips and silencing his words of remonstration (Isa 6:1–7). While the "coal" that God put on the prophet's lips prepared him for a vocation of proclamation (vv. 6–7), a key lesson from this story is that sharing best begins in a posture of silence and a thoughtful response. Physical silence can lead us into a place of spiritual peace. Christ taught that what defiles us is what comes out of our mouths (Matt 15:11), which explains the many ways that Buddhist and Christian interactions have been contexts of tiresome defilement instead of restorative healing. Words, of course, will be necessary, even to appreciate silence—as silence is only meaningful in relation to language. With a Buddhist's attitude of nonduality (a prerequisite to insight), we will not need to separate ourselves from the other. The goal is to be concise in our speaking as we progress towards trust in genuine friendships. The Bible shows that it was the confusion of languages that were the result of the failure known by the tower builders of Babel (Gen 11:1–9).

"Listenology" (learning about other faiths beyond one's own), the gift of listening, has the potential to clarify our own perspectives. Perhaps differences are magnified when we try to say too much about the differences that exist in the world. Raimundo Panikkar reminds us that not only is the Buddha silent, but "his response is silence as well . . . The Buddha makes no reply because he eliminates the question. It is not that he does not respond

---

48. Larkin, *Tap Dancing in Zen*, 85.
49. Lefebure, *The Buddha and the Christ*, xvii.

to what is asked. Rather, strictly speaking, nothing is asked. The Buddha silences our anxieties, the thirst to know, to go, to get there, to possess, and to be capable."[50] Truth may not always be expressed in silence, but words can carry the virus of isolating, prideful assertion.

Both Buddhism and Christianity call us to look at the world in ways beyond mental reasoning alone. Spiritual maturity may lead to openness to new ideas while it leads to a stronger sense of inward certainty. Reason and openness are not mutually contradictory: We need to express our reasonableness through our openness. Faith includes both mystery and humility, but neither Christianity nor Buddhism suggests that the path of life is fundamentally antirational. In fact, a state of openness offers one the potential to reason and gain a deeper appreciation of truth.

Buddhists have found Buddha to be a secure refuge. Christians have experienced Christ as our Risen Savior. Buddhists and Christians have found safety from evil through faith and inner peace. Gifts of salvation or enlightenment cannot be taken away because these are experiences and not dogmatically didactic messages, but truths lived. Perhaps we best express the reality of our faiths, and their healing powers, when we share the "silent love" of listening.[51]

SHARING THE SAME PATH

Christians or Buddhists are often saying the same things to one another about our spiritual journeys. This should not be surprising because we share similar experiences even though we walk on distinct pathways. Our parents, and those we trusted, told us many of the same things about our world. As children, we accepted the assumptions passed down from generation to generation. While we may assume that these views are chosen based on discovered truths, many of these are rooted in familial or cultural legacies. Then, as we move forward in life, our experiences confirm our choices and faith commitments. Along the way, we learn more about ourselves and the world and assume that what we are learning relates to our faith and convictions. As we come to learn about our true selves and learn to share our voice, we also learn how faith helps us provide a larger context to understand these discoveries. Different paths—same results: a coherent way to give form to the meaning of our daily lives.

Lineage, according to Nietzsche, is a way to find significance and make sense of our reality. For Christians, God has come to earth through

50. Panikkar, *The Silence of God*, 148.
51. Carmody, *What Are They Saying about Non- Christian Faith?*, 45.

the prophetic lineage from Adam through the prophets and kings of revelation. The earthly lineage of Jesus points to his heavenly lineage. In contrast, the earthly lineage of a man, Siddhartha, brings him to the discovery of an inherently eternal lineage—the Buddha-nature. The lineage for Buddha consists of hundreds of previous revelations of the truth without beginning or end. For Buddhism, lineage does not segue into an ongoing thread that promises an afterlife because the Buddha offers us an infinite now. Linear time creates its own salvation, whereas the Buddha teaches what is already apparent: The fundamental relationship between the transcendent and the imminent.

Words can often blur what is obvious. Once, on a plane from Sao Paulo, Brazil, I playfully asked my seatmate, a student from Clemson University in South Carolina, if she had ever been to *Nova Iorque?* She said no, and that she had never heard of such a place. In fact, the flight we shared was, at that moment, approaching New York. She had failed to recognize the Portuguese name for the city displayed on the in-flight monitors in front of us. Her comments reminded me of a movie I saw, titled *God and Allah Need to Talk*, based on a comment that some people love God but hate Allah. This conversation also reminded me of an event that happened to my oldest son while he was attending a Baptist school in Carlisle, Pennsylvania. His teacher, speaking of Brazil, said only 1 percent of Brazilians were "Christian," meaning born-again. My son responded, at the risk of getting expelled: "Excuse me, but I thought almost everyone in Brazil was a Christian?" It is easy to lose sight of obvious facts when our minds are filled with conceptualities and limiting assumptions.

What emerges in shared involvement between our faiths are new paths out of a dense, historical thicket. Harboring misconceptions (or focusing on labels) will get us nowhere going forward. Genuine interfaith engagement is much more about relational dynamics than about theoretical abstractions. Such interactions should not be sequestered to the detachment of libraries and classrooms. Intellectual, organizational, and conceptualizing models that are filtered to live only in the petri dishes of familiar theologies may provide some self-satisfaction to those interested in protecting (or promoting) their own egos. These tiny platelets, however, are not capable of carrying fresh water from the well to dry and thirsty villagers. Because Buddhism strives to learn and listen, dialogue will encourage humility and acceptance. Because Christianity is committed to serving as Christ's witnesses (Matt 28:20), dialogue will also be a place of humility and acceptance. Christians accept that all have sinned (Rom 3:23), but that God has given us the gift of grace (Rom 6:23). Christ, who unites all things in himself (Eph 1:10), and who reconciles the world to himself (2 Cor 5:19), calls us to be ministers of reconciliation. To borrow a phrase from Graham Greene, this process will be a "journey without maps." One limitation we should overcome is our fear of moving beyond the security of what we already think we understand. Sometimes we are hesitant to leave the secure cocoons of our own making to risk multifaith interactions that promise nothing but uncertainty. I hope to encourage Christians and Buddhists to resolve to trust our own voices even if this path surprises others.

HOW IS THE BABY?

There is a story, from ancient Japan, told about a little girl, nine years of age, who was asked by her mother to care for her infant sibling while the mother completed an errand. The girl sat peacefully with her brother in the warm sunlight of the garden until, suddenly, a fierce wolf appeared and attacked the two children. The little girl only had a moment to protect her little brother from attack. Neighbors heard horrific cries and ran to see a ravenous wolf tearing into the girl. She was bleeding profusely. Soon, her blood soaked the earth. Before dying, the little girl only had the strength to ask one question: "How is the baby?" Lifting her corpse, the villagers only then discovered her brother, smiling and unaffected, safe underneath her tattered body.[52]

Buddhist–Christian interactions are meetings of unpredictable discoveries that take place within life's fluid currents. The newborn infant of our partnerships will take on a life of its own, marked by both laughter and tears. Christians meeting Buddhists along the way, the truth, and the life will face many challenges in our interactions. Even in these, we should continue to find a "Middle Path" of loving engagement and empathetic nurture. We share the same road.

---

52. Hasegawa, *The Cave of Poison Grass*, 2.

Glossary of Selected Buddhist Terms

Anatman (Pali: *anatta*)—A doctrine taught by the Buddha that contradicts the notion of a pure, eternal, subtle self, or *atman*. This idea eliminates grasping onto a self, which constitutes the fundamental ignorance binding sentient beings to the suffering of conditioned existence.

Bodhisattva (Pali: *Bodhisatta*)—This Mahayana concept teaches that some beings are bodhisattva who have developed an unbiased compassion for all and, even though they are on the way to perfect Buddhahood, delay that realization to serve the well-being of others, to help them attain enlightenment.

Buddha—A Buddha is an "awakened one." Persons who have awakened have attained liberation from all faults and the perfection of all qualities. This allows them to be fully capable of benefiting others.

Buddhahood—Buddhahood is the state of complete liberation where all faults have been purified and all virtues have been attained.

Deer Park Sermon—This is the first sermon given by the Buddha after he had finished meditating beneath a *pipal* tree. The sermon was given in Sarnath on the outskirts of Varanasi to the ascetics with whom he had once practiced rigorous austerities. He preached to them to embrace a "middle path" and avoid the extremes of carnality and asceticism.

Dhammapada—This is the most well-known of all Buddhist scriptures. It contains 423 verses and outlines the key ideas of Buddha's teachings about humanity's plight.

Dharma (Pali: *Dhamma*)—The term comes from the word meaning "to hold." Teaching provides the "truth" or the "way," of the Buddha's message. The Tibetan equivalent *chos* means "transformation" and refers to the power of words to change a person's life.

Dukha (Pali: *dukkha*)—Often translated "suffering," *dukka* is the First Noble Truth speaking of the transitory nature of life and the need to realize that there is no satisfaction through grasping. Suffering refers to both physical pain as well as psychological and emotional afflictions. Teachers refer to three levels of suffering: (1) the suffering from painful experiences, (2) the suffering from immutability and inevitable change, and (3) the suffering of conditioned existence. *Dukka* refers to the basic state of a person feeling dissatisfied with life and under a cloud of delusion from their unenlightened way of perception.

Eightfold Path—The Fourth Noble Truth has eight dimensions: (1) right understanding, (2) right thought, (3) right speech, (4) right action, (5) right livelihood, (6) right effort, (7) right mindfulness, and (8) right concentration. These form the basis for a genuine spiritual path.

Emptiness—The doctrine of emptiness, or *shunyata*, is first found in the *Perfection of Wisdom Sutras* of the Mahayana canon. The concept is also part of Therevada Buddhism and appears in Pali texts as *sunnatta*. It refers to the absence of inherent existence in persons/things.

Enlightenment—This English word describes a state of perfect inward awakening. The Tibetan term *jang chup* means "one who has purified obscurations and is perfectly realized."

Five Aggregates—All physical and mental phenomena are classified under the heading of five aggregates, or *skandhas*. These five aggregates are form, feeling, perception, volition, and consciousness. This is what could be called a person's individual's sense of self or identity.

Four Noble Truths—(1) Suffering (*dukha*) exists; (2) the origin of suffering is attachment; (3) there can be an end to suffering; and (4) there is a path to take to end suffering. These truths deal with both the origin of suffering (the cause) and the truth of suffering (the effect). The True Path leads to liberation and explains how humanity relates to Samsara and Nirvana.

Geshe—A Tibetan term that translated means "spiritual friend."

Hinayana—This term means "lesser vehicle" and is used by Mahayana teachers to distinguish Theravadan Buddhists from themselves. Most scholars dismiss this distinction as artificial and somewhat pejorative. It is used to describe the Southeast Asian Buddhists of Myanmar, Sri Lanka, Vietnam, Thailand, and Cambodia.

Impermanence (Sanskrit: *Anitya*; Pali: *Anicca*)—The view that humans do not have a fixed, distinct identity. This view embraces both the transient nature of things as well as the many changes that constantly take place in the physical world. Nothing endures through time, and the process of change is never-ending.

Glossary of Selected Buddhist Terms

Interdependence (Sanskrit: *pratityasamutpada*)—This is the idea that anything that is real necessarily exists in dependence on something else. This idea is closely tied to the emphasis on emptiness and the truth that all things are causally interdependent as well as empty of any intrinsic or distinct nature. Objects/beings exist only in relation to other objects or beings.

Karma—This is a key concept in both Buddhism and the Vedic Traditions that stresses how all actions have specific consequences. This relates to both acts and the memory of any acts. It can also generally refer to the idea that all actions will inevitably have resultant effects.

Mahayana—This term refers to the "great vehicle" and names one of the two major traditions of Buddhism. It is associated with the Buddhism of China, Japan, Tibet, and Korea. Although one strand of Buddhism takes its name from the "great vehicle," both Mahayana and Theravada Buddhism teach that Buddha is compassionate and that all Buddhists can win enlightenment.

Maitreya—This is the name, which means "loving one," of the coming Buddha, the embodiment of the loving-kindness of all the Buddhas. There is also a Bodhisattva Maitreya as well as a historical person by the same name, who is the author of several important Mahayana texts.

Mandala—One of any number of cosmic symbols designed to display certain concentric circles and symmetries: a contemplative visual tool in meditation practice.

Method—This refers to all the dimensions of the path that promote a sense of compassion and the altruistic actions of the bodhisattva. A genuine spiritual path should be a balance of both wisdom and method.

Metta—If compassion is the will to share in the suffering of others, *metta*, or loving-kindness, is the aspiration that wishes others to be happy; *metta* is truly altruistic and other-regarding.

Nirvana (Pali: *Nibbana*)—This term means "passed beyond pain and sorrow," it refers to a total freedom from suffering and its origins. Therefore, *nirvana* is sometimes also known as *nirodha* (true cessation) or *moksha* (release).

No-self—The Buddhist teaching about no-self, or selflessness, is also translated as "no-soul." It is a key idea that explains how an unenlightened, conditioned existence is rooted in a false belief in the existence of a permanent, enduring self.

Pali Canon—The Buddhist canon, called the *Tripitaka* (the "three baskets"), is the primary set of discourses used by the Theravada tradition.

Prajna (Pali: *panna*)—This term means "wind" or "breath" and is usually translated "wisdom" in both Theravada and Mahayana Buddhism. It refers to the various forms of subtle energy that animate a person. These psychological forces travel throughout the body and dramatically affect physical and mental well-being. The study of these is a major focus of the Tantric traditions of Tibet.

Pure Land—This term refers to the vision of Mahayanists of a pure state filled with compassion and wisdom. It is a realm where the teachings and presence of the Buddha fill the entire environment. The Pure Land sects of Buddhism are primarily found in Japan and in China and they focus on how a person can be reborn into the Pure Land after physical death.

Samadhi—This term describes the art of meditative stabilization. Practitioners are called upon to single-pointedly concentrate on a designated object without distraction. When *samadhi* is perfected, a person will be able to attain the cultivation of tranquil abiding, which is also known as *samatha*.

Samsara—This term refers to the unenlightened cycle of conditioned existence in which all beings find themselves until freed from the power of their karma and false delusions about the nature of reality. The Fourth Noble Truth teaches that it is possible to experience the cessation of conditioned existence, or *samsara*, through a state of liberation known as Nirvana.

Sangha—This term refers to both the community of faithful practitioners of the Buddhist message worldwide as well as to communities of ordained monks and nuns.

Suffering (Sanskrit: *dukka*; Pali: *dukkha*)—Suffering refers to both physical pain as well as psychological and emotional afflictions. Teachers refer to three levels of suffering: (1) the suffering from painful experiences, (2) the suffering from immutability and inevitable change, and (3) the suffering of conditioned existence. This refers to the basic state of a person feeling dissatisfied with life and under a cloud of delusion from their unenlightened way of perception.

Sutra—(Pali: *sutta*) This term describes any of the preserved writings of Lord Buddha. It is often seen as a suffix to a host of writings regarded by communities as authentic works of enlightened insight (e.g. *The Heart of Wisdom Sutra*).

Tantra—This term means "continuum," and describes esoteric methods that bring deeper insight. Sometimes, the tantric path is contrasted to the sutra path, used by most Buddhists to learn truth. It is a term frequently cited in reference to Tibetan or *Vajrayana* Buddhism.

Theravada Tradition—This is the term used by the Orthodox Buddhists of Southern Asia to describe their own way of understanding the message of Buddha. Theravada predominates in the monastic communities of Cambodia, Sri Lanka, Thailand, Myanmar, and Vietnam.

Three Jewels—Buddhists are encouraged to cherish the Three Jewels of refuge: the life of Lord Buddha, Buddha-Dharma (doctrine), and the Buddha-Sangha (spiritual community). Each is a refuge for those who seek liberation. These three are called jewels because they are precious.

Vajrayana Buddhism—This term can also be translated as the "diamond vehicle." Vajrayana refers to the forms of Tibetan Buddhism that often focus on a host of esoteric, tantric aspects.

Wisdom—Together with method, wisdom is seen as one of the two vital aspects of the Buddhist path. Without both wisdom and method together, many Buddhists say that enlightenment is not likely. The Sanskrit term *prajna* is often translated as "wisdom," although "insight" is perhaps a more accurate translation. This refers to the active awareness of things as they are without any delusion. Wisdom is something to be sought through strengthening an active cognitive process.

Bibliography

Abe, Masao. *Buddhism and Interfaith Dialogue*. Edited by Stephen Heine. Honolulu: University of Hawaii Press, 1995.

———. "Spirituality and Liberation: A Buddhist–Christian Conversation." *Horizons* 15 (1988) 347–64.

Adeney, Frances S. "How I, as a Christian, Have Learned from Buddhist Practice or 'The Frog Sat on the Lily Pad . . . Not Waiting.'" *Buddhist–Christian Studies* 21 (2001) 33–36.

Alcoholics Anonymous. *Twelve Steps and Twelve Traditions*. New York: Alcoholics Anonymous, 1953.

Amore, Roy, and Julia Ching. "The Buddhist Tradition." In *World Religions*. Vol. 2, *Eastern Traditions*, edited by Willard G. Oxotoby, 198–315. 2nd ed. Don Mills, Oxford: Oxford University Press, 2002.

Anderson, Norman. *Christianity and World Religions: The Challenge of Pluralism*. 2nd ed. Leicester, UK: Inter-Varsity, 1984.

Appleton, George. *On the Eightfold Path: Christian Presence amid Buddhism*. New York: Christian Presence Series. Oxford University Press, 1961.

Ariarajah, S. Wesley. *Not Without My Neighbour: Issues in Interfaith Relations*. Risk Book Series 85. Geneva: WCC Publications, 1999.

Armstrong, Karen. *Buddha*. Penguin Lives Series. New York: Penguin Putnam, 2001.

Arthur, Chris. "Maitreya, the Buddhist Messiah?" In *The Coming Deliverer: Millennial Themes in World Religions*, edited by Fiona Bowie, with Christopher Deacy, 43–59. Religion, Culture, and Society. Cardiff: University of Wales Press, 1997.

Autry, James A., and Stephen Mitchell. "Giving Up Control." In *Mountains Are Mountains and Rivers Are Rivers: Applying Eastern Teaching to Everyday Life*, edited by Ilana Rabinowicz, 111–13. New York: Hyperion, 1999.

Augustine, Morris J. "The Sociology of Knowledge and Buddhist–Christian Forms of Faith, Practice and Knowledge." *Japanese Journal of Religious Studies* 8 (1981) 237–60.

Balani, Laju M. "Thich Nhât Hanh on Buddhist–Christian Dialogue." PhD diss., Baylor University, 2005.

Batchelor, Martine, trans. *The Path of Compassion: The Bodhisattva Precepts*. Sacred Literature Series. Published in cooperation with the International Sacred Literature Trust. Walnut Creek, CA: Alta Mira, 2004.

Batchelor, Stephen. *Buddhism without Beliefs: A Contemporary Guide to Awakening*. New York: Riverhead, 1997.

———. "The Trials of Dandaron: "Stalin's Liquidation of Russian Buddhists in the Great Purges." *Tricycle* 1/3 (Spring 1992). https://tricycle.org/magazine/trials-dandaron/.

Beck, Charlotte Joko. *Everyday Zen: Love and Work*. New York: HarperOne, 1989.

Berger, Peter, and Anton Zijderveld. *In Praise of Doubt: How to Have Convictions without Becoming a Fanatic*. New York: HarperCollins, 2009.

Berrigan, Daniel, and Thich Nhât Hanh. *The Raft Is not the Shore*. Beacon Paperback 523. Boston: Beacon, 1975.

Berthrong, John. "Third North American Buddhist–Christian Theological Encounter." *Journal of Ecumenical Studies* 23 (1986) 775–76.

———. "Trends in Contemporary Buddhist–Christian Dialogue." *Ecumenical Trends* 14 (1985) 135–37.

Berzin, Alexander. *Developing Balanced Sensitivity: Practical Buddhist Exercises for Daily Life*. Ithaca, NY: Snow Lion, 1998.

Black, Patrick. "Contemplation on Buddhist–Christian Dialogue: One Student's Perspective." In *The Cross and the Lotus: Christianity and Buddhism in Dialogue* edited by G. W. Houston, 109–19. New Delhi: Banarsidass, 1985.

Blahuta, Jason. "On the Futility of a Buddhist–Christian Dialogue." *Religious Humanism* 35 (2001) 15–34.

Blyth R. H. *Games Zen Masters Play*. New York: Penguin, 1976.

Bobilin, Robert. *Revolution from Below: Buddhist and Christian Movements for Justice in Asia*. Lanham, MD: University Press of America, 1998.

Bodhi, Bhikku, trans. *The Connected Discourses of the Buddha: A New Translation of the Samyutta Nikaya*. Boston: Wisdom, 2003.

———, ed. *In the Buddha's Words: An Anthology of Discourses from the Pali Canon*. Boston: Wisdom, 2005.

Boeke, Richard F. "The UUA, the IARF, and the Buddhist/Christian Dialogue." *Journal of Ecumenical Studies* 24 (1987) 511–12.

Míguez Bonino, José. "The Uniqueness of Christ and the Plurality of Humankind." In *Interfaith Theology: A Reader*, edited by Daniel Cohn-Sherbok, Oxford: Oneworld, 2001.

Borg, Marcus, and Ray Riegert, eds. *Jesus and Buddha: The Parallel Sayings*. Berkeley: Ulysses, 1997.

Bowers, Russell H., Jr. *Someone or Nothing? Nishitani's "Religion and Nothingness" as a Foundation for Christian-Buddhist Dialogue*. Asian Thought and Culture 27. New York: Lang, 1995.

Bowie, Fiona, with Christopher Deacy, eds. *The Coming Deliverer: Millennial Themes in World Religions*. Religion, Culture and Society. Cardiff: University of Wales Press, 1997.

Brown, Brian. "Toward a Buddhist Ecological Cosmology." In *Worldviews and Ecology: Religion Philosophy and the Environment* edited by Mary Evelyn Tucker and John A. Grim, 124–37. Ecology and Justice. Maryknoll, NY: Orbis, 1994.

Brown, Margrethe B. J. "Consultation on Dialogue between Men of Living Faiths: A Conversation between Hindus, Buddhists, Christians and Muslims." *Journal of Ecumenical Studies* 7 (1970) 906–7.

Brück, Michael von, and Whalen Lai. *Buddhismus und Christentum: Geschichte, Konfrontation, Dialogue*. Munich: Beck, 1997.

Bruns, J. Edgar. *The Christian Buddhism of St. John*. New York: Paulist, 1971.

Bstan-'dzin-rgya-mtsho, Dalai Lama XIV. *Answers: Discussions with Western Buddhists.* Edited by José Ignacio Cabezón. Ithaca, NY: Snow Lion, 2001.

———. *Buddha Nature: Death and the Eternal Soul in Buddhism.* Woodside, CA: Bluestar, 1997.

———. *The Compassionate Life.* Boston: Wisdom, 2003.

———. *Essence of the Heart Sutra: The Dalai Lama's Heart of Wisdom Teachings.* Translated and edited by Geshe Thupten Jinpa. Boston: Wisdom, 2005.

———. *Freedom in Exile: The Autobiography of the Dahlai Lama.* New York: HarperCollins, 1990.

———. *The Good Heart: A Buddhist Perspective on the Teachings of Jesus.* Translated and annotated by Geshe Thupten Jinpa. Edited by Robert Kiely. Boston: Wisdom, 1998 (1996).

———. *Opening the Eye of New Awareness.* Rev. ed. Translated by Donald S. Lopez, with Jeffrey Hopkins. Boston: Wisdom, 1999.

Bradbury, Ray. *Fahrenheit 451.* New York: Simon & Schuster, 1967.

Brunner, Emil. "Revelation and Reason." In *Interfaith Theology: A Reader,* edited by Daniel Cohn-Sherbok, 49–50. Oxford: Oneworld, 2001.

Bruteau, Beatrice. *What We Can Learn from the East.* New York: Crossroad, 1995.

Buddha Groove (website). "*Namaste*: Meaning, Origin, and Its Use in Yoga." *Balance* (blog). https://blog.buddhagroove.com/meaning-of-namaste/.

Buri, Fritz. *The Buddha-Christ as the Lord of the True Self: The Religious Philosophy of the Kyoto School and Christianity.* Translated with an introduction by Harold H. Oliver. Macon, GA: Mercer University Press, 1997.

Cabezón, Jose Ignacio. "A God, Not a Savior." In *Buddhists Talk about Jesus, Christians Talk about the Buddha,* edited by Rita M Gross and Terry C. Muck, 17–31. New York: Continuum, 2000.

———. "Homosexuality and Buddhism." In *Homosexuality and World Religions,* edited by Arlene Swidler, 81–102. Valley Forge, PA: Trinity, 1993.

Callaway, Tucker N. *Japanese Buddhism and Christianity.* Tokyo: Shinkyo Shuppansha, 1957.

Campbell, June. *Traveller in Space: Gender Identity and Tibetan Buddhism.* Rev. ed. London: Continuum, 2002.

Camps, Arnulf. *Partners in Dialogue: Christianity and Other World Religions.* Translated by John Drury. Maryknoll, NY: Orbis, 1983.

Carmody, Denise Lardner. *What Are They Saying about Non-Christian Faith?* Ramsey, NJ: Paulist, 1982.

Carmody, Denise Lardner, and John Tully Carmody. *Serene Compassion: A Christian Appreciation of Buddhist Holiness.* New York: Oxford University Press, 1996.

Carroll, Lewis. *The Annotated Alice: Alice's Adventures in Wonderland & Through the Looking Glass.* Original illustrations by John Tenniel. Introduction and notes by Martin Gardner. New York: Norton. 1999.

Carus, Paul. *Buddhism and Its Christian Critics.* Chicago: Open Court, 1897

Chappell, David W. "New Horizons for Buddhist-Christian Encounter." *Council of Societies for the Study of Religion Bulletin* 22/3 (1993) 66–71.

Chabra, Meenakashi. "Redefining and Expanding the Self in Conflict Resolution." In *Buddhist Women and Social Justice: Ideals Challenges and Achievements,* edited by Karma Lekshe Tsomo, 89–99. SUNY Series in Feminist Philosophy. Albany: State University of New York Press, 2004.

Chakravarti, Uma. *The Social Dimensions of Early Buddhism*. New Delhi: Oxford University Press, 1987.
Chetwynd, Tom. *Zen and the Kingdom of Heaven: Reflections on the Tradition of Meditation in Christianity and Zen Buddhism*. Boston: Wisdom, 2001.
Ching, Julia. *Chinese Religions*. London: Macmillan, 1993.
Chung, Paul S. "Martin Luther and Shinran: The Presence of Christ in Justification and Salvation in a Buddhist-Christian Context." *Asia Journal of Theology* 18 (2004) 295–309.
Chödrön, Pema. *When Things Fall Apart: Heart Advice for Difficult Times*. 20th anniversary ed. Boulder, CO: Shambhala, 2016.
Chögyam, Ngakpa, and Khandro Dechen. *Roaring Silence: Discovering the Mind of Dzogchen*. Boston: Shambhala; distributed in the US by Random House, 2002.
Christ, Carol P., ed. *Diving Deep and Surfacing: Women Writers on Spiritual Quest*. 3rd ed., with a new afterword. Boston: Beacon, 1995.
Clasper, Paul. *Eastern Paths and the Christian Way*. Maryknoll, NY: Orbis, 1980.
———. "Buddhist-Christian Encounter in Burma." *Review & Expositor* 58 (1961) 35–49.
Cleary, Thomas. *Entry into the Inconceivable: An Introduction to Hua-yen Buddhism*. Honolulu: University of Hawaii Press, 1983.
———, trans. *Zen and the Art of Insight*, from *Prajñaparamita Heart Sutra*. Boston: Shambhala, 1999.
Cobb, John B., Jr. *Beyond Dialogue: Toward a Mutual Transformation of Christianity and Buddhism*. Philadelphia: Fortress, 1982.
———. "The Buddhist-Christian Dialogue since 1946: The Christian Side." In *Religious Issues and Interreligious Dialogues*, edited by Charles Wei-Hsun Fu and Gerhard E. Spiegler, 571–611. New York: Greenwood, 1989.
———. "Buddhist Emptiness and the Christian God." *Journal of the American Academy of Religion* 45/1 (March 1977) 11–25.
Cobb, John B., Jr., and Christopher Ives, eds. *The Emptying God: A Buddhist-Jewish-Christian Conversation*. Faith Meets Faith Series. Maaryknoll, NY: Orbis, 1990.
———, eds. *The Emptying God: A Buddhist-Jewish-Christian Conversation*. 1990. Reprint, Eugene, OR: Wipf & Stock, 2005.
Cohn-Sherbok, Daniel, ed. *Interfaith Theology: A Reader*. Oxford: Oneworld, 2001.
Cole, Alan. *Text as Father: Paternal Seductions in Early Mahayana Buddhist Literature*. Berkeley: University of California Press, 2005.
Coleman, James William. *The New Buddhism: The Western Transformation of an Ancient Tradition*. Oxford: Oxford University Press, 2001.
Conner, James. "5th Buddhist-Christian Meditation Conference at Naropa." *Journal of Ecumenical Studies* 22 (1985) 880–81.
Conze, Edward, ed. *Concise Encyclopedia of Living Faiths*. London: Hutchinson, 1982.
Cook, Francis H. "The Second Buddhist-Christian Theological Encounter: A Report." *Eastern Buddhist* 19 (1986) 127–34.
Coomaraswamy, Ananda K. *Buddha and the Gospel of Buddhism*. New York: Harper & Row, 1964.
Corless, Roger, J. *The Vision of Buddhism: The Space under the Tree*. New York: Paragon, 1989.
Corless, Roger, and Paul F. Knitter, eds. *Buddhist Emptiness and Christian Trinity: Essays and Explorations*. New York: Paulist, 1990.

Cornille, Catherine. "Dynamics of Multiple Belonging." In *Many Mansions? Multiple Religious Belonging and Christian Identity*, edited by Catherine Cornille, 1–6. Faith Meets Faith Series. Maryknoll, NY: Orbis, 2002.

Covell, Ralph R. *Confucius, the Buddha, and Christ: A History of the Gospel in Chinese*. American Society of Missiology Series 11. Maryknoll, NY: Orbis, 1986.

Coward, Harold G. "The Possibility of Paradigm Choice in Buddhist–Christian Dialogue." *Journal of Ecumenical Studies* 25 (1988) 370–82.

Cowell, Alan. "Pope, in Sri Lanka, Seeks to Soothe Buddhist Critics." *New York Times*, January 21, 1995.

Cracknell, Kenneth. *Towards a New Relationship: Christians and People of Other Faiths*. London: Epworth, 1986.

Cragg, Kenneth, *The Christ and the Faiths: Theology in Cross-Reference*. Philadelphia: Westminster, 1986.

———. *To Meet and to Greet: Faith with Faith*. London: Epworth, 1992.

Crosby, Donald A. *Living with Ambiguity: Religious Naturalism and the Menace of Evil*. Albany: State University of New York Press, 2008.

Crossan, John Dominic. *God and Empire: Jesus against Rome, Then and Now*. New York: HarperCollins, 2007.

Cruz, Robert, ed. "The Pope and Buddhism: That New Chapter in Buddhist–Christian Dialogue." Special issue, *Dialogue* 22 (1995) 1–96, 104–24.

Dagyab, Loden Sherap. *Buddhist Symbols in Tibetan Culture*. Boston: Wisdom, 1995.

Davis, Richard H. "Religions of India in Practice." In *Asian Religions in Practice: An Introduction*, edited by Daniel S. Lopez Jr., 8–55. Princeton Readings in Religions. Princeton: Princeton University Press, 1999.

D'Costa, Gavin. *The Meeting of Religions and the Trinity*. Faith Meets Faith Series. Maryknoll, NY: Orbis, 2000.

Derrett, J. Duncan M. *Two Masters: The Buddha and Jesus*. Northamptonshire: Pilkington, 1995.

De Silva, Lynn A., ed. "Buddhist–Christian Renewal and the Future of Humanity: Creative Transformation." Special issue, *Dialogue* 8 (1981).

———. *The Problem of the Self in Buddhism and Christianity*. Library of Philosophy and Religion. New York: Barnes & Noble, 1979.

———. "Buddhist–Christian Dialogue." In *Inter-Religious Dialogue*, edited by Herbert Jai Singh, 170–203. Bangalore: Christian Institute for the Study of Religion and Society, 1967.

Desjardins, Michael. *Peace, Violence, and the New Testament*. The Biblical Seminar. Sheffield, England: Sheffield Academic, 1997.

Dhamma, Rewata. *The First Discourse of the Buddha*. Boston: Wisdom, 1997.

Dharmasiri, Gunapala. *A Buddhist Critique of the Christian Concept of God*. Antioch, CA: Golden Leaves, 1988.

Dorje, Rig'dzin. *Dangerous Friend: The Teacher-Student Relationship in Vajrayana Buddhism*. Boston: Shambhala, 2001.

Dragpa, Chokyi Nyima. *Uniting Wisdom and Compassion: Illuminating the Thirty-Seven Practices of a Bodhisattva*. Translated by Heidi I. Koppl. Boston: Wisdom, 2004.

Dreuille, Mayeul de. *From East to West: A History of Monasticism*. New York: Crossroad, 1999.

Dumoulin, Heinrich. *Christianity Meets Buddhism*. Translated by John C. Maraldo. Religious Encounter: East and West. LaSalle, IL: Open Court, 1974.

Dupuis, Jacques. *Christianity and the Religions: From Confrontation to Dialogue.* Translated by Phillip Berryman. Maryknoll, NY: Orbis, 2002.

Dutcher-Walls, Tim. "Being Hyphenated: Reflections of a Buddhist–Christian." *Dialog* 40 (2001) 270–73.

Earhart, H. Byron, ed. *Religion in the Japanese Experience: Sources and Interpretations.* 2nd ed. Religious Life in History Series. Belmont, CA: Wadsworth, 1997.

Eckel, Malcolm David. "Perspectives on the Buddhist–Christian Dialogue." *The Christ and the Bodhisattva*, edited by Donald S. Lopez, Sr. and Steven C. Rockefeller, 43–62. SUNY Series in Buddhist Studies. Albany: State University of New York Press, 1987.

Eilert, Håkan. *Boundlessness: Studies in Karl Ludvig Reichelt's Missionary Thinking with Special Regard to the Buddhist–Christian Encounter.* Studia Missionalia Upsaliensia 24. Århus, Denmark: Aros, 1974.

Elinor, Robert. *Buddha & Christ: Images of Wholeness.* Cambridge: Lutterworth, 2000.

Fa-tsang. "Cultivation of Contemplation of the Inner Meaning of the Hua-yen: The Ending of Delusion and Return to the Source." In *Entry into the Inconceivable: An Introduction to Hua-yen Buddhism*, edited by Thomas Cleary, 147–69. Honolulu: University of Hawaii Press, 1983.

Fields, Rick. *How the Swans Came to the Lake: A Narrative History of Buddhism in America.* Boston: Shambhala, 1992.

Fischer, Norman, "On Questioning." In *Mountains Are Mountains and Rivers Are Rivers: Applying Eastern Teachings to Everyday Life*, edited by Ilana Rabinowicz, 17–20. New York: Hyperion, 1999.

Fischer, Norman, et al. *Benedict's Dharma: Buddhists Reflect on the Rule of Saint Benedict.* Edited by Patrick Henry. With a new translation of the Rule by Patrick Barry and an introduction to the Rule by Mary Margaret Funk. New York: Riverhead, 2001.

Fisher, Mary Pat, ed. *An Anthology of Living Religions.* 2nd ed. Upper Saddle River, NJ: Prentice-Hall, 2008.

Florida, Robert E. *The Buddhist Tradition.* Human Rights and the World's Major Religions 5. Westport, CT: Praeger, 2005.

———. "What Does Comparative Religion Compare? The Buddhist–Christian Example." *Studies in Religion* 19 (1990) 163–71.

Ford, J. Massyngbaerde. *My Enemy Is My Guest: Jesus and Violence in Luke.* Maryknoll, NY: Orbis, 1984.

Fredericks, James L. *Buddhists and Christians: Through Comparative Theology to Solidarity.* Faith Meets Faith Series. Maryknoll, NY: Orbis, 2004.

———. "The Cross and the Begging Bowl: Deconstructing the Cosmology of Violence." *Buddhist-Christian Studies* 18 (1998) 155–67.

———. *Faith among Faiths: Christian Theology and Non-Christian Religions.* New York: Paulist, 1999.

Fry, C. George, et al. *Great Asian Religions.* Grand Rapids: Baker, 1984.

Garbe, Richard. *India and Christendom: The Historical Connections between Their Religions.* Translated by Lydia Gillingham Robinson. La Salle, IL: Open Court, 1959.

Garvey, John. *Seeds of the Word: Orthodox Thinking on Other Religions.* Foundations Series. Crestwood, NY: St Vladimir's Seminary Press, 2005.

Geffré, Claude, and Mariasusai Dhavamony, eds. *Buddhism and Christianity.* Concilium 116. New York: Seabury, 1979.

Bibliography

Girard, Rene. *Things Hidden Since the Foundation of the World*. Translated by Stephen Bann and Michael Metteer. Stanford: Stanford University Press, 1987.

Goldberg, Ellen. "Buddhism in the West: Transplantation and Innovation." In *Buddhism in World Cultures: Comparative Perspectives*, edited by Stephen C. Berkwitz, 285–310. ABC-CLIO Religion in Contemporary Cultures Series. Santa Barbara, CA: ABC-CLIO, 2006.

Gombrich, Richard F. *How Buddhism Began: The Conditioned Genesis of the Early Teachings*. Jordan Lectures in Comparative Religion 17. London: Athlone, 1996.

Govinda, Lama Anagarika. *A Living Buddhism for the West*. Translated by Maurice Walshe. Boston: Shambhala, 1990.

Graham, Dom Aelred. *Zen Catholicism*. New York: Crossroad, 1994.

Griffiths, Paul J., ed. *Christianity through Non-Christian Eyes*. Faith Meets Faith Series. Maryknoll, NY: Orbis, 1990.

———. "On the Possible Future of the Buddhist–Christian Interaction." In *Japanese Buddhism: Its Tradition, New Religions, and Interactions with Christianity*, edited by Minoru Kiyota et al., 145–61. Los Angeles: Buddhist Books, 1987.

———. *Problems of Religious Diversity*. Exploring the Philosophy of Religion. Oxford: Blackwell, 2001.

Gross, Rita M. "Meditating on Jesus" in *Buddhists Talk about Jesus, Christians Talk about the Buddha*, edited by Rita M. Gross and Terry C. Muck, 32–51. New York: Continuum, 2000.

———. "Some Reflections about Community and Survival." In *Buddhist-Christian Studies* 23 (2003) 3–19.

Gross, Rita M., and Terry C. Muck, eds. *Christians Talk about Buddhist Meditation, Buddhists Talk about Christian Prayer*. New York: Continuum, 2003.

———, eds. *Buddhists Talk about Jesus, Christians Talk about the Buddha*. New York: Continuum, 2000.

Gross, Rita M., and Rosemary Radford Ruether. *Religious Feminism and the Future of the Planet: A Christian-Buddhist Conversation*. New York: Continuum, 2001.

Guenther, Herbert, and Leslie S. Kawamura, trans. *Mind in Buddhist Psychology: A Translation of "The Necklace of Clear Understanding," by Ye-shes rgyal-mtshan*. Tibetan Translation Series. Emeryville, CA: Dharma, 1975.

Habito, Ruben L. F. *Experiencing Buddhism: Ways of Wisdom and Compassion*. Faith Meets Faith Series. Maryknoll, NY: Orbis, 2005.

———. "Maria Kannon Zen: Explorations in Buddhist Christian Practice." *Dialogue* 19–20 (1994) 145–56.

———. "On Dharmakara as Ultimate Reality: Prolegomenon for a Buddhist–Christian Dialogue." *Japanese Journal of Religious Studies* 12 (1985) 233–52.

Hall, Dorothy Judd. "Wallace Stevens's Spiritual Voyage: A Buddhist–Christian Path to Conversion." In *Seeing into the Life of Things: Essays on Literature and Religious Experience*, edited by John L. Mahoney, 277–304. Studies in Religion and Literature 1. New York: Fordham University Press, 1998.

Harris, Elizabeth J. "Buddhist–Christian Encounter: Achievements and Hopes in the Sri Lankan Experience." *A Great Commission: Christian Hope and Religious Diversity; Papers in Honor of Kenneth Cracknell on His 65th Birthday*, edited by Martin Forward et al., 351–69. Oxford: Lang, 2000.

Harvey, Andrew, Foreword. In *Dhammapada: Annotated & Explained*, ix–xvi. Annotated by Jack Maguire. Translated by Max Muller. Revised by Jack Maguire. SkyLight Illuminations. Woodstock, VT: SkyLight Paths, 2002.

Harvey, Peter. *Introduction to Buddhism: Teachings, History, and Practices*. Cambridge: Cambridge University Press, 1990.

Hasegawa, Seikan. *The Cave of Poison Grass: Essays on the Hannya Sutra*. Companions of Zen Training. Arlington, VA: Great Ocean, 1975.

Haynes, Jeff. *Religion in Third World Politics*. Issues in Third World Politics. Buckingham, UK: Open University Press, 1993.

He, Jianming. "Buddhist–Christian Encounter in Modern China: A Case Study of Ren Jian Jue Banyuekan." *Ching Feng* 1 (2000) 121–42.

Heng Sure. "Filial Respect and Buddhist Meditation." *Religion East and West* 1 (2010) 57–65.

Hoebrichts, Joan Hogetsu. "Bringing Zen Practice Home." *Journal of Religion & Health* 43 (2004) 201–16.

Humphreys, Christmas. *Buddhism: An Introduction*. Hammondsworth, UK: Penguin, 1981.

Hunter, Louise H. *Buddhism in Hawaii: Its Impact on a Yankee Community*. Honolulu: University of Hawaii, 1971.

Ingram, Paul O. *Buddhist–Christian Dialogue in an Age of Science*. Lanham, MD: Rowman & Littlefield, 2008.

———. "'Fruit Salad Can Be Delicious': The Practice of Buddhist–Christian Dialogue." *Cross Currents* 50 (2000–2001) 541–49.

———. *The Modern Buddhist–Christian Dialogue: Two Universalistic Religions in Transformation*. Studies in Comparative Religion, 2. Lewiston, NY: Mellen, 1988.

———. *Wrestling with the Ox: A Theology of Religious Experience*. 1997. Reprint, Eugene, OR: Wipf & Stock, 2006.

Ingram, Paul O., and David R. Loy. "The Self and Suffering: A Buddhist–Christian Conversation." *Dialog* 44 (2005) 98–107.

Ingram, Paul O., and Frederick J. Streng, eds. *Buddhist–Christian Dialogue: Mutual Renewal and Transformation*. 1986. Reprint, Eugene, OR: Wipf & Stock, 2007.

Ives, Christopher, ed. *Divine Emptiness and Historical Fullness: A Buddhist-Jewish-Christian Conversation with Masao Abe*. Valley Forge, PA: Trinity, 1995.

James, Robison B. *Tillich and World Religions: Encountering Other Faiths Today*. Macon, GA: Mercer University Press, 2003.

Jinkins, Michael. *Christianity, Tolerance, and Pluralism: A Theological Engagement with Isaiah Berlin's Social Theory*. Routledge Studies in Religion 7. London: Routledge, 2004.

Johnston, William. *Christian Zen*. New York: Harper & Row, 1971.

———. *Lord, Teach Us to Pray: Christian Zen and the Inner Eye of Love*. London: Collins, 1990.

———. *The Mirror Mind: Zen-Christian Dialogue*. New York: Fordham Press, 1990.

Jones, Charles B. *The View from Mars Hill: Christianity in the Landscape of World Religions*. Cambridge: Cowley, 2005.

Jones, James W. *The Mirror of God: Christian Faith as Spiritual Practice; Lessons from Buddhism and Psychotherapy*. New York: Palgrave Macmillan, 2003.

Jones, Ken. *The New Social Face of Buddhism: A Call to Action*. Boston: Wisdom, 2003

Kabat-Zinn, Jon. *Wherever You Go, There You Are: Mindfulness Meditation for Everyday Life*. Rev., 10th anniversary ed. New York: Hyperion, 2005.

Kadowaki, J. K. *Zen and the Bible*. Translated by Joan Rieck. Maryknoll, NY: Orbis, 2002.

Karentzky, Patricia Eichenbaum. *The Life of the Buddha: Ancient Scriptural and Pictorial Traditions*. Lanham, MD: University Press of America, 1992.

Kasimow, Harold, et al., eds. *Beside Still Waters: Jews Christians and the Way of the Buddha*. Boston: Wisdom, 2003.

Kaza, Stephanie. "Finding Safe Harbor: Buddhist Sexual Ethics in America." *Buddhist-Christian Studies* 24 (2004) 23–35.

Keel, Hee-Sung. "vesus the Bodhisattva: Christology from a Buddhist Perspective—Interreligious Encounters in Korea." *Buddhist-Christian Studies* 16 (1996) 169–85.

Keithley, Alan. *Into Every Life a Little Zen Must Fall: A Christian Philosopher Looks to Alan Watts and the East*. A Wisdom East-West Book. Grey Series. London: Wisdom, 1986.

Keller, Catherine. "Scoop Up the Water and the Moon Is in Your Hands: On Feminist Theology and Dynamic Self-Emptying." In *The Emptying God: A Buddhist-Jewish-Christian Conversation*, edited by John B. Cobb Jr. and Christopher Ives, 102–15. Faith Meets Faith Series. Maryknoll, NY: Orbis, 1990.

Kennedy, Robert E. *Zen Gifts to Christians*. London: Continuum, 2000.

———. *Zen Spirit, Christian Spirit: The Place of Zen in Christian Life*. New York: Continuum, 1995.

Khandu Lama. "Trafficking in Buddhist Girls: Empowerment through Prevention." In *Buddhist Women and Social Justice: Ideals Challenges and Achievements* edited by Karma Lekshe Tsomo, 165–91. SUNY Series in Feminist Philosophy. Albany: State University of New York Press, 2004.

Kim, Sebastian C. H., ed. *Christian Theology in Asia*. Cambridge: Cambridge University Press, 2008.

Kinahan, Timothy. *A Deep but Dazzling Darkness: A Christian Theology in an Inter-Faith Perspective*. Blackrock, Ireland: Columba, 2005.

King, Sallie B. *Being Benevolence: The Social Ethics of Engaged Buddhism*. Topics in Contemporary Buddhism. Honolulu: University of Hawaii Press, 2005.

———. "They Who Burned Themselves for Peace: Quaker and Buddhist Self-Immolators during the Vietnam War." *Buddhist-Christian Studies* 20 (2000) 127–50.

King, Sallie, and Paul O. Ingram, eds. *The Sound of Liberating Truth: Buddhist-Christian Dialogues in Honor of Frederick J. Streng*. 1999. Reprint, Eugene: OR: Wipf and Stock, 2006.

King, Winston. "Buddhist-Christian Dialogue." In *Religions in Dialogue: East and West Meet*, edited by Zacharias P. Thundy and Kuncheria Pathil, 261–69. Lanham, MD: University Press of America, 1985.

———. *Buddhism and Christianity: Some Bridges of Understanding*. Philadelphia: Westminster, 1962.

Kinnard, Jacob. *The Emergence of Buddhism*. Greenwood Guides to Historic Events of the Ancient World. Westport, CT: Greenwood, 2006.

Kipling, Rudyard. "If." In *Kipling: A Selection of His Stories and Poems*, edited by John Beecroft, 2:432–33. Illustrated by Richard M. Powers. 2 vols. 1892. Reprint, New York: Doubleday, 1956.

Kjellberg, Seppo. *Urban Ecotheology*. Utrecht: International Books, 2000.

Kloppenborg, Ria. "A Buddhist-Christian Encounter in Sri Lanka: The Pānadura Veda." In *Religion: Empirical Studies; A Collection to Mark the 50th Anniversary of the British Association for the Study of Religions*, edited by Steven Sutcliffe, 179–91. London: Routledge, 2004.

Knitter, Paul F. *Jesus and the Other Names: Christian Mission and Global Responsibility*. Maryknoll, NY: Orbis, 1996.

———. "Spirituality and Liberation: A Buddhist-Christian Conversation." *Horizons* 15 (1988) 347–64.

Kohn, Michael H., trans. *The Shambhala Dictionary of Buddhism and Zen*. Boston: Shambhala, 1991.

König, Franz Cardinal. *Open to God, Open to the World*. Edited by Christa Pongratz-Lippitt. London: Burns & Oates, 2005.

Kornfield, Jack. *After the Ecstasy, the Laundry: How the Heart Grows Wise on the Spiritual Path*. New York: Bantam, 2000.

Koyama, Kosuke. *No Handle on the Cross: An Asian Meditation on the Crucified Mind*. Maryknoll, NY: Orbis, 1977.

———. *Water Buffalo Theology*. 25th anniversary ed. Maryknoll, NY: Orbis, 1999.

Kubose, Gyomay. *Zen Koans*. Chicago: Regnery, 1973.

Küng, Hans and Karl-Josef Kuschel, eds. *A Global Ethic: The Declaration of the Parliament of the World's Religions*. London: SCM, 1993.

Lai, Pan Chiu. "Buddhist-Christian Complementarity Perspective of Quantum Physics." *Studies in Interreligious Dialogue* 12 (2002) 148–64.

———. "Cobb's Theory of Inter-Religious Dialogue and the Buddhist-Christian Encounter in China." *Ching Feng* 40 (1997) 261–90.

Lai, Whalen W. "The Buddhist-Christian Dialogue in China." In *Religious Issues and Interreligious Dialogues* edited by Charles Wei-Hsun Fu and Gerhard E. Spiegler, 613–31. Westport, CT: Greenwood, 1989.

Lai, Whalen W., and Michael von Bruck. *Christianity and Buddhism: A Multicultural History of Their Dialogue*. Translated by Phyllis Jestice. Faith Meets Faith Series. Maryknoll, NY: Orbis, 2001.

Lande, Aasulv. "Interreligious Fellowship: A Kind of Pilgrimage?" *Swedish Missiological Themes* 90 (2002) 5–16.

Lande, Aasulv, et al., eds. *Christian Perceptions of Buddhism: Proceedings of the European Network of Buddhist-Christian Studies' Conference Held in Lund May 2001*. Uppsala: Swedish Institute of Missionary Research, 2002.

Lardner, Lorne, ed. *The Wheel of Great Compassion: The Practice of the Prayer Wheel in Tibetan Buddhism*. Translated by Lama Thubten Zopa, Rinpoche et al. Boston: Wisdom, 2000.

Largen, Kristin Johnston. *What Christians Can Learn from Buddhism: Rethinking Salvation*. Facets. Minneapolis: Fortress, 2009.

Larkin, Geri. *Tap Dancing in Zen*. Berkeley: Celestial Arts, 2000.

Lee, Archie C. C. "Cross-Textual Hermeneutics and Identity in Multi-scriptural Asia." In *Christian Theology in Asia*, edited by Sebastian C. H. Kim, 179–204. Cambridge: Cambridge University Press, 2008.

Lefebure, Leo D. *The Buddha and the Christ: Explorations in Buddhist and Christian Dialogue*. Faith Meets Faith Series. Maryknoll, NY: Orbis, 1993.

———. "Divergence, Convergence: Buddhist-Christian Encounters." *Christian Century* 113 (1996) 964–73.

Leighton, Taigen Daniel. *Bodhisattva Archetypes: Classic Buddhist Guides to Awakening and Their Modern Expression.* New York: Penguin, 1998.
Leighton, Taigen Daniel, and Yi Wu, trans. "Cultivating the Empty Field," by Hongzhi Zheng Jue. In *The Art of Just Sitting: Essential Writings on the Zen Practice of Shikantaza*, edited by John Daido Loori, xxvii–xxxii. 2nd ed. Boston: Wisdom, 2004.
Leong, Kenneth S. *The Zen Teachings of Jesus.* Rev. and exp. ed. New York: Crossroad, 2001.
Lewis, C. S. *Mere Christianity.* Rev. ed. 1961. Reprint, New York: HarperCollins, 2001.
Ling, Trevor Oswald. "The Buddhist-Christian Encounter: The Christian Encounter: 2." *Theology* 69 (1966) 358–65.
———. *Buddhism, Imperialism, and War: Burma and Thailand in Modern History.* London: Allen & Unwin, 1979.
Loori, John Daido. *The Zen of Creativity: Cultivating Your Artistic Life.* New York: Ballantine, 2005.
Lopez, Donald S., Jr., ed. *Modern Buddhism: Readings for the Unenlightened.* London: Penguin, 2002.
Lopez, Donald S., Jr., and Steven C. Rockefeller, eds. *The Christ and the Bodhisattva.* SUNY Series in Buddhist Studies. Albany: State University of New York Press, 1987.
Losel, Thubten. "Buddhist-Christian Dialogue—A Prolegomena." In *Interreligious Dialogue* edited by M. Darrol Bryant and Frank K. Flinn, 191–97. New York: Paragon.
Loy, David R. "Dead Words, Living Words, and Healing Words: The Disseminations of Dogen and Eckhart." In *Healing Deconstruction: Postmodern Thought in Buddhism and Christianity*, edited by David Loy, 33–51. Reflection and Theory in the Study of Religion 3. Atlanta: Scholars, 1996.
———. *The Great Awakening: A Buddhist Social Theory.* Boston: Wisdom, 2003.
———, ed. *Healing Deconstruction: Postmodern Thought in Buddhism and Christianity.* American Academy of Religion 3. Reflection and Theory in the Study of Religion. 3. Atlanta: Scholars, 1996.
Luz, Ulrich, and Axel Michaels. *Encountering Jesus & Buddha: Their Lives and Teachings.* Translated by Linda M. Maloney. Minneapolis: Fortress, 2006.
MacInnes, Elaine. *Zen Contemplation for Christians.* Lanham, MD: Sheed & Ward, 2003.
Magliola, Robert. *On Deconstructing Life-Worlds: Buddhism, Christianity, Culture.* American Academy of Religion Cultural Criticism, Series 3. Atlanta: Scholars, 1997.
Malalgoda, Kitsiri. "Buddhist-Christian Confrontation in Ceylon, 1800–1880." *Social Compass* 20 (1973) 171–200.
Matthews, Warren. *World Religions.* 6th ed. Belmont, CA: Wadsworth, 2007.
Matthiessen, Peter. *Nine-Headed Dragon River: Zen Journals, 1962–1982.* Boston: Shambhala, 1986.
Maraldo, John C. "The Hermeneutics of Practice in Dogen and Francis of Assisi: An Exercise in Buddhist-Christian Dialogue." *Eastern Buddhist* 14/2 (1981) 22–46.
Masuzawa, Tomoko. *The Invention of World Religions, or, How European Universalism Was Preserved in the Language of Pluralism.* Chicago: University of Chicago Press, 2005.

May, John D'Arcy. "Conversion and Religious Identity in Buddhism and Christianity: Sixth Study Conference of the European Network of Buddhist–Christian Studies, Arch Abbey of St. Ottilien, Germany, 10–13 June 2005." *Studies in Interreligious Dialogue* 15 (2005) 240–43.

———. *Meaning, Consensus, and Dialogue in Buddhist–Christian Communication: A Study in the Construction of Meaning*. Studies in the Intercultural History of Christianity 31. Berne, Switzerland: Lang, 1984.

———. "'Rights of the Earth' and 'Care for the Earth': Two Paradigms for a Buddhist–Christian Ecological Ethic." *Horizons* 21 (1994) 48–61.

———. *Transcendence and Violence: The Encounter of Buddhist, Christian, and Primal Traditions*. New York: Continuum, 2003.

Mayer, John R. "The Buddhist–Christian Dialogue: Secularity and Transformation." *Japanese Religions* 14/2 (1986) 1–18.

McDaniel, Jay B. "The Garden of Eden, the Fall, and the Life of Christ: A Christian Approach to Ecology." In *Worldviews and Ecology: Religion Philosophy and the Environment*, edited by, Mary Evelyn Tucker and John A. Grim, 71–81. Ecology and Justice. Maryknoll, NY: Orbis, 1994.

———. *Of God and Pelicans: A Theology of Reverence for Life*. Louisville: Westminster John Knox, 1989.

McDermott, Gerald R. *Can Evangelicals Learn from World Religions? Jesus, Revelation & Religious Traditions*. Downers Grove, IL: InterVarsity, 2000.

———. *God's Rivals: Why Has God Allowed Different Religions? Insights from the Bible and the Early Church*. Downers Grove, IL: IVP Academic, 2007.

Merton, Thomas. *Zen and the Birds of Appetite*. A New Directions Book. New York: New Directions, 1968.

Metcalf, Franz. *What Would Buddha Do? 101 Answers to Life's Daily Dilemmas*. Berkeley, CA: Seastone, 1999.

Mieder, Wolfgang, ed. *The Prentice-Hall Encyclopedia of World Proverbs*. New York: MJF Books, 1996.

Milarepa. *Drinking the Mountain Stream: Songs of Tibet's Beloved Saint Milarepa*. Rev. ed. Translated by Lama Kunga Rinpoche and Brian Cutillo. Boston: Wisdom, 1995.

Mitchell, Donald W. *Buddhism: Introducing the Buddhist Experience*. New York: Oxford, 2002.

———. "The 'Place' of the Self in Christian Spirituality: A Response to the Buddhist–Christian Dialogue." *Japanese Religions* 13/3 (1984) 2–26.

———. "Society for Buddhist–Christian Studies Is Formed." *Journal of Ecumenical Studies* 25 (1988) 149–51.

———. *Spirituality and Emptiness: The Dynamics of Spiritual Life in Buddhism and Christianity*. New York: Paulist, 1991.

Mitchell, Donald W., and James A. Wiseman, eds. *The Gethsemani Encounter: A Dialogue on the Spiritual Life by Buddhist and Christian Monastics*. New York: Continuum, 1998.

Moltmann, Jürgen. "God Is Unselfish Love." In *The Emptying God: A Buddhist–Jewish–Christian Conversation*, 116–24. 1990. Reprint, Eugene, OR: Wipf & Stock, 2005.

Mommaers, Paul, and Jan Van Bragt. *Mysticism, Buddhist and Christian: Encounters with Jan van Ruusbroec*. Nanzan Studies in Religion and Culture. New York: Crossroad, 1995.

Muck, Terry. "Images of the Buddha." In *Buddhists Talk about Jesus, Christians Talk about the Buddha*, edited by Rita M. and Terry C. Muck, 95–106. New York: Continuum, 2000.

Muggeridge, Malcolm. *Something Beautiful for God: Mother Teresa of Calcutta*. Norwich England: Collins/Fontana, 1972.

———. *Something Beautiful for God: Mother Teresa of Calcutta*. New York: Harper & Row, 1986.

Muller, Max, trans. *Dhammapada: Annotated & Explained*. Annotated and revised by Jack Maguire. SkyLight Illuminations. Woodstock, VT: SkyLight Paths, 2002.

Nakagawa, Yoshiharu. "The Child as Compassionate Bodhisattva and as Human Sufferer/Spiritual Seeker: Intertwined Buddhist Images." In *Nurturing Child and Adolescent Spirituality: Perspectives from the World's Religious Traditions*, edited by Karen Marie Yust et al. 33–42. Lanham, MD: Rowman & Littlefield, 2006.

Nakamura, Hajime. *Buddhism in Comparative Light*. 2nd, rev. ed. New Delhi: Banarsidass, 1986.

Nakasone, Ronald Y. "Differing States of Mind." In *The Transforming Spiritual Landscape: Buddhist-Christian Encounters*, edited by Ronald Y. Nakasone, 31–38. Fremont, CA: Dharma Cloud, 2005.

———, ed. *The Transforming Spiritual Landscape: Buddhist-Christian Encounters*. Fremont, CA: Dharma Cloud, 2005.

Namdrol, Khenpo Rinpoche. *The Practice of Vajrakilaya: Our Teachings*. Ithaca, NY: Snow Lion, 1999.

Nasu, Eisho. "Fabian Fucan: From Evangelist to Apostate." In *The Transforming Spiritual Landscape: Buddhist-Christian Encounters*, edited by Ronald Y. Nakasone, 51–60. Fremont, CA: Dharma Cloud, 2005.

Neill, Stephen. *Christian Faith and Other Faiths: The Christian Dialogue with Other Religions*. 2nd ed. New York: Oxford University Press, 1970.

Nhât Hahn, Thich. *A Joyful Path: Community, Transformation, and Peace*. Berkeley: Parallax, 1994.

———. *Living Buddha, Living Christ*. New York: Riverhead, 2007.

———. *The Path of Return Continues the Journey*. Berkeley: Parallax, 1993.

———. *Teachings on Love*. 2nd ed. Berkeley, CA: Parallax, 2002.

Nhât Hahn, Thich, and Daniel Berrigan. *The Raft Is Not the Shore: Conversations toward a Buddhist-Christian Awareness*. Maryknoll, NY: Orbis, 2001.

Nielsen, Niels C., Jr. "*Analogia Entis* as the Basis of Buddhist-Christian Dialogue." *Modern Theology* 3 (1987) 345–57.

Niles, D. T. *Buddhism and the Claims of Christ*. Richmond, VA: John Knox, 1967.

Nobuhara, Tokiyuki. "*Sunyata, Kenosis*, and *Jihi* or Friendly Compassionate Love: Toward a Buddhist-Christian Theology of Loyalty." *Japanese Religions* 15/4 (1989) 50–66.

Norbu, Thinley. *White Sail: Crossing the Waves of Ocean Mind to the Serene Continent of the Triple Gems*. Boston: Shambhala, 1992.

Northup, Lesley A. *Ritualizing Women: Patterns of Spirituality*. Cleveland: Pilgrim, 1997.

Novak, Philip. *The World's Wisdom: Sacred Texts of the World's Religions*. San Francisco: HarperSanFrancisco, 1994.

Nyanasobhano, Bhikkhu. *Landscapes of Wonder: Discovering Buddhist Dhamma in the World around Us*. Boston: Wisdom, 1998.

Odin, Steve. "Kenōsis as Founadation for Buddhist-Christian Dialogue." *Eastern Buddhist* 20 (1987) 34–61.
Ogden, Schubert M. "Christian Identity and Genuine Openness to the Religious Beliefs of Others." *Buddhist-Christian Studies* 25 (2005) 21–27.
———. *Is There Only One True Religion or Are There Many?* Dallas: Southern Methodist University Press, 1992.
Oh, Kang-nam. "Buddhahood and Metanoia: The Buddhist-Christian Dialogue in Korea." *Journal of Dharma* 20 (1995) 223–38.
O'Hanlon, Daniel J. "Third International Buddhist-Christian Conference." *Journal of Ecumenical Studies* 24 (1987) 513–14.
Palihawadana, Mahinda. "A Buddhist Response: Religion Beyond Ideology and Power." In *Christian Faith in a Religiously Plural World*, edited by Donald G. Dawe and John B. Carman, 34–45. Maryknoll, NY: Orbis, 1978.
Pallis, Marco. *A Buddhist Spectrum: Contributions to Buddhist-Christian Dialogue*. London: Allen & Unwin, 1980.
Panikkar, Raimundo. *The Silence of God: The Answer of the Buddha*. Translated from the Italian by Robert R. Barr. Faith Meets Faith Series. Maryknoll, NY: Orbis, 1989.
Pannenburg, Wolfhart. *Systematic Theology*. Vol. 1. Translated by Geoffrey W. Bromiley. 3 vols. Grand Rapids: Eerdmans, 1991.
———. *Theology and the Philosophy of Science*. Translated by Francis McDonagh. Philadelphia: Westminster, 1976.
Patterson, Orlando. *Rituals of Blood: Consequences of Slavery in Two American Centuries*. Washington, DC: Civitas/CounterPoint, 1998.
Pennington, M. Basil, OSCO. "A Source of Hope, an Instrument of Peace." In *Spiritual Perspectives on America's Role as Superpower*, 205–14. Woodstock, VT: SkyLight Paths, 2003.
Phan, Peter C. *Being Religious Interreligiously: Asian Perspectives on Interfaith Dialogue*. Maryknoll, NY: Orbis, 2004.
Pieris, Aloysius, ed. "Buddhists and Christians on Peace and Justice: Minjung Buddhism and Minjung Theology." Special issue, *Dialogue* 16/1–3 (1989).
———. "Cross-Scripture Reading in Buddhist-Christian Dialogue: A Search for the Right Method." *Dialogue* 31 (2004) 69–104.
———. *Fire and Water: Basic Issues in Asian Buddhism and Christianity*. Faith Meets Faith Series. Maryknoll, NY: Orbis, 1995.
———. "Lakshmi and Lynn: Woman and Man in Buddhist-Christian Dialogue." *Dialogue* 19–20 (1992–1993) i–vi.
———. *Love Meets Wisdom: A Christian Experience of Buddhism*. Faith Meets Faith Series. Maryknoll, NY: Orbis, 1988.
Pope, Alexander. "Essay on Criticism." In *Pope's Essay on Man, and Essay on Criticism* edited by Joseph Seaburry, 65–87. The Silver Series of English Classics. New York: Silver, Burdett, 1900.
Preece, Rob. *The Wisdom of Imperfection: The Challenge of Individuation in Buddhist Life*. Ithaca, NY: Snow Lion, 2006.
Queen, Christopher, "Glassman Roshi and the Peacemaker Order: Three Encounters." In *Engaged Buddhism in the West*, edited by Christopher S. Queen, 95–127. Boston: Wisdom, 2000.
Race, Alan. *Christians and Religious Pluralism: Patterns in the Christian Theology of Religions*. London: SCM, 1983.

Ratnasekera, Leopold. "Towards a Buddhist-Christian Dialogue: Some Bridges of Understanding." *SEDOS Bulletin* 35 (2003) 85–88.
Rawcliffe, Rosemary, dir. *The Great 14th: Tenzin Gyatso, the 14th Dalai Lama in His Own Words*. Starring the Dalai Lama. Produced by Frame of Mind Films.
Ray, Reginald. "From Dialogue to Mutual Transformation: The Third Buddhist-Christian Theological Encounter." *Eastern Buddhist* 20 (1987) 115–27.
Raymaker, John. *Buddhist-Christian Logic of the Heart: Nishida's Kyoto School and Lonergan's "Spiritual Genome" as World Bridge*. Lanham, MD: University Press of America, 2002.
———. *Empowering Philosophy and Science with the Art of Love: Lonergan and Deleuze in the Light of Buddhist-Christian Ethics*. Lanham, MD: University Press of America, 2006.
Reader, Ian, et al. *Japanese Religions: Past and Present*. Honolulu: University of Hawaii Press, 1995 (1993).
Reat, N. Ross. "Buddhist-Christian Dialogue: Whether, Whence, and Why." In *Perspectives on Language and Text: Essays and Poems in Honor of Francis I. Andersen's Sixtieth Birthday, July 28, 1985*, edited by Edgar W. Conrad and Edward G. Newing, 425–32. Winona Lake, IN: Eisenbrauns, 1987.
Reilly, Richard. "Compassion as Justice." *Buddhist-Christian Studies* 26 (2006) 13–31.
Riegert, Ray, and Thomas Moore, eds. *The Lost Sutras of Jesus: Unlocking the Ancient Wisdom of the Xian Christia Monks*. Translated by Jon Babcock. Berkeley, CA: Seastone, 2003.
Ro, Bong Rin and Mark C. Albrecht. *God in Asian Contexts: Communicating the God of the Bible in Asia*. Asia Evangelical Theological Library 3. Taichung, Taiwan: Asia Theological Association, 1988.
Rocha, Cristina. *Zen in Brazil: The Quest for Cosmopolitan Modernity*. Topics in Contemporary Buddhism. Honolulu: University of Hawaii Press, 2006.
Ross, Nancy Wilson. *Buddhism: A Way of Life and Thought*. New York: Vintage, 1981.
———. *Buddhism: A Way of Life and Thought*. New York: Knopf, 1981.
Ruland, Vernon. *Imagining the Sacred: Soundings in World Religions*. Faith Meets Faith Series. Maryknoll, NY: Orbis, 1998.
Ryan, Thomas. "Buddhist and Catholic Monks Talk about Celibacy." *Buddhist-Christian Studies* 27 (2007) 143–45.
Sangharakshita, Bhikshu Sthavira. *Alternative Traditions*. Glasgow: Windhorse, 1986.
Schmidt-Leukel, Perry, ed. *Buddhism and Christianity in Dialogue*. The Gerald Weisfeld Lectures 2004. London: SCM, 2005.
———, ed. *Buddhism, Christianity and the Question of Creation: Karmic or Divine?* Aldershot, UK: Ashgate, 2006.
———. "War and Peace in Buddhism." In *War and Peace in World Religions*, edited by Perry Schmidt-Leukel, 33–56. The Gerald Weisfeld Lectures 2003. London: SCM, 2004.
———, ed., in cooperation with Thomas Josef Götz and Gerhard Köberlin. *Buddhist Perceptions of Jesus*. St. Ottilien: EOS, 2001.
———. *"Den Löwen brüllen hören": zur Hermeneutik eines christlichen Verständnisses der buddhistischen Heilsbotschaft*. Beiträge zur ökumenischen Theologie 23. Paderborn: Schöning, 1992.
Schneider, David. *Street Zen: The Life and Work of Issan Dorsey*. Boston: Shambhala, 1993.

Schwager, Raymund. *Must There Be Scapegoats? Violence and Redemption in the Bible.* Translated by Maria L. Assad. San Francisco: Harper & Row, 1987.

Senauke, Alan. "Personal Notes on Buddhism in America Today." In *The Transforming Spiritual Landscape: Buddhist–Christian Encounters*, edited by Ronald Y. Nakasone, 101–6. Fremont, CA: Dharma Cloud, 2005.

Shakespeare, William. *King Henry IV, Part 2.* Edited by Barbara Mowat and Paul Werstine. The New Folger Library Shakespeare. New York: Washington Square, 1999.

Sheard, Robert B. *Interreligious Dialogue in the Catholic Church since Vatican II: An Historical and Theological Study.* Toronto Studies in Theology 31. Lewiston, NY: Mellen, 1987.

Shenk, Calvin E. *Who Do You Say That I Am? Christians Encounter Other Religions.* Scottdale, PA.: Herald, 1997.

Shrobe, Richard. *Don't-Know Mind: The Spirit of Korean Zen.* Boston: Shambhala, 2004.

Siegmund, Georg. *Buddhism and Christianity: A Preface to Dialogue.* Translated by Mary Francis McCarthy. Tuscaloosa: University of Alabama Press, 1980.

Simmer-Brown, Judith. "Remedying Globalization and Consumerism: Joining the Inner and Outer Journey's in 'Perfect Balance.'" *Buddhist–Christian Studies* 22 (2002) 31–46.

Simpkins, C. Alexander, and Annellen Simpkins. *Simple Buddhism: A Guide to Enlightened Living.* Boston: Tuttle, 2000.

Sister Kristine (Thich Nu Pho-Chau). "Life as a Vietnamese Nun." In *Blue Jean Buddha: Voices of Young Buddhists,* edited by Sumi D. Loundon, 52–58. Boston: Wisdom, 2001.

Sivaraksa, Sulak. "Buddhist–Christian Encounter." *Japan Christian Quarterly* 53 (1987) 204–7.

Smart, Ninian. *Buddhism and Christianity: Rivals and Allies.* Library of Philosophy and Religion. London: Macmillan, 1993.

Smith, Jean. *The Beginner's Guide to Walking the Buddha's Eightfold Path.* New York: Bell Tower, 2002.

Soares-Prabhu, George M. *The Dharma of Jesus.* Edited by Francis X. D'Sa. Maryknoll, NY: Orbis, 2003.

So, Yuen-tai. "William Johnston's Contemplation Approach to Buddhist–Christian Dialogue." *Ching Feng* 42/1–2 (1999) 83–110.

Society for Buddhist–Christian Studies. *Resources for Buddhist–Christian Encounter: An Annotated Bibliography.* Wofford Heights, CA: Multifaith Resources, 1993.

Song, C. S. *Tell Us Our Names: Story Theology from an Asian Perspective.* Maryknoll, NY: Orbis, 1985.

———. *Theology from the Womb of Asia.* Maryknoll, NY: Orbis, 1993.

Spae, Joseph J. *Buddhist–Christian Empathy.* Chicago: Chicago: Institute of Theology and Culture, 1980.

———, ed. "The Buddhist–Christian Encounter." Special issue, *Pro Mundi Vita Bulletin* 67 (1977).

Sparks, Irving Alan. "Buddha and Christ: A Functional Analysis." *Numen* 13 (1966) 190–204.

Steindl-Rast, David. "A Shift in Buddhist–Christian Dialogue." *Areopagus* 2/1 (1988) 18–20.

Streeter, Burnett Hillman. *The Buddha and the Christ: An Exploration of the Meaning of the Universe and of the Purpose of Human Life.* The Bampton Lectures for 1932. Port Washington, NY: Kennikat, 1970.

Strong, John. "A Family Quest: The Buddha, Yashodhara, and Rahula in the Mulasarvastivada Vinaya." In *Sacred Biography in the Buddhist Traditions of South and Southeast Asia,* edited by Juliane Schober, 113–28. Honolulu: University of Hawaii Press, 1997.

Stultz, J. Anthony. Lecture delivered at the Blue Mountain Lotus Society, in Harrisburg, PA, on April 2004.

Sumner, George. *The First and the Last: The Claim of Jesus Christ and the Claims of Other Religious Traditions.* Grand Rapids: Eerdmans, 2004.

Sundara, Sister Ajahn. "Women in Theravada Buddhism." On *Discovering Sacred Texts* (a British Library blog), September 23, 2019. https://www.bl.uk/sacred-texts/articles/women-in-theravada-buddhism/.

Suzuki, Daisetz Teitaro. *Buddha of Infinite Light.* Revised with an introduction and notes by Taitetsu Unno. Boston: Shambhala, 1998 (1970).

———. *An Introduction to Zen Buddhism.* New York: Grove, 1964.

———. *Mysticism: Christian and Buddhist; The Eastern and the Western Way.* New York: Collier, 1962.

Swearer, Donald K. "Buddha Loves Me! This I Know, for the Dharma Tells Me So." *Buddhist–Christian Studies* 19 (1999) 113–20.

Swick, David. *Thunder and Ocean: Shambhala & Buddhism in Nova Scotia.* Lawrencetown Beach, NS: Pottersfield, 1996.

Swidler, Arlene, ed. *Homosexuality and World Religions.* Valley Forge, PA: Trinity, 1993.

Tachibana, Shundo. *The Ethics of Buddhism.* 1929. Reprint, London: Curzon, 1992.

Tashi Tsering, Geshe. *The Four Noble Truths.* The Foundation of Buddhist Thought. 1. Boston: Wisdom, 2005.

Tennent, Timothy C. *Christianity at the Religious Roundtable: Evangelicalism in Conversation with Hinduism Buddhism and Islam.* Grand Rapids: Baker Academic, 2002.

Thelle, Notto R. *Buddhism and Christianity in Japan: From Conflict to Dialogue, 1854–1899.* Honolulu: University of Hawaii Press, 1987.

———. "Buddhist–Christian Encounter: From Animosity to Dialogue." *Japan Christian Quarterly* 42 (1976) 96–104.

———. "From Animosity to Dialogue: Vital Issues of the Buddhist–Christian Encounter in Japan." *Temenos* 13 (1977) 175–88.

———. "Zen for Missionaries: A Report of a Seminar for Missionaries at Eiheiji." *Japanese Religions* 12 (1981) 65–71.

Thera, A. Dhammika. "The Silent Stream: Contemplation and Buddhist–Christian Dialogue." *Dialogue* 11 (1984) 15–23.

Thera, Nyanaponika. *The Vision of Dhamma: Buddhist Writings of Nyanaponika Thera.* Edited with an introduction by Bhikkhu Bodhi. London: Rider, 1986.

Thomas, M. M. *Risking Christ for Christ's Sake: Towards an Ecumenical Theology of Pluralism.* Geneva: WCC Publications, 1987.

Thundy, Zacharias P. *Buddha and Christ: Nativity Stories and Indian Traditions.* Studies in the History of Religions 60. Leiden: Brill, 1993.

Thurston, Bonnie Bowman. "The Conquered Self: Emptiness and God in a Buddhist–Christian Dialogue." *Japanese Journal of Religious Studies* 12 (1985) 343–53.

Tillich, Paul. *Christianity and the Encounter of World Religions. Fortress Texts in Modern Theology*. Fortress Texts in Modern Theology. Minneapolis: Fortress, 1994.
Tin, Pe Maung. "Certain Factors in the Buddhist–Christian Encounter." *South East Asia Journal of Theology* 3/2 (1961) 27–33.
Tracy, David W. "Some Aspects of the Buddhist–Christian Dialogue." In *The Christian Understanding of God Today*, edited by James M. Byrne, 145–53. Trinity College Dublin Studies in Theology. Dublin: Columba, 1993.
Trapnell, Judson B. "Suffering and Compassion: A Jewish–Buddhist–Christian Dialogue." *Horizons* 27 (2000) 98–113.
Trungpa, Chögyam. *Dharma Art*. Edited by Judith L. Lief. Dharma Ocean Series. Boston: Shambhala, 1996.
Tshongkhapa. *Tantric Ethics: An Explanation of the Precepts for Buddhist Vajrayana Practice*. Translated by Gareth Sparham. Boston: Wisdom, 2005.
Ueki, Masatoshi. *Gender Equality in Buddhism*. Asian Thought and Culture 46. New York: Lang, 2001.
Unno, Taitetsu. *River of Fire, River of Water: An Introduction to the Pure Land Tradition of Shin Buddhism*. New York: Doubleday, 1998.
US Congressional-Executive Commission on China. *Special Report: Tibetan Self-Immolation—Rising Frequency, Wider Spread, Greater Diversity*, August 22, 2012. https://www.cecc.gov/publications/issue-papers/special-report-tibetan-self-immolation-rising-frequency-wider-spread/.
Valkenberg, Paul, "Jacques Dupuis as a Theologian with a Reversed Mission: Some Remarks on His Controversial Theology of Religious Pluralism." In *"Mission Is a Must": Intercultural Theology and the Mission of the Church*, edited by Frans Wissen and Peter Nissen, 147–58. Kerk en Theologie in Context 40. Amsterdam: Rodopi, 2002.
Victoria, Brian Daizen. *Zen at War*. 2nd ed. War and Peace Library. Lanham, MD: Rowan & Littlefield, 2006.
Vidyasagara, Vijaya. "The Marxist Movement and the Buddhist–Christian Dialogue in Sri Lanka: A Comment." *Dialogue* 10/2–3 (1985) 16–28.
Vroom, Hendrik M. *No Other Gods: Christian Belief in Dialogue with Buddhism, Hinduism, and Islam*. Translated by Lucy Jansen. Grand Rapids: Eerdmans, 1996.
———. "How May We Compare Ideas of Transcendence? On the Method of Comparative Theology." In *Comparative Theology: Essays for Keith Ward*, edited by T. W. Bartel, 66–76. London: SPCK, 2003.
Waldenfels, Hans. *Absolute Nothingness: Foundations for a Buddhist–Christian Dialogue*. Translated by J. W. Heisig. New York: Paulist, 1980.
Warner, Jisho, "What Do Lesbians Do in the Daytime?" In *Being Bodies: Buddhist Women on the Paradox of Embodiment*, edited by Lenore Friedman and Susan Moon, 110–14. Boston: Shambhala, 1997.
Watts, Alan. *Buddhism: The Religion of No-Religion: The Edited Transcripts*. Boston: Tuttle, 1996.
———. *The Wisdom of Insecurity: A Message for an Age of Anxiety*. New York: Vintage, 1951.
Weerasingha, Tissa. "Buddhism through Christian Eyes." In *God in Asian Contexts: Communicating the God of the Bible in Asia*, edited by Bong Rin Ro and Mark C. Albrecht, 145–64. Taichung, Taiwan: Asia Theological Association, 1988.

West, Elizabeth. *Happiness Here and Now: The Eightfold Path of Jesus; Revisited with Buddhist Insights*. New York: Continuum, 2000.

Wiesel, Elie. *The Gates of the Forest*. Translated by Frances Frenaye. New York: Holt, Rinehart & Winston, 1966.

Wiles, Maurice. *Christian Theology and Inter-religious Dialogue*. London: SCM, 1992.

Wood, Ralph C. *Preaching and Professing: Sermons by a Teacher Seeking to Proclaim the Gospel*. Grand Rapids: Eerdmans, 2009.

Wright, Arthur F. *Buddhism in Chinese History*. Stanford Studies in the Civilizations of Eastern Asia. Stanford: Stanford University Press, 1971.

Yagi, Seiichi. "An Unhappy Dialogue: Problems of Reversibility and Irreversibility in Buddhist–Christian Discussions." *Japanese Religions* 14 (1987) 2–13.

Yagi, Seiichi, and Leonard Swidler. *A Bridge to Buddhist–Christian Dialogue*. New York: Paulist, 1990.

Young, Richard Fox, and Gintota Parana Vidanage Somaratna. *Vain Debates: The Buddhist–Christian Controversies of Nineteenth-Century Ceylon*. Indologisches Institut. Sammlung De Nobili. Publications of the De Nobili Research Library. Vienna: Gerold, 1996.

Yu, Chai-shin. *Early Buddhism and Christianity: A Comparative Study of the Founders' Authority, the Community, and the Discipline*. New Delhi: Banarsidass, 1981.

Zornberg, Avivah Gottlieb. *Moses: A Human Life*. Jewish Lives. New Haven: Yale University Press, 2016.

www.ingramcontent.com/pod-product-compliance
Lightning Source LLC
Chambersburg PA
CBHW031357230426
43670CB00006B/571